# WOMEN, GENDER, AND CONDITIONAL CASH TRANSFERS

Conditional Cash Transfer (CCT) Programs have been widely used throughout less economically developed countries to fight poverty and foster socioeconomic development. In *Women, Gender, and Conditional Cash Transfers*, a multidisciplinary group of feminist scholars use in-depth interviews, survey data analysis, and ethnographic and archival research to explore the extent to which *Bolsa Família*, the largest CCT program in the world, contributes to foster gender justice, women's autonomy, and to improve gender relations.

Comprising nine chapters, written by authors from different regions of Brazil, this book captures perspectives from across Brazil to explain *Bolsa Família* according to regional social inequalities and provide historical, and up-to-date, insights into this program from a feminist perspective. The authors are able to contribute and move beyond conventional feminist knowledge on CCTs, through considering questions of gender raised in the specialized literature in relation to *Bolsa Família* and by addressing concerns of intersectional categories such as race, ethnicity, age and geographic location.

*Women, Gender, and Conditional Cash Transfers* will be of great interest not only to scholars of Latin American politics, but also to students of development policy, public policy, and gender.

**Teresa Sacchet** is a professor at the Graduate Program in Interdisciplinary Studies on Women, Gender and Feminism, at the Federal University of Bahia, Brazil. She specializes on topics related to feminism, democratic theories, political institutions, political parties, quotas, electoral system, electoral financing, and public policies with a focus on gender and racial issues.

**Silvana Mariano** is a professor at the Department of Social Sciences at the State University of Londrina, Brazil. She specializes in the field of Sociology, with an emphasis on Gender Studies, working mainly on the following themes: gender, feminism, public policies and citizenship.

**Cássia Maria Carloto** is a professor at the State University of Londrina, Brazil and the leader of the Gender, Public Policies, and Family research group at the same institution. She has conducted research on women's participation in Conditional Cash Transfer programs since 2003, focusing particularly on *Bolsa Família*.

'A much needed feminist critical review of *Bolsa Familia* that might enlighten Conditional Cash Transfers Program's analysis and improve them to better impact on women's lives and gender equality.'

**Corina Rodríguez Enríquez**, *FLACSO Argentina*

'This book makes an essential contribution to studies of gender (and race) within conditional cash transfer (CCT) programmes. It offers a detailed examination of the best-known CCT, Brazil's *Bolsa Família*, showing how it has been both essential and insufficient for the amelioration of extreme poverty, and how it has built upon, and shifted, gender roles in the country. This is an essential resource to scholars and students working in this field.'

**Alfredo Saad-Filho**, *King's College London*

# WOMEN, GENDER, AND CONDITIONAL CASH TRANSFERS

## Interdisciplinary Perspectives from Studies of *Bolsa Família*

*Edited by Teresa Sacchet, Silvana Mariano and Cássia Maria Carloto*

NEW YORK AND LONDON

First published 2021
by Routledge
52 Vanderbilt Avenue, New York, NY 10017

and by Routledge
2 Park Square, Milton Park, Abingdon, Oxon OX14 4RN

*Routledge is an imprint of the Taylor & Francis Group, an informa business*



*Library of Congress Cataloging-in-Publication Data*
A catalog record for this title has been requested

ISBN: 978-0-367-25115-4 (hbk)
ISBN: 978-0-367-25116-1 (pbk)
ISBN: 978-0-429-28613-1 (ebk)

Typeset in Bembo
by Taylor & Francis Books

**To women living in poverty who have to fight daily for their own and their family's survival, particularly women from *Bolsa Família* who take part in this book with their histories and experience.**

# CONTENTS

# ILLUSTRATIONS

## Figures



## Tables

# CONTRIBUTORS

**Cássia Maria Carloto** Social Worker and Professor at the Department of Social Work and the Postgraduate Program in Social Work and Social Policy of the State University of Londrina, Brazil. Leader of the Gender, Public Policies, and Family research group. She has conducted research on women's participation in Conditional Cash Transfer programs since 2003, focusing particularly on *Bolsa Família.*

**Fábio Domingues Waltenberg** is an associate professor of Economics at the Universidade Federal Fluminense (UFF), Brazil, and a researcher at the Center for Studies on Inequality and Development (CEDE). He is a member of the Graduate Program in Economics of UFF, which he coordinated between 2015 and 2017. He holds BA and MA degrees in Economics from the Universidade de São Paulo, Brazil, and a PhD in Economics from the Université Catholique de Louvain, Belgium, obtained in 2007. He is currently a senior Post-Doctoral Researcher at the Chair on Inequalities at the Brazilian Institute of Advanced Studies, Universidade Federal do Rio de Janeiro, and coordinates the Brazilian team involved in the evaluation of a Universal Basic Income program in Maricá. His research focuses on economic analyses of social policies, with emphasis on economics of education and cash transfer policies.

**Josimara Delgado** Social Worker and professor at the Postgraduate Program in Interdisciplinary Studies on Women, Gender, and Feminism, Federal University of Bahia, Brazil. Her research focuses on the relationship between class, gender, and generation; social protection, public policies, social service, and *Bolsa Família.*

**Luana Passos** is a researcher at the Family Economics Study Group and Gender (GeFam). She holds BA degrees in Economics from the Universidade Estadual de

Feira de Santana, Brazil, and MA and PhD degrees in Economics from the Universidade Federal Fluminense, Brazil. She was Post-Doctoral Researcher in the Universidade Federal de Minas Gerais, Brazil. Her research interests include Labor Economics, Gender Relations, Feminist Economics, and Tax Justice. PNPD/ CAPES Fellow during the time of preparation of this chapter.

**Mani Tebet A. de Marins** Adjunct Professor of Sociology at the Federal Rural University of Rio de Janeiro, Brazil. Professor at the Postgraduate Program in Public Policies in Human Rights at the same institution. She has conducted research and published on the following themes: inequality, public policies, education, race and gender relations, and *Bolsa Família.*

**Márcia Santana Tavares** Social worker, professor of the Postgraduate Program in Interdisciplinary Studies on Women, Gender, and Feminisms at Federal University of Bahia, Brazil; researcher at the Center for Interdisciplinary Studies on Women; member of the Observatory for the Application of the Maria da Penha Law (UFBA). Her research interests include: gender relations, practices and social representations; management, monitoring and evaluation of public policies, with a focus on gender and violence against women, social service and *Bolsa Família.*

**Márcio Ferreira de Souza** Sociologist and associate professor at the Federal University of Uberlândia (UFU), Brazil. In sociology, he specializes, in particular, in gender studies, Brazilian social thought, sociology of the use of time, and sociology of emotions.

**Silvana Mariano** Sociologist, professor at the Department of Social Sciences and coordinator of the Postgraduate Program in Sociology at the State University of Londrina, Brazil. She has experience in political sociology, with emphasis on Gender Studies, working mainly in the following subjects: gender, feminism, family-programs, privacy control laws, citizenship, and *Bolsa Família* from a gender perspective.

**Simone Wajnman** is Full Professor of Demography at CEDEPLAR, Universidade Federal de Minas Gerais (UFMG), Brazil, where she teaches courses on demographic methods, economic demography, and family demography. She holds a BA in Economics, and both an MA and PhD in Demography from UFMG. In 2001 she was a visiting fellow at the Office of Population Research at Princeton University. She was Secretary and Vice-President of Brazilian Association of Population Studies and Member of the advisory council of CNPq, Brazil, and Editor in Chief of Brazilian Journal of Demographic Studies. Her research encompasses economic and family demography; demographic aspects of poverty and inequality, female labor force participation, and gender inequality.

**Teresa Sacchet** Political scientist, professor at the Postgraduate Program in Interdisciplinary Studies on Women, Gender, and Feminisms, Federal University of Bahia, and researcher at the Research Center for Public Policy, University of São Paulo, Brazil. She specializes on topics related to: feminism, democratic theories, political institutions, political parties, quotas, electoral system, electoral financing, and public policies with a focus on gender and racial issues.

# ACRONYMS

| | |
|---|---|
| BF | *Bolsa Família* (Family Grant) |
| PBF | Programa *Bolsa Família* (Family Grant Program) |
| BPC | Benefício de Prestação Continuada (Continuous Cash Benefit) |
| Cadastro Único | Cadastro Único de Programas Sociais do Governo Federal (Single Registry of Social Programs of the Federal Government) |
| CEF | Caixa Econômica Federal (Federal Savings Bank) |
| CCT | Conditional Cash Transfers |
| CRAS | Centro de Referência de Assistência Social (Reference Center for Social Assistance) |
| GDP | Gross Domestic Product |
| IBGE | Instituto Brasileiro de Geografia e Estatística (Brazilian Institute of Geography and Statistics) |
| MDS | Ministério do Desenvolvimento Social e Combate à Fome (Ministry of Social Development and Fight Against Hunger) |
| PBSM | Plano Brasil sem Miséria (Brazil Without Extreme Poverty Plan) |
| PETI | Programa de Erradicação do Trabalho Infantil (Eradication of Child Labor Program) |
| PNAD | Pesquisa Nacional de Amostra por Domicílio (National Household Sample Survey) |
| PNAS | Política Nacional de Assistência Social (National Social Assistance Policy) |
| SUAS | Sistema Único de Assistência Social (Unified Social Assistance System) |
| SUS | Sistema Único de Saúde (Unified Health System) |

# ACKNOWLEDGMENTS

This book arose from our desire to build bridges: between researchers of different subject areas who investigate the *Bolsa Família* Program in Brazil from feminist perspectives and between these researchers and an international audience. Teresa Sacchet was the first to instigate the proposal, and following a consensus between the three organizers and a clear interest from Routledge, we contacted and established dialogues with Brazilian researchers from various regions of the country, resulting in a team of authors who have contributed to this collection of chapters.

We understood that a book on gender research on the *Bolsa Família* Program, which is the largest and is considered the most important cash transfer program (CCT) in the world, could contribute towards internal reflection, and enrich studies in this perspective in other countries. We perceived that although there were various academic works on CCTs and gender, very few focused specifically on the *Bolsa Família* Program.

For approximately two years, this team of scholars has exchanged information and held intensive discussions on each item of research presented in the collection. This collective endeavor was to make the book unified. We were very happy to achieve this objective and, as the organizers, are grateful for the commitment and dedication of each author who has taken part in this project.

We would like to thank Routledge for the opportunity and their confidence in us, especially the editors Natalja Mortensen and Charlie Baker, who were always very enthusiastic about this project and understanding of our difficulties and responsive to our requests and questions.

We would like to thank the Beatrice Bain Research Group, at the Department of Gender and Women's Studies, University of California, Berkeley, where the initiative for this book started, as part of a research project conducted by Teresa Sacchet.

We would like to thank the universities in which the organizers of this collection have worked in recent years and that provided the institutional conditions to conduct this research: the State University of Londrina (UEL) and Federal University of Bahia (UFBA). Brazilian public universities are our main locus to undertake advanced research.

We would like to thank the people who assisted with the translations and revisions of the chapters of this book: Omar Al Jamal, Christine Eida, David Rodgers, Fraser Robinson, and Lina Penati Ferreira.

Finally, we are especially grateful to all our respondents: The women who receive *Bolsa Família*, civil servants, social workers, and public authorities, without whom the content, analyses and reflections presented in this book would not be possible.

# 1

# INTRODUCTION

## *Bolsa Família* in a Political Context

*Teresa Sacchet*

This chapter introduces the topic of Conditional Cash Transfers (CCTs) in general, and the Brazilian CCT program, *Bolsa Família* (BF) (Family Grant), in particular; it provides a brief historical perspective of the latter's development, to identify recent changes, and to present the main arguments put forward in each chapter. Brazil has recently experienced major political turmoil, exemplified in the deposition of a democratically elected president and the coming to power of the far-right after 13 years of being governed by a center left government. As a consequence, it has seen a significant reduction in public spending, and reshaping in public policy guidelines. BF has been a part of this process, but changes to the program are not always explained in chapters of this book, since the research on which they are based was usually carried out either prior or during these changes. The contextualization and update provided in this chapter on the program's developments should help to locate discussions, analysis, and findings in this book.

Poverty alleviation programs, such as CCT, are the main policy initiatives put forward by governments in Latin America in recent decades to combat poverty. They consist of the transfer of a variable sum, related to the family size and level of destitution, to families that fall below the lines of poverty and extreme poverty. They were initially implemented by left and center left governments in the region, but given their success in reducing poverty at a low cost, they became more widespread. Mexican and Brazilian CCTs were amongst the first implemented on a national scale, and have been used as models for other countries in the region, and elsewhere.

Contemporary CCTs emerged in Latin America in the 1990s, as specific social protection policy models, in response to a particular political and economic configuration. The 1980s and early 1990s in Latin America was a period with marginal economic growth, and Structural Adjustment Programs significantly reduced the countries' social spending. There was a reduction in state responsibility for social protection, and an increase in the role played by the market, the family, and the community (Jenson 2009; Molyneux 2006). Fast-spreading neoliberalism also resulted in setbacks in employment rights, and an increase in social inequality and poverty in the region.

In this context, CCTs were presented as a policy alternative to alleviate poverty. Its rationale was influenced by a new development paradigm, referred to by some as "inclusive liberalism" (Porter and Craig 2004), which emerged in the region in the 1990s, marked by a social policy orientation distanced from universal social rights and towards a focus on excluded social groups. It was built upon the idea of a "social investment," whereby the state plays a key role, as a social investor, helping people out of poverty through cash transfers, and initiatives that aim to promote human development (Jenson 2009; Morel, Palier, and Palme 2009). This targeted, pro-poor approach to social policy has been encouraged, and sometimes financially supported by development agencies and international financial institutions.

Alvarez (2014) argues that in this new phase of neoliberalism, a "perverse confluence of gender" occurred whereby, on the one hand, some specific issues of the feminist agenda were incorporated into the programs of political parties, governments, and international development agencies in Latin America and, on the other hand, women were included on the "new poverty agenda," as a means of better integrating them into a more effective and efficient "market development." In CCTs cash is usually transferred to female heads of households, who must then comply with conditionalities, in order to remain on the program. Since its inception, women have made up more than 90% of *Bolsa Família* recipients. As argued by a number of feminists, this focus on women hinges on a reified and essentialized notion of women as good mothers (Molyneux 2006), and on the actual role they tend to play as family caregivers. Given that by looking after their families well women maximize returns from investment on social protection programs, transferring the allowance to them is rational from a public management perspective and, as such, their altruistic behavior has been welcomed and encouraged by public officials and authorities, as highlighted in most chapters of this book. Targeting women carries the contradiction of being welcomed, providing them with access to financial resources (or a little more), however it reinforces traditional gender roles and relations. From a gender equality perspective, this reproduction of gender norms, and the essentialization of women as mothers has numerous drawbacks, which are explored in the chapters of this book.

## *Bolsa Família*

*Bolsa Família* was implemented in 2003, in the first Workers' Party (*Partido dos Trabalhadores* – PT) government. After a decade of economic fluctuations, marked by periods of high inflation, the privatization of public industries, and devaluation of the national currency, the last years of Fernando Henrique Cardoso's administration were critical in defining the result of the 2002 elections. They marked the return of high inflation, an increase in unemployment rates, a reduction in income, and impoverishment of the population. In this context, a party founded by trade unions, new social movements, and left-wing intellectuals succeeded in winning the presidential election. The PT saw its main leader, Luiz Inácio Lula da Silva (Lula), become president after three failed bids for the office. Lula marked his emotional inaugural speech both by talking about the prejudices he had faced in politics due to his working-class background and poor childhood as a north-eastern migrant, and by vowing to better distribute wealth, and end poverty. Indeed, although his administrations did not promote major structural reforms, the levels of inequality fell considerably during his two terms in government (Pochmann 2011) and the fight to end hunger and poverty became his hallmark.

BF, like most CCTs, was proposed as an initiative to combat poverty, and to help people out of it, through human development initiatives. It has been widely acclaimed in academic studies for its positive influence on social and economic indicators, and recommended as a model for other countries (Jenson 2009; Barrientos 2011, 2013). Its high international profile was evinced, with the creation of the World Without Poverty (WWP) initiative, in 2014. WWP is a joint project between Brazilian governmental institutions, namely, the then *Ministério do Desenvolvimento Social e Combate à Fome* (MDS) (Ministry of Social Development and Fight Against Hunger) – now called the *Ministério da Cidadania* (Ministry of Citizenship) –, the Instituto de Pesquisas Econômicas Aplicadas (IPEA) (Institute of Applied Economic Research), the Centro Internacional de Políticas para o Crescimento Inclusivo (IPC-IG) (International Policy Centre for Inclusive Growth), and the World Bank, which has the aim of documenting the Brazilian experience of poverty reduction, and disseminating this knowledge to other countries. However, the program approaches women and gender issues from the same perspective as most other CCTs and, therefore, is not a model to be adopted by those interested in promoting gender justice.

In 2011, Dilma Rousseff, also from the PT, succeeded Lula, and expanded the idea of investing in sustainable ways out of poverty, by setting up the *Plano Brasil sem Miséria* (PBSM) (Brazil Without Extreme Poverty Plan). With the slogan "the end of poverty is only a beginning," PBSM introduced initiatives around three main axes: providing extra income to families living in extreme poverty (complementing *Bolsa Família*); securing access to public services – education and health in particular; and promoting productive inclusion initiatives through capacity building and credit, to increase employment opportunities among poor families (Costa 2013). Thus, PBSM aimed to expand on a process started by *Bolsa Família*, intended to alleviate poverty through cash transfers, and increase the alternatives it had proposed for people to escape poverty, through productive inclusion and credit. This strategy worked well during Dilma Rousseff's first term in government, but started to weaken at the beginning of her second term. With the fiscal crises of this period, the government reduced PBSM initiatives in areas such as vocational training, credit for agricultural production, and the provision of cisterns to communities that suffered from droughts, among others. BF was not directly affected, but nor was there any increase in the number of families assisted by the program.

Dilma Rousseff's second term in government was short-lived. She beat Aécio Neves, from the Brazilian Social Democracy Party, in the 2014 presidential election by only a small percentage of votes – a little over 3%. The day after the election, Neves started legal proceedings contesting its result, and then commissioned an impeachment petition that was filled by three lawyers in the Chamber of Deputies, and led to a coordinated action between members of the legislative and judicial powers and businesses for Rousseff's removal from government. In August 2016, after the impeachment vote was passed in the Chamber of Deputies, she had to vacate her position, so that her trial could continue in the Senate. In December the same year, she was finally deposed from the presidency, through the consolidation of an impeachment process that today is described, even by its proponents, as a coup.[1]

Since the beginning of Rousseff's second term, there have been major economic and social policy adjustments, which have had a greater negative effect on the economically worse off. Changes were accelerated when Michel Temer, Rousseff's vice president, took over the presidency in August 2016, and have further intensified under Jair Messias Bolsonaro's administration. Under Temer and Bolsonaro, there have been cuts in employment rights, income, social security, and investment in public policies. A labor reform in 2017 introduced changes to employment rules, which resulted in a reduction in salaries, and produced both decreases in formal employment rates and job deregulation that drove an increase in informal jobs and subcontracting.

High unemployment rates marked Michel Temer's government, reaching 12.3% at the end of his term in 2018. With Bolsonaro, at the end of the first year of his administration in 2019, this had dropped to 11.9%, but job informality had rocketed (Nery 2019). One of the major setbacks, in terms of social rights, was the 20-year freeze in public spending, approved by a Constitutional Amendment in late 2016. This has further damaged the country's already weak education, health, and social assistance systems, increasing inequality, and putting extra pressure on women in poverty who, in order to remain on the BF program, have to comply with conditionalities.

Higher unemployment rates means that more people need social protection from the state. However, instead of an increase, we have seen a decline in investment in social assistance programs, such as *Bolsa Família*. Even if the present federal administration has hidden the actual figures, in order to avoid criticism, the number of people awaiting access to BF has increased dramatically (Rossi 2020; Capetti and Martins 2020).[2] A focus on reducing, rather than granting the benefit, particularly through the narrative of combating fraud used by Temer and

Bolsonaro's administrations, has increased the costs of remaining on the program for women. They now have to report any minor change in their, or their family's, occupations and update their information on the *Cadastro Único de Programas Sociais do Governo Federal* (Single Registry of Social Programs of the Federal Government) more frequently, to prevent their allowance from being suspended – see more on this topic in Chapter 3. Cuts in social service spending have also affected them, since mobile outreach services, designed specifically to reach those living in distant locations, have now been significantly reduced.

Complying with such increasing demands to remain on the program is particularly difficult for those who live far away from the city centers, where the main BF offices are usually located, such as *quilombo* residents, riverside communities, and indigenous people. These people sometimes have to travel long distances, but they lack the means to do this, including paying for public transportation. According to a public authority, which I spoke to about recent changes in the program, people from more remote indigenous communities sometimes have to travel for up to three weeks to receive the allowance. Constant requests for database updates make it harder for people from these communities to remain on the program. Thus, changes to BF have particularly penalized the most vulnerable who lack the means to meet such increasing demands.

Although initiatives implemented during the PT government had drawbacks from a gender perspective, they played an important role in alleviating material poverty, becoming an option for those who could count on little else for survival. However, since President Dilma Rousseff's impeachment, there has been a significant reduction in the program, and its complementary policies, making it difficult for BF to fulfill even its most basic objective of fighting hunger, let alone fostering human development. From a gender equality perspective, a policy that was already lacking with the center left, has deteriorated under the recent right and far-right administrations.

The book has nine chapters, written by authors from different academic institutions, and regions of Brazil, whose work encompasses scholarly fields, such as political science, economics, sociology, and social work. Some of the authors have also had experience in public management. Chapters explores different, but related, dimensions of *Bolsa Família* from gender and feminist perspectives informed by theoretical perspectives and concepts (mostly feminists) of these different academic areas, and feminist approaches to CCTs. They seek to explore key issues in this debate, focusing on the institutional design and experience of implementing this policy, on the relationship of BF recipients with the program and their experience of living in poverty, and on the impact of BF on dimensions considered key to promote gender justice and women's autonomy. Their analyses follow qualitative and quantitative research methods and use both primary data from interviews, ethnography and surveys, and secondary data obtained from academic studies, official databases, and government reports. These studies either adopt a nationwide perspective, or focus on the experience of some specific states or municipalities.

Issues discussed in the book from a gender perspective also take into account the intersectionality of women's experiences related to race, ethnicity, age, and geographical location. Brazil is a country of immense social inequality, which is further compounded by geographic differences between the north and south. The organizers of this book sought to capture, and reflect on these regional differences, by including chapters from authors who have lived and conducted research in different regions of the country. Therefore, the book also aims to provide a contribution to the subject of CCTs and gender, from the perspective of local scholars from different regions of Brazil.

Chapter 2, "*Bolsa Família*: Background, operation, and gender issues," follows this introductory chapter. It is written by myself, Silvana Mariano, and Cássia Carloto and provides further information on the economic, political, and social context in which *Bolsa Família* emerged, explains how it operates, and introduces key ideological perspectives and concepts, which have supported the role women play in it. A key argument presented, and which underlays those of many other chapters, is that although necessary as a measure to alleviate poverty, BF is limited as a project to combat poverty, due to the fact that such an endeavor requires structural changes not seen in previous and recent governments. Also, the focus on the family as a unit adopted by this program overlooks inherent issues of gender inequality.

Chapter 3, "Beyond Distribution: Issues of Gender Justice in the Fight Against Poverty in Brazil," written by me, focuses on the limits of *Bolsa Família*, and complementary policies, to promote human development. I claim that a policy that makes women responsible for conditionalities, and does not invest in initiatives to enhance their capabilities, cannot be considered an endeavor that promotes human development. CCTs may only be considered a human development policy if women are removed from the equation. Based on feminist theories of gender justice, I put forward the argument that ignoring cultural and political issues related to poverty means that key sources of inequality between social groups, essential for defining and fighting poverty, are erased from policy planning, limiting the program's ability both to increase capabilities and to foster gender justice. The analysis presented is based on primary and secondary research material, and my direct experience with this program, working as a policy adviser and coordinator of the MDS Committee on Gender and Women's Policy between 2011 and 2014.

Chapter 4, "The *Bolsa Família* Program in Bahia: Intersections of Class, Gender, Race, and Generations," by Josimara Delgado and Márcia Tavares, presents an intersectional analysis of BF in Bahia, a state located in the poorest northeast region of Brazil. Their work demonstrates a higher rate of informal employment, and dependency on the state in this region, particularly among black women. The vast majority of those receiving BF in Bahia are black women, in families that have been working informally or in low paid, low status jobs for generations, with limited access to goods and services. The authors argue that the program's familist focus does not take into account intersectionalities of class, gender, race, and generation, thus making black women more susceptible to vulnerabilities that prevent them from overcoming poverty and exclusion. The authors argue that fighting poverty requires a gender perspective that takes intersectionality into account. They claim that cash transfer policies are part of a process of dismantling fundamental universal policies, such as health, education and social security.

Chapter 5, "The *Bolsa Família* Program: Reflections on its Role in Social Protection and Gender Relations in Brazil," by Luana Passos, Simone Wajnman, and Fábio Waltenberg, adopts an economic perspective to analyze the effects of BF's imposition of conditionalities both on female participation in the labour market and gender relations in the family. They argue that BF carries the virtues, limitations, contradictions, and dilemmas of targeted policies. On the one hand, it meets multiple objectives in an incomplete welfare state, of a middle-income country marked by social inequalities and permeated by an informal labor market, but on the other hand, since it requires female recipients to fulfill conditionalities that increase their family-domestic chores, it produces drawbacks that impinge on female autonomy. Their analysis is based on research they carried out in 2017, and on data from the Continuous National Household Sample Survey of the Brazilian Institute of Geography and Statistics.

Chapter 6, "Gender and Autonomy of Women in Poverty: An Investigation into the *Bolsa Família* Program," by Silvana Mariano and Márcio Ferreira de Souza, analyzes issues of empowerment relating to women who receive BF. It has two main objectives: firstly, to understand women's perceptions of policy concepts, such as rights and citizenship, to uncover how they interpret their relationship with the state, access to public policies, and their agency within this process; and secondly, to measure the autonomy of these women, linked to their ability to make decisions within the domestic sphere, and in aspects relating to their own individualization. The analyses are based on data obtained from both open and closed interviews in municipalities of different sizes in the state of Paraná (south of Brazil). The authors claim that the prevalence of answers that cite rights associated to public policies, in particular, social rights, and criticisms of the quality of these policies, indicates politicization among beneficiaries to some degree. However, this politicization has not contributed to changes in gender relations within the family.

Chapter 7, "Conditionalities in the *Bolsa Família* Program and women's use of time in domestic family work," by Cássia Maria Carloto, discusses conditionalities, and the way they can increase women's workloads, and cause stress for women living with poor public service provisions, who fear losing the allowance. Her analysis is based on interviews carried out with female BF recipients, social policy managers, and education, social assistance, and health agents. The chapter provides context and through direct citation from women recipients of *Bolsa Família* themselves is able to supports the author's claims that the conditionalities required by BF in a context of poor-quality public services, such as education, health, and social assistance, lead to psychological distress and increase the workload of women, who are already overburdened by domestic chores.

Chapter 8 "Stigmas and Controls on *Bolsa Família* Beneficiary Women," by Mani Tebet A. de Marins, presents a sociological analysis of the BF program, examining the justification criteria used by beneficiaries to explain the fact that they "deserve" the benefit and how they view themselves as BF recipients. The analysis includes discussions on the relationship between beneficiaries and non-beneficiaries in their communities, and conflicts that arise among them from the fact that some people, even when they qualify for receiving BF, are not included on the program. The chapter considers the extent to which women suffer embarrassment, controls, and (social, gender-based, and racial) discrimination, because of their dependence on the state. Analysis in this chapter is based on participant observation, in-depth interviews with beneficiaries, and other people associated with the program, in a suburb of the metropolitan region of Rio de Janeiro.

"Conclusions", is written by Silvana Mariano and Cássia Carloto and gives an overview of the main arguments, findings, and conclusions of each chapter in the book, highlighting the connections between them. Among other things, it claims that targeting the poor is limited, in terms of achieving poverty alleviation. It also reaffirms claims made throughout the book that the familistic perspective in which this program is built, perceives women as a means to an end, producing drawbacks for their autonomy. Recent political and policy developments have resulted in cuts in public expenditure, reduction of the state, and democratic setbacks, increasing the pressures placed on women.

I trust this book provides an important contribution to the debate on CCTs and gender. By considering gender issues raised in specialized literature in relation to *Bolsa Família*, the largest and arguably most influential CCT program in the world, as well as addressing intersectional issues, chapters in this book address and complement conventional feminist knowledge on CCTs, women and gender relations.

## Notes

1 Michel Temer, Dilma Rousseff's vice president from the Brazilian Democratic Movement Party, who took over when she was ousted, was widely accused by Rousseff's supporters of having helped the opposition to organize and gather support for her removal from office. He always both denied his involvement in it and argued that the process that had led to her ousting was not a coup, as claimed by Rousseff's supporters. However, when interviewed on a TV program (Roda Viva program, of Cultura TV) on September 16, 2019, he used the word coup three times to refer to her impeachment. In one of these mentions, he ascertained: "I never supported or made any effort for the coup to happen" (Congresso em Foco 2019; Redação 2019). Janaina Paschoal (a jurist and law professor during Rousseff's impeachment, and now also a State Deputy) who, alongside two other jurists, played a critical role filling the petition that started the impeachment procedures, has also, on a number of occasions hinted at the fact that Rousseff was impeached not because of the reasons officially presented. On September

12, 2019, she tweeted: "Does anyone believe Dilma fell because of accounting issues?" This manifestation heated again the debate in the media concerning Rousseff's ousting, strengthening the claim of those that considered it as being a coup. The main claim made against Dilma Rousseff that led to her impeachment was administrative misconduct and charges of manipulating the federal budget.

2 In order to gain access to the latest data on the number of people receiving and waiting to access BF, the newspaper *O Globo* had to turn to the Information Access Law, which assures people the right to information on government spending and general data.

## References


Alvarez, Sonia E. 2014. "Para além da Sociedade Civil: Reflexões sobre o campo feminista. Dossiê O Gênero da Política: Feminismos, Estado e Eleições." *Cadernos Pagu*, no. 43: 13–56. https://doi.org/10.1590/0104-8333201400430013.

Barrientos, Armando. 2011. "Social Protection and Poverty." *International Journal of Social Welfare* 20, no. 3: 240–249.

Barrientos, Armando. 2013. "Human development income transfers in the longer term." Working Paper, no. 116. Brasília: International Policy Center for Inclusive Growth.

Capetti, Pedroa and Elisa Martins. 2020. "Bolsa Família volta a ter fila; são quase 500 mil famílias à espera do benefício." *O Globo*, January 27, 2020. https://oglobo.globo.com/economia/bolsa-familia-volta-ter-fila-sao-quase-500-mil-familias-espera-do-beneficio-1-24212924.

Congresso em Foco. 2019. "Veja o vídeo em que Temer admite 'golpe' e entenda o contexto". *Congresso em Foco*, September 17, 2019. https://congressoemfoco.uol.com.br/video/veja-o-video-em-que-temer-admite-golpe-e-entenda-o-contexto/.

Costa, Patricia Vieira da. 2013. "Um outro Brasil é Possível." In *O fim da Miséria é só um começo. Plano Brasil Sem Miséria: 2 anos*, edited by MDS (Ministério do Desenvolvimento Social e Combate à Fome), 4–5. Brasília: MDS.

Jenson, Jane. 2009. "Lost in translation: the social investment perspective and gender equality." *Social Politics* 16, no. 4: 446–483.

Molyneux, Maxine. 2006. "Mothers at the Service of the New Poverty Agenda: Progresa/Oportunidades, Mexico's Conditional Transfer Programme." *Social Policy & Administration* 40, no. 4: 425–449. https://doi.org/10.1111/j.1467-9515.2006.00497.x.

Morel, Nathalie, Bruno Palier, and Joakim Palme. 2009. *What Future for Social Investment?* Stockholm: Institute for Future Studies.

Nery, Carmen. 2019. "Extreme poverty affects 13.5 million persons and hits highest level in seven years." *Summary of Social Indicators, IBGE*. November 6, 2019. https://agenciadenoticias.ibge.gov.br/en/agencia-news/2184-news-agency/news/25895-extreme-poverty-affects-13-5-million-persons-and-hits-highest-level-in-seven-years.

Pochmann, Márcio. 2011. "Políticas sociais e padrão de mudanças no Brasil durante o governo Lula." *SER Social* 13, no. 28: 12–40. https://doi.org/10.26512/ser_social.v13i28.12681.

Porter, Doug and David Craig. 2004. "The third way and the third world: poverty reduction and social inclusion in the rise of 'inclusive' liberalism." *Review of International Political Economy* 1, no. 2: 387–423.

Redação. 2019. "*Temer admite que impeachment de Dilma foi golpe no Roda Viva.*" Revista Forum, September 16, 2019. https://revistaforum.com.br/politica/temer-admite-que-impeachment-de-dilma-foi-golpe-no-roda-viva/.

Rossi, Marina. 2020. "Governo Bolsonaro não explica tamanho real da fila do Bolsa Família." *El Pais*, January 31, 2020. https://brasil.elpais.com/brasil/2020-01-31/governo-bolsonaro-nao-explica-tamanho-real-da-fila-do-bolsa-familia.html.

# 2

# *BOLSA FAMÍLIA*

## Background, Operation, and Gender Issues

*Teresa Sacchet, Silvana Mariano, and Cássia Maria Carloto*

### Introduction

Despite being the ninth economy in the world in 2019, Brazil has a history of inequality and poverty that dates back to the period of colonization and slavery. The last century witnessed moments of firm state commitment and investments to economically develop the country. However, social issues were neglected, and income inequality was presented as a temporary evil, needed for the process of economic growth. Thus, we reach the 1990s with an immense number of people living on the margins of this development, in a situation of destitution and poverty. The Gini index, which in 1960 was 0.535, had risen to 0.607 by 1990 (IBGE 2019b).

Conditional cash transfer (CCT) policies emerged in Brazil and Latin America during this time, with the goal of combating the poverty, which was increasing in the region, and promoting social development. Globally, this process converged with the diffusion of the language of the rights, extensively reiterated at international conferences during the 1990s, and with the dissemination of human rights and development agendas. Throughout the 1990s, with the support of UN development agencies, and other international organizations, the idea of social protection as a right of citizenship, against the risks and needs that produce a low quality of life, became recognized and strengthened. Actions to combat poverty, often with targeted programs, rose to prominence as a strategy for these policies, in a context of job insecurity, observed not only in Latin America and the Global South, but also in the majority of countries, as a consequence of the accelerated globalization process and economic liberalization observed since the 1990s.

A common trait of these policies is the instrumental inclusion of women. The preference for women is due to a specific perception of family and gender relations, where women are more responsible for managing the household economy and, consequently, transferring the benefit to them is considered a way of more effectively managing the program's resources. While payment of the benefit to women may represent a way of guaranteeing them an income, or additional income, feminists have raised important questions that should be considered in program analyses.

We have three main objectives in this chapter. One is to present a historical discussion on the process of the country's economic and social developments that helps to contextualize the emergence of cash transfer policies in Brazil. The second objective is to present the *Bolsa Família* Program (PBF) (Family Grant Program), its structure, operation, and institutional liaison, and to introduce the way women are included in this program. Lastly, we explore how Brazilian social policies, including the *Bolsa Família* Program, approach the family unit, and the functions socially assigned to women in the domestic space. These objectives will be pursued in three different sections, and developed in the order the objectives were presented. In this chapter, we argue that the Brazilian selection of a social protection model centered on cash transfer does not tackle historical and structural obstacles, crucial for reducing social inequalities in general, and gender differences, in particular, with relevant limitations for its inclusion as a policy with a gender perspective.

## The Economic, Social, and Political Background to the *Bolsa Família* Program

Historically, social policy in Brazil was considered less as a way of reducing inequality and increasing the citizenship of the less privileged classes, and more as a way of supporting economic growth, and promoting social stability. In search of this growth, the country took various routes, guided by different models, in which the social issue took second place, and social policies operated as important ancillary instruments, supporting the exclusion process produced by the system. As a general rule, economic and social development in Brazil were presented as separate processes.

The 19$^{th}$-century Brazilian economy, like the other Latin American countries, was predominantly based on exports, making the economic development process face outwards and being dependent on the more economic developed countries' demands. The export of a few agricultural products made this economy vulnerable to successive international crises and price fluctuations (Corrêa and Simioni 2011). Given this vulnerability and external dependence, the traditional export model fell into a deep crisis following the 1930s depression, forcing the national economy to re-focus and meet the demands of an emerging domestic market.

From 1930, the country sought to establish an import substitution industrialization (ISI) system, along the lines of a developmental state. Through public investment in infrastructure, generally financed by international loans, the country invested in the construction of a national industry that continued to expand until the 1980s (Draibe 1993). During this time, there was a sharp decline in agricultural activities, and an intense migration process of people to the larger cities, attracted by the job opportunities offered by the manufacturing industry. Many were not absorbed by these jobs, especially those without specialized skills, and they settled in the periphery areas of large cities, in precarious housing and social conditions.

Despite the increase in formal job opportunities, pay and income inequalities increased, particularly during the military regime – between 1964 and 1985. The country had moments of high economic development, known as the period of the "Brazilian economic miracle" (1968–1973), with economic growth rates of over 10% per year. The productive and upper middle classes were supported by reduced labor rights, a lowered minimum salary, job flexibility, fiscal incentives, credit, subsidized healthcare, housing loans, and free university education (Saad-Filho 2015). While the economy grew at astonishing rates, the concentration of income increased. Through official advertisements, the government announced that the "cake needed to be larger, so it could then be divided," propagating the idea that a condition for economic growth was the concentration of income and wealth. By the end of the regime, in 1985, the richest 10% held half the national income (Saad-Filho 2015). Income concentration was sustained through a policy of repression and torture of those opposing the regime, control over unions, and censorship of the press.

From the 1930s, the first movements to build a social protection system in Brazil began (Silva 1995; Draibe 1993). The move from an agrarian export to an industrialization substitution model required the state to pay attention to the working classes that were growing. In this period, there were significant changes to labor and welfare legislation, as well as smaller healthcare and education initiatives (Draibe 1993). However, as with the economy, it was during the period of the military dictatorship, in 1964, that there was a leap in the development of social protection in the country, driven by the increase in industrialization and urbanization. During this period, a selective social protection system was introduced, in education, healthcare, social assistance, welfare, and housing. According to Draibe, a Brazilian welfare state standard was created, with tinges of corporatism and clientelism, heavily based on assistentialism, and it was fragmented, and intermittent (Draibe 1993). According to Silva, the expansion of social protection during the Brazilian military dictatorship had the goal of making programs and social services contribute to minimizing the intense repression of the working classes and the population at large (Silva 2007). The population on the margins of "development" during this period, which was firmly structured on the concentration of income, was supported by a number of specific policies, such as the expansion of allowances and pensions to the rural population, allowances for people with disabilities, and funeral assistance, etc. (Saad-Filho 2015).

The Brazilian economic miracle was short-lived. The 1973 international oil crisis brought to light the weaknesses of the import substitution and income concentration model, producing inflation and, in a short time, external debt and an inflationary surge disrupted the regime's economic success. Following surges of popular protests, many led by women, followed by a re-democratization process that began in the late 1970s, expansion of the free union movement (known as *Novo Sindicalismo* or New Unionism), and establishment of new political parties, the military regime came to an end in 1985. The new social and political actors of the period demanded greater political participation and the expansion of public policies.

With re-democratization in Brazil, and other countries in the region, civil society underwent a period of political rediscovery, with notable action from social movements at the public sphere (Alvarez 1988; Costa 1994; Pinto 2006). This period is characterized by the resurgence of far-reaching social movements, established from a multiplicity of issues, demands, and topics, including unions, grassroots and neighborhood organizations, women's, environmental and student movements, basic ecclesial communities, and other forms of association. The women's movements took a leading role in the re-democratization of Brazil. The actions of civil society, through social movements, contributed towards the dissemination of a new concept of citizenship – active citizenship, that made its way to the core of a large part of social and political thinking (Paoli 2002).

In 1988, Brazil built a new Constitution, in which a welfare system was more properly established. The Constitution defined the equality of citizenship and social rights as universal. The state was considered responsible for providing social protection, allowances, housing, education, and healthcare. Measures were defined to ensure the expansion of labor rights, such as limiting the working week to 44 hours, workplace safety, the payment of overtime and vacations, maternity and paternity leave, the right to union membership and to strike (Coutinho 2013; Fagnani 2005). Social security policy was based on health, welfare, and social assistance policies, representing a move forward, in terms of social protection (Silva 2007). Social assistance policy became a constitutionally guaranteed right, in contrast to the culture of favors, and establishing that all people, even those outside the labor force, would have the right to social protection from the state. The first discussions on cash transfer began in this context.

Following promulgation of the Constitution, Brazil entered a rapid implementation phase of neoliberal policies during the 1990s, which began with President Fernando Collor de Melo's (1990–1992) government, and they were developed during Itamar Franco's (1992–1994) and Fernando Henrique Cardoso's (1995–2002) governments. There was a transformation in the employment standards in the country, with substantial consequences for social policies, the effects of which were felt differently by men and women, with a stronger negative impact on the latter. These transformations resulted in a significant decline in jobs in manufacturing activities, cuts in wages and jobs, outsourcing, and informalization of the labor market (Pochmann 2003; Baltar 2014; Saad-Filho 2015). Poverty spread throughout the country as a consequence.

The neoliberal reforms of these governments, with their ideologies and views on cuts in public spending, defined changes in Brazilian social policies, which began to focus on the more impoverished sectors of society, through poverty alleviation programs, in contradiction to the universal rights defined in the Constitution. As Saad-Filho argues (2015, 1229) "in essence, the Constitution created a Swedish-type universal welfare state, while the reforms curtailed, privatized and individualized social provision."

In the place of policies that contributed to a better distribution, and universal public service systems funded by progressive taxation, a minimal state was being installed, where individual provision was the recommendation, through insurance and private loans. CCTs arose as transitional measures, to support sections of the population that had historically been on the sidelines of successive, exclusionary socioeconomic development models and that, although they were workers, were unable to meet their own and their family's basic needs (Fagnani 2014). Poverty was gradually defining social policies in the country, with CCTs performing a dual role: preventing extreme poverty and, at the same time, supporting their precarious inclusion in the labor market.

The model to combat poverty, formulated within a context of adjustments, received strong criticism, including: i) reducing the problem of inequality to a problem of poverty; ii) the emphasis on palliative aspects, to the detriment of structural ones that produce and reproduce poverty and inequality; iii) depoliticization of the issue of poverty, in favor of a technical or managerial discourse; iv) instrumental use of reproductive obligations socially attributed to women; v) the priority given to targeted policies, to the detriment of universal ones, and vi) the adoption of conditionalities, to the detriment of the affirmation of rights (Telles 1999; Stein 2000; Mariano 2008). The combination of these different factors, pointed out by critics, has resulted in policies with little capacity to reduce social inequalities in Brazil. According to Lena Lavinas (2004, 67), their "objective is not to end poverty, but to ensure a minimum level of social reproduction that mitigates the ravishing effects of adjustment policies."

With the PT's arrival in the federal government in 2003, there was an expectation that the new center-left government's policy would promote a structural change capable of transforming a social context that historically defined the country as being one of the most unequal in the world. However, although this period saw an improvement in the lower social classes' living conditions, due to government efforts to implement cash transfer policies, the same dedication was not allocated to expanding and improving universal policies, and promoting the structural changes that would have been key in decreasing social inequalities in the country.

In recent decades, the financialization processes, typical of neoliberalism, became a significant tendency in a large number of countries around the world. Lavinas (2017) highlights that this process needs to be understood, to interpret the current economic, political, and social situation. Studies show that there was economic growth in Brazil between 2004 and 2013, due to the increase in consumption by low-income families. However, Lavinas argues that this increase in consumption was less to do with a real increase in these families' incomes, and more with the ease of accessing credit. People and families became indebted, made easier by purchases in installments with high interest rates, and accelerated access to private healthcare, education, and social security services. The limit on consumption imposed by income disparities began to have little importance, with easy access to credit, albeit associated with one of the highest interest rates in the world. Thus, indebtedness was then used as an indicator of social inclusion, and debt renegotiation an alternative to the economic exclusion that limited access to consumption. However, the strategy of development through increased consumption, financed by high-interest rates, was unable to guarantee economic growth for long, and one of its side effects was de-industrialization and an increase in the export of commodities (Lavinas 2017).

One of the recent project's central problems is that there was nothing to combat the structural factors that generate poverty. The cash transfer initiative, and corresponding credit incentives for micro-entrepreneurship, started to be adopted as a safe path towards social development, and the alleviation of poverty. In this perspective, an improvement in people's living conditions only means access to survival conditions, rather than the construction of conditions for citizenship, and more effective participation in society.

## Development, Structure, and Management of *Bolsa Família*

Conditional cash transfer programs started to be more effectively promoted in Brazil in 1995, with the implementation of pioneering experiences at the municipal level, in some cities around the country: Campinas (São Paulo), Ribeirão Preto (São Paulo), Santos (São Paulo), and Brasília (Federal District). In 1996, the first cash transfer experiences began at the federal level, with the creation of the *Programa de Erradicação do Trabalho Infantil* (PETI) (Eradication of Child Labor Program) and reformulation of the *Benefício de Prestação Continuada* (BPC) (Continuous Cash Benefit).[1] In 1997, National Congress approved Law no. 9.533, which enabled the federal government to sign agreements with all the municipalities, so they could implement cash transfer programs. This law included conditionalities in the areas of health, education, and labor. In 2001, new federal programs emerged, such as *Bolsa Escola* and *Bolsa Alimentação* (school and food payments), which were introduced in a decentralized way in most Brazilian municipalities (Silva 2007). *Bolsa Escola*, introduced by Law no. 10.219, of April 11, 2001, had the objectives of enabling children and adolescents to have access to school, including families in their children's educational process, and reducing dropout rates and child labor.

In October 2003, the *Bolsa Família* Program was established by the president, Luiz Inácio Lula da Silva, through Provisional Measure 132, which was later changed into Law 10.836. Decree 5.209, of September 17, 2004, determined that the program's aim was to unify procedures to administer and execute cash transfer actions, and federal government registration. Therefore, there was a significant increase in the federal cash transfer budget, in comparison with prior investments. The Ministry of Social Development and Fight Against Hunger (now the Ministry of Citizenship) was created in January 2004, with the central goal of unifying cash transfer initiatives. Cash transfer policy became the central axis of social protection in the country.

One of the main focuses of BF is targeting families living in poverty and extreme poverty, which is calculated from income limits. It has been observed that most developing countries have prioritized this target, with the justification of financial limitations, more efficient spending, and, from some perspectives, greater social justice. The idea is that this strategy has a greater impact on alleviating poverty, since it concentrates its actions on the most deprived. Cobo (2012) highlights that targeting uses a variety of instruments, to select and classify individuals who meet the programs' eligibility criteria. This also includes self-targeting and an evaluation of the individual or family. Silva (2016) argues that "targeting," in general terms, can be understood as directing resources and programs to certain population groups, considered vulnerable within society. They are adopted in countries with larger economic and poverty issues, especially in the neoliberal context, in which limiting public policy expenditure guides the adoption of targeted social policies.

Families' access to BF initially takes place with registration on the *Cadastro Único de Programas Sociais do Governo Federal, or Cadastro Único,* (Single Registry of Social Programs of the Federal Government), system which was established in July 2001, and regulated in June 2007. The Special Department for Social Development within the Ministry of Citizenship, *Caixa Econômica Federal* (CEF) (Federal Savings Bank), and the municipal governments manage and operationalize *Cadastro Único*. This registration is the gateway to social programs at federal, state, and municipal levels. It is also an instrument for identification and the socioeconomic characterization of low-income families. Information is collected on the following aspects through this registration: income; number of people living in the household; housing conditions; conditions to access labor; and the existence of any disabilities that may affect family members. Families may register on *Cadastro Único* if they have a monthly income per person equal or lower than half a minimum salary, if their monthly income does not exceed three minimum salaries, and also if their income is higher than three minimum salaries, provided, in this last case, that their registration is linked to inclusion in programs in the three levels of government (municipal, state, and federal).

Once included on *Cadastro Único*, to be eligible for BF, the family must meet the program's specific rules, and is also dependent on the availability of federal government funding, and the quota of resources allocated to the municipality in which they are registered. BF classifies the beneficiary families in two groups; one follows the poverty criterion, and the other, the extreme poverty criterion. Poor families have a per capita income of between BRL 89.01[2] and 178.00. Families in this income bracket, with children or adolescents aged up to 17, benefit from the program. BF considers families in extreme poverty to be those with a per capita income of up to BRL 89.00 per month. For these families, income is the only criteria for eligibility. These values are less than the World Bank's classification for extreme poverty, which is USD 1.90 per day, or approximately BRL 145.00 per month. In September 2019, there were 27,796,543 families on *Cadastro Único*, of which 13.505.758 received *Bolsa Família* (SAGI n.d.).

Not all those eligible for the benefit receive it. But sometimes people and BF agents do not know about the necessary criteria. The lack of knowledge on the inclusion criteria may also generate conflict and distrust among residents of the same region or neighborhood who live in the same conditions of poverty.

At the federal level the Ministry of Citizenship is responsible for coordinating, following-up, and supervising the management, implementation, and execution of *Cadastro Único*, issuing operational instructions, training staff, evaluating quality, and adopting oversight and control procedures. CEF is responsible for processing the information collected and paying the benefit. Payment is made through a magnetic card, issued by CEF to the holder of the benefit, from a bank account. The municipality is responsible for processing family registration, by joining the *Sistema Único de Assistência Social* (SUAS) (Unified Social Assistance System), which is the institution responsible for management of the *Política Nacional de Assistência Social* (PNAS) (National Social Assistance Policy). SUAS acts within the municipalities through the *Centro de Referência de Assistência Social* (CRAS) (Reference Centers for Social Assistance).

The "family" is the unit of reference for registration on *Cadastro Único*, and the program recognizes it as a nuclear unit, with one or more people, who contribute towards its income, or have their expenses met by it, and all reside within the same household. They do not need to be blood related. The families who are identified for specific registration are: indigenous people, *quilombola* residents, homeless families, families residing in collective households, families with hospitalized relatives, in shelters, or are in detention for more than 12 months, Roma families, families belonging to *terreiro* communities,[3] extractivist families, small-scale fishing families, family farmers, families who live from collecting recyclable materials, families living in riverside communities, families settled through land reform, and families living in camps. The person responsible for the family unit must belong to the family, reside in the household, be over the age of 16, and preferably be a woman (SAGI n.d.).

Identification of a household with a family is a controversial option. Saraceno (1997, 17) evaluates that living together, under the same roof, is one of the simplest and most obvious indicators of the existence of a family. However, it is not a sufficient characterization, since not all the people who live together may be considered, and/or self-define as families. There are various household arrangements, including relatives other than children, hindering the establishment of a standard family. The multiplicity of family typologies, from the perspective of its structure, does not only create difficulties for scholars, but also for legislators, administrators, and executors of public policies, caught between the need to set clear criteria, and the observation of an empirical variety, which a growing segment of the population is moving towards (Saraceno 1997). This debate refers to the criticism made of the familistic approach (discussed in more detail later in this chapter), which is predominant in cash transfer programs. On implementation of BF, there were frequent occurrences of variations in the combination between family and household. In these variations, groups of people who live in the same household self-classify as distinct families, especially when they do not share daily financial expenses, such as food. On the other hand, people who live in different households self-classify as family, especially when they share financial commitments.

When registering on *Cadastro Único*, self-declaration is considered sufficient information to demonstrate the family income. However, remaining on the program is dependent on fulfilling conditionalities, and the results ascertained by the federal government, by cross-checking various databases, with data on work and income. If an adult family member obtains a job that places the family income slightly above the established limit, the family may be excluded. According to Cobo (2012, 187), "this occurs without observing other conditions of poverty that still affect the family, or even waiting for the investment made in the education of children and adolescents, in terms of completing basic education."

According to the Summary of Social Indicators, disseminated by the *Instituto Brasileiro de Geografia e Estatística* (IBGE) (IBGE 2019a) (Brazilian Institute of Geography and Statistics), the total number of people living in extreme poverty has been growing since the economic crisis began in 2015. In 2018, 52.5 million people, 72.7% of whom were black or brown, were below the poverty line. In contrast with the growth of poverty, the percentage of families who receive *Bolsa Família* has been decreasing for seven years, falling from 15.9% in 2012, to 13.7% in 2018 (IBGE 2019a). In the federal government's general budget, approved for 2020, the expectation is a reduction in BF expenditure, in comparison to 2019. Control over public spending was the main argument for the measure, thus reinforcing the residual nature of this type of selective targeting. As Silva argues (2016, 57), it is residualist targeting, based on market justice "which reduces social policies to residual actions, targeting the sectors that are on the margins of inclusive economic processes." Table 2.1 demonstrates the distribution of benefits in different regions of the country.

Table 2.1 shows that the northeast of the country houses the largest population living in extreme poverty. It has always been the region with the lowest human development indexes in the country: characterized by drought, a lack of public services, and low formal employment rates. Data from the Brazilian Institute of Social and Economic Analysis, presented by Silva (Ibase 2008, cited by Silva

**TABLE 2.1** Benefit distribution per region

| *Region* | *Families* | *Total BRL* | *Benefit Average BRL* |
|---|---|---|---|
| Northeast | 6,942,227 | 1,272,592,651.00 | 183.31 |
| North | 1,750,691 | 350,513,873.00 | 200.21 |
| left-West | 653,506 | 102,436,811.00 | 156.75 |
| Southeast | 3,553,154 | 587,847,630.00 | 165.44 |
| South | 836,763 | 132,288,231.00 | 158.10 |
| Total | 13,736,341 | 2,445,679,196.00 | 178.04 |

Source: Ministry of Social Development and Fight against Hunger, 2018. Prepared by the authors.

2016, 176), shows that the main use of the benefit in this region is for food (87%), indicating that the majority of recipients need this income as a way to meet their basic needs. With regards to the average value paid, the north region presents the highest average; the largest riverside communities and indigenous populations are located in this region.

BF conditionalities are limited to education, health, and social assistance. For healthcare, families must follow up weighing and vaccinating children aged under seven. Pregnant women and nursing mothers must attend regular appointments at basic healthcare units. For education, families must keep children in school, have an attendance rate of above 85% for children and adolescents aged up to 15, and a minimum of 75% for adolescents aged between 16 and 17. For social assistance, children and adolescents aged up to 15, in at-risk situations, or removed from child labor by PETI, must participate in Socialization and Bond Strengthening Services, with a minimum attendance of 85% of the monthly allocation, and update their registration every two years.

Families who do not fulfill these conditionalities are penalized in the following way: on the first occasion they do not comply, they receive a warning; the second time, they have the benefit blocked for 30 days; if they remain non-complaint, it will be suspended for 60 days; after this, if the non-compliance continues, the benefit will be cancelled. Table 2.2 demonstrates the sanctions received by the families.

The family is informed of the penalty they will receive for non-compliance with the conditionalities via a notification, which can be written correspondence or a message on the benefit bank statement. The person responsible for the family may appeal to the municipal administrator, if they believe there has been a mistake. The administrator is responsible for making an evaluation and decision. In the case of non-compliance with conditionalities for adolescents aged between 16 and 17, only the young person's benefit will be blocked/cancelled, with no impact on the remainder of the value received by the family. If the benefit is cancelled for non-compliance of conditionalities, the family can only return to the program after 180 days.

**TABLE 2.2** Sanctions for not fulfilling conditionalities

| *Non-compliance* | *Sanction* | *Effect* |
|---|---|---|
| 1st occasion | Warning | The family receives a warning but it does not affect or alter receipt of the benefit. |
| 2nd occasion | Block | The family has the benefit blocked for 30 days but receives the accumulated value the following month. |
| 3rd occasion | 1st Suspension | The family has the benefit suspended for 60 days, and does not receive a back payment. |
| 4th occasion | 2nd Suspension | The family has the benefit blocked for 60 days and does not receive a back payment. |
| 5th occasion | Cancellation | The family has the benefit cancelled. |

Source: Ministry of Social Development and Figth against Hunger, 2014. Prepared by the authors.

CRAS follows up the beneficiaries who do not fulfill the conditionalities. One obstacle is that CRAS technicians are only informed of this when the family is already facing some form of sanction, via quarterly reports received from the federal government, which impedes preventive action. Another challenge is the difficulty in establishing intersectoral management of the public policies involved in the conditionalities, through liaison between health, education, and social assistance. The lack of this kind of work negatively affects the service provided to the families, fragmenting actions and not meeting their needs. Women are the ones most affected by program deficiencies.

These rules, and the way that BF operates, incorporate a familistic focus. In its actions, the family is a word used as a euphemism for women. In other words, those who assist the state to fulfill its role are, in fact, women, and not families, as we will demonstrate in the following section.

## Women, *Bolsa Família*, and Familism in Brazil

There is a commonly used expression in Brazil: "poverty has a gender and color." According to the criteria adopted by the World Bank in 2017, the country was classified as upper-middle income, with a poverty line suggested by the bank of USD 5.50 per day in purchasing power parity. Using this criterion, that year IBGE estimated that 26.5% of the population was under the poverty line, the equivalent of 55 million people. In the same group were 56.9% of households headed by women without a spouse, and with children aged under 14, and 64.4% of households headed by black or brown women without a spouse, and with children. With regards to income from employment, in 2017, white people received, an average of 72.5% more than black or brown people, and men received an average of 29.7% more than women. Monetary poverty has a greater effect on black or brown people, women, children, and adolescents aged under 14 (IBGE 2018b).

In order to understand the monetary poverty of Brazilian women, it is important to consider the interconnections between productive and reproductive labor. Women work more hours than men (adding together paid and unpaid working hours) and, despite having more education, they receive lower salaries. In 2016, women aged 14 or over dedicated an average of 20.9 hours per week to the care of others and/or household chores, while men dedicated 11.1 hours (IBGE 2018a). In 2017, the proportion of children aged under three who went to school or day care in the country was 30.4% (IBGE 2018a). Based on 2013 data from the *Pesquisa Nacional de Amostra por Domicílio* (PNAD) (National Household Sample Survey), Medeiros and Pinheiro (2018) noted that when adding together paid and unpaid work, women worked approximately three hours a week more than men. Considering the division between paid and unpaid work, a gender bias is noted with the use of time: in paid work, men work an average of 13 hours per week more than women; in unpaid work, women spend an average of 17 hours more than men. This data shows the negative effect for women, resulting from gendered and racial division in the allocation of "productive" work and distribution of "reproductive" work.

As noted in the Interviewer Manual of the *Secretaria de Avaliação e Gestão da Informação* (SAGI), BF does not recognize domestic, unpaid activities performed by women, for the benefit of other family members, as work. This rule hides a significant percentage of female labor under the label "housewife" (SAGI 2011). Relying on housewives' efforts is a fundamental asset for these programs to meet their targets.

The racial issue in the country is a key conditioning factor to understand poverty. Black women occupy positions with a lower social prestige and wages, have less access to social security benefits, and are over-represented in the population living in poverty. An example of this condition is the allocation of these women in domestic labor. In 2015, 18% of working black women were engaged in domestic labor, while the percentage of white women was 10.3% (IPEA, n.d.).[4] Domestic labor perfectly illustrates the intersections of gender, class, and race inequalities, and the adoption of paid domestic labor is often a delegation strategy that enables white, middle-class women with higher levels of education to access jobs with a higher social prestige and better salaries (Bruschini and Lombardi 2000; Hirata and Kergoat 2007).

Historically, Brazilian social policies responded to poverty based on the familistic approach, which has produced more noteworthy effects for women. We use familism to define the approach adopted by social policies that allocate a central position to families and, often, almost exclusively, in the provision of protection and care of its members. In this approach, if the family fails, public policies act as auxiliary devices (Castilho and Carloto 2010; Moser and Mulinari 2017).

However, who is the family that allegedly cares for, protects, and seeks assistance when it is needed? According to feminist interpretations, familistic policies are characterized as considering the family, and women, as synonyms and, consequently, these terms are used interchangeably (Jelin 1995; Molyneux 2007; Castilho and Carloto 2010).

*Familism* sees women from the position of mother and carer, taking them as representatives of the domestic group in matters related to social assistance. Familistic policies uncritically assume the female responsibilities related to the tasks of social reproduction, and reinforces them (Jelin 1995). As Elizabeth Jelin (1995) points out, a special and central issue is that *familism* guides policies and actions that replace the concern for empowering women, with the defense of policies that reinforce the family. A characteristic of these policies is the reference to poverty without any connection to a criticism of female subordination, even when the feminization of poverty is invoked (Jelin 1995; Molyneux 2007; Miguel 2016).

The reinforcement of family by social policies also involves the ideological and moral character present in the defense of certain family arrangements, notably the nuclear family, made up of spouses of opposite sexes and the children from that union. The alleged "structured family," in addition to having this composition, would have the necessary means to meet its members' needs, not requiring social assistance. Something that differs from this hegemonic model in Brazilian society is derogatorily called an "unstructured family" (Goldani 1993; Fonseca 2005). In defense of the family, as an alleged way to ensure social order, political and theoretical principles are proposed that legitimize female subordination and, therefore, male domination.

In general, these policies combine the familistic and maternalistic approaches. Women are understood from their link to motherhood and, thus, "mother" is also a word that state agents use as synonymous with woman. Therefore, family, mother, and woman are indistinct expressions. Adopting a feminist perspective, in order to analyze these experiences, requires a deconstruction of these associations because they naturalize, essentialize and create an amalgam among them, erecting obstacles against a change in the status given to women (Carloto and Mariano 2010).

Familism and maternalism are approaches that have applied to Brazilian policies for women for many years. This was the focus when mother-child protection programs were the main actions directed towards them (Lavinas 1996). The family, motherhood, and the various ways of being a woman underwent significant transformations, especially since the 1970s. However, the political, moral, and instrumental conceptions included in social policies did not always follow these changes. BF has inherited this cultural and institutional tradition because it enables the instrumental use of women's work.

BF's instrumentality of women's role in domestic spaces contributes towards the program's efficacy and efficiency. Women tend to use the benefit to improve their family's living conditions, especially their children's, with food, clothing, the purchase of school supplies, furniture for the house, and construction materials to improve the physical conditions of the house, thus contributing towards alleviating poverty (Mariano and Carloto 2011). The characteristic of gender is useful for the program's success; however, it may generate undesired consequences in several aspects. Women are among the main victims of poverty and hunger, to a large extent due to factors related to racial inequalities, and gender inequalities. Not using this information as data that should be taken into account by the program is not only bad for female recipients of the benefit, but also compromises fulfilling part of its goals, as Teresa Sacchet explores in chapter three of this book.

## Final Considerations

The discussions presented in this chapter led us to several conclusions. Historically, Brazilian economic development did not effectively contribute towards reducing inequalities. The level of social inequality, measured by the Gini index, is higher today than it was almost 60 years ago: from 0.535 in 1960 to 0.545 in 2018 (IBGE 2019b). Gender and racial inequalities remain, and are demonstrated by poverty and unemployment rates, salary differences, and types of job. However, beyond these material issues, they are also perpetuated in the way women, the majority of whom are black, are included in social programs that seek to reduce poverty, such as *Bolsa Família*, from a traditional gender perspective, in which they are considered as having the main responsibility for the family.

BF represented an advance in relation to previous programs, insofar as a cash transfer provided the families with greater autonomy for use of the benefit. Nevertheless, this achievement coexists with limitations, such as low investments in universal social policies, especially education and healthcare; a conservative approach towards the adoption of familism and maternalism; a residual targeting model, with a low poverty line and high selectivity among the public that meets the program's income criteria; and conditionalities, a requirement that currently performs the moral role of socially and politically legitimizing cash transfers to the poorest, at the expense of the time of the women who receive the benefit.

Despite the advances that we have indicated, the Brazilian decision to adopt cash transfers as the main pillar of the social protection system is flawed because it does not deal with the central, structural issues that generate poverty and inequalities. Poverty reduction policies are also important for women, insofar as they are the ones who usually have to deal with its consequences within the family. However, one of the program's limitations is not considering and effectively incorporating the way in which gender and racial inequalities affect poverty, in the design and implementation of its policies.

## Notes

1 The *Benefício de Prestação Continuada* (BPC) (Continuous Cash Benefit) is a cash benefit of one minimum salary for people of any age with disabilities or for the elderly, aged over 65, who have long-term difficulties, of a physical, mental, intellectual, or sensory nature and who, for this reason, have difficulties in fully participating and interacting in society. For this benefit to be granted, the family's monthly income must be up to ¼ of the minimum salary per person (INSS 2020).
2 The average annual sales price of the commercial dollar in 2018: BRL 3.65. Source: Central Bank of Brazil.
3 Traditional peoples and communities of African descent are defined as groups that are organized through civilizing values, and a worldview brought to the country by Africans transferred here during the system of slavery, which enabled an African civilizing continuation in Brazil, forming their own territories, characterized by a community experience, receptivity and providing services to the community (SEPPIR 2013, 12).
4 Available at http://www.ipea.gov.br/retrato/indicadores_trabalho_domestico_remunerado.html. Accessed September 15, 2019.

## References

Alvarez, Sonia. 1988. "Politizando as Relações de Gênero e Engendrando a Democracia." In *Democratizando o Brasil*, edited by Alfred Stepan, 315–380. Rio de Janeiro: Paz e Terra.

Baltar, Paulo. 2014. "Crescimento da Economia e Mercado de Trabalho no Brasil." In *Presente e Futuro do Desenvolvimento Brasileiro*, edited by André Bojikian Calixtre, André Martins Biancarelli, and Marcos Antonio Macedo Cintra, 423–468. Brasília: IPEA.

Bruschini, Cristina and Maria Rosa Lombardi. 2000. "A Bipolaridade do Trabalho Feminino no Brasil Contemporâneo." *Cadernos de Pesquisa* 110: 67–104. https://doi.org/10.1590/S0100-15742000000200003.

Carloto, Cassia Maria and Silvana Mariano. 2010. "No Meio do Caminho entre o Privado e o Público: Um Debate sobre o Papel das Mulheres na Política de Assistência Social." *Revista Estudos Feministas* 18, no. 2: 451–471. https://doi.org/10.1590/S0104-026X2010000200009.

Castilho, Cleide de Fátima Viana, and Cássia Maria Carloto. 2010. "O Familismo na Política de Assistência Social: Um Reforço À Desigualdade de Gênero." Work presented in I Simpósio sobre Estudos de Gênero e Políticas Públicas, Londrina, Brasil.

Cobo, Bárbara. 2012. *Políticas Focalizadas de Transferência de Renda: Contextos e Desafios*. São Paulo: Cortez.

Corrêa, Vanessa Petrelli and Monica Simioni (Eds). 2011. *Desenvolvimento e Igualdade: homenagem aos 80 anos de Maria da Conceição Tavares*. Rio de Janeiro: IPEA.

Costa, Sergio. 1994. "Esfera Pública, Redescoberta da Sociedade Civil e Movimentos Sociais no Brasil: Uma Abordagem Tentativa." *Novos Estudos* 38, no. 1: 138–152.

Coutinho, Diogo R. 2013. "Decentralization and Coordination in Social Law and Policy." In *Law and the New Developmental State*, edited by David M. Trubek et al., 253–288. Cambridge: Cambridge University Press. https://doi.org/10.1017/CBO9781139381888.011.

Draibe, Sônia M. 1993. "The Welfare State no Brasil: Características e Perspectivas." *Caderno de Pesquisa* 8: 1–50.

Fagnani, Eduardo. 2005. "Política Social no Brasil (1964–2002)" ["Social Policy in Brazil (1964–2002)"]. PhD dissertation, Universidade Estadual de Campinas.

Fagnani, Eduardo. 2014. "Política Social e Desigualdade Social." *Texto para Discussão* 238: 1–7.

Fonseca, Claudia. 2005. "Concepções de Família e Práticas de Intervenção: Uma Contribuição Antropológica." *Saúde e Sociedade* 14, no. 2: 50–59. https://doi.org/10.1590/S0104-12902005000200006.

Goldani, Ana Maria. 1993. "As Famílias no Brasil Contemporâneo e o Mito da Desestruturação." *Cadernos Pagu* 1, no. 1: 68–110.

Hirata, Helena and Daniele Kergoat. 2007. "Novas Configurações da Divisão Sexual do Trabalho." *Cadernos de Pesquisa* 37, no. 132: 595–609. https://doi.org/10.1590/S0100-15742007000300005.

IBGE (Instituto Brasileiro de Geografia e Estatística). 2018a. "Estatísticas de gênero." https://www.ibge.gov.br/apps/snig/v1/?loc=0.

IBGE (Instituto Brasileiro de Geografia e Estatística). 2018b. *Síntese de indicadores sociais: uma análise das condições de vida da população brasileira 2018*. Rio de Janeiro: IBGE.

IBGE (Instituto Brasileiro de Geografia e Estatística). 2019a. *Síntese de indicadores sociais: uma análise das condições de vida da população brasileira 2019*. Rio de Janeiro: IBGE.

IBGE (Instituto Brasileiro de Geografia e Estatística). 2019b. "Pnad Contínua 2018: 10% da população concentram 43,1% da massa de rendimentos do país." https://agenciadenoticias.ibge.gov.br/agencia-sala-de-imprensa/2013-agencia-de-noticias/releases/25700-pnad-continua-2018-10-da-populacao-concentram-43-1-da-massa-de-rendimentos-do-pais.

INSS (Instituto Nacional de Seguro Social). "BPC (Benefício de Prestação Continuada)." n.d. https://www.inss.gov.br/tag/bpc/.

IPEA (Instituto de Pesquisa Econômica e Aplicada). n.d. "Retrato das Desigualdades de Gênero e Raça." http://www.ipea.gov.br/retrato/indicadores_trabalho_domestico_remunerado.html.

Jelin, Elizabeth. 1995. "Familia y Género: Notas para el Debate." *Revista Estudos Feministas* 2, no 3: 395–413. https://doi.org/10.1590/%25x.

Lavinas, Lena. 1996. "As Mulheres no Universo da Pobreza: O Caso Brasileiro." *Revista Estudos Feministas* 4, no. 2: 464–479. https://doi.org/10.1590/%25x.

Lavinas, Lena. 2004. "Universalizando Direitos." *Observatório da Cidadania* 59, 67–74.

Lavinas, Lena. 2017. *The Takeover of Social Policy by Financialization: The Brazilian Paradox*. New York: Palgrave Macmillan.

Mariano, Silvana and Cassia Maria Carloto. 2011. "Gênero e Combate à Pobreza no Programa Bolsa Família." In *Faces da Desigualdade de Gênero e Raça no Brasil*, edited by Alinne Bonetti, and Maria Aparecida de Abreu, 61–78. Brasília: IPEA.

Mariano, Silvana. 2008. "Feminismo, Estado e Proteção Social: a Cidadania das Mulheres Pobres." PhD dissertation, Universidade Estadual de Campinas.

MDS (Ministério de Desenvolvimento Social e Combate à Fome). 2018. "Bolsa Família beneficia mais de 13.7 milhões de família em junho." http://mds.gov.br/area-de-imprensa/noticias/2018/junho/bolsa-familia-beneficia-mais-de-13-7-milhoes-de-familias-em-junho.

MDS (Ministério de Desenvolvimento Social e Combate à Fome). n.d. "Bolsa Família." https://aplicacoes.mds.gov.br/sagirmps/bolsafamilia/.

Medeiros, Marcelo and Luana Simões Pinheiro. 2018. "Desigualdades de Gênero em Tempo de Trabalho Pago e Não-Pago no Brasil, 2013." *Sociedade e Estado* 33, no. 1: 161–188. https://doi.org/10.1590/s0102-699220183301007.

Miguel, Antonia Celeste. 2016. "Familismo, Maternalismo e Políticas Sociais: o Caso da Política Nacional de Microcrédito do Governo Lula." PhD dissertation, Universidade Federal de São Carlos.

Molyneux, Maxine. 2007. *Change and Continuity in Social Protection in Latin America*. Ginebra: Unrisd.

Moser, Liliane and Bruna Aparecida Pavoski Mulinari. 2017. "Proteção Social e Família: o Caráter Familista da Política Social no Brasil." Work presented in II Seminário Nacional de Serviço Social, Trabalho e Políticas Sociais, Florianópolis, Brasil.

Paoli, Maria Celia. 2002. "Empresas e Responsabilidade Social: os Enredamentos da Cidadania no Brasil." In *Democratizar a Democracia: os Caminhos da Democracia Participativa*, edited by Boaventura de Sousa Santos, 373–418. Rio de Janeiro: Civilização Brasileira.

Pinto, Celia Regina Jardim. 2006. "As ONGS e a Política no Brasil: Presença de Novos Atores." *Dados-Revista de Ciências Sociais* 49, no. 3: 651–670. https://doi.org/10.1590/S0011-52582006000300008.

Pochmann, Marcio. 2003. "Sobre a Nova Condição de Agregado Social no Brasil" ["On the New Condition of Social Aggregate in Brazil"]. *Revista Paranaense de Desenvolvimento* 105, no.1: 5–23.

Saad-Filho, Alfredo. 2015. "Social Policy for Neoliberalism: The Bolsa Família Programme in Brazil." *Development and Change* 46, no. 6: 1227–1252. https://doi.org/10.1111/dech.12199.

SAGI (Secretaria de Avaliação e Gestão da Informação). 2011. *Manual do Entrevistador*. Third edition. Brasília: MDS.

SAGI (Secretaria de Avaliação e Gestão da Informação). n.d. "Relatório sobre o Bolsa Família e Cadastro Único." https://aplicacoes.mds.gov.br/sagi/RIv3/geral/relatorio_form.php?p_ibge=&area=0&ano_pesquisa=&mes_pesquisa=&saida=pdf&relatorio=153&ms=623,460,587,589,450,448,1237.

Saraceno, Chiara. 1997. *Sociologia da Família*. Lisboa: Editorial Estampa.

SEPPIR (Secretaria de Políticas de Promoção da Igualdade Racial). 2013. *Plano Nacional de Desenvolvimento Sustentável de Povos e Comunidades Tradicionais de Matriz Africana*. First edition. Brasília, Federal District.

Silva, Maria Ozanira da Silva. 1995. "Origem e desenvolvimento do Welfare State." *Revista de Políticas Públicas* 1, no. 1: 1–23.

Silva, Maria Ozanira da Silva. 2007. "O Bolsa Família: Problematizando Questões Centrais na Política de Transferência de Renda no Brasil." *Ciência e Saúde Coletiva* 12, no. 6: 1429–1439. https://doi.org/10.1590/S1413-81232007000600006.

Silva, Maria Ozanira da Silva (Ed.). 2016. *O Bolsa Família: Verso e Reverso*. Campinas: Papel Social.

Stein, Rosa Helena. 2000. "A (Nova) Questão Social e as Estratégias para seu Enfrentamento." *Ser Social* 6, no. 1: 133–168. https://doi.org/10.26512/ser_social.v0i6.12853.

Telles, Vera Silva. 1999. "A 'Nova Questão Social' Brasileira: ou Como as Figuras de Nosso Atraso Viraram Símbolo de Nossa Modernidade." *Caderno CRH* 12, no. 30: 85–110.

# 3

# BEYOND DISTRIBUTION

## Issues of Gender Justice in Fighting Poverty in Brazil[1]

*Teresa Sacchet*

### Introduction

Conditional cash transfer (CCTs) programs, such as *Bolsa Família* (BF), are the most common response offered by Latin American governments to the issue of poverty in the region. Developed in the 1990s as a specific model of social protection, CCTs were implemented within a very particular political and economic environment. After the so-called lost decade, which marked the 1980s in Latin America with marginal economic growth and with structural adjustment programs that led to a reduction in spending on universal social policies, a phase of targeted public policy took off in the 1990s and grew over the decades that followed. In addition to cuts to social spending, the international scenario of rapidly expanding neoliberalism led to setbacks in labor and social rights that have exacerbated socioeconomic inequalities (Draibe 1993).[2] In this context, current models of CCT were developed with a twofold purpose: on the one hand, to protect the most vulnerable social strata from the impact of market failures on their income and consumption of goods and services – while at the same time creating conditions for their financial independence via human development (HD) initiatives – and, on the other hand, to provide conditions conducive to economic growth and capitalist reforms.

Although some components of this policy model may vary from country to country, they maintain similar foundations and designs. In addition to income transfer, which varies according to the family's level of income and composition, they tend to focus on the family, transferring cash to female heads of households, and to be accompanied by human development initiatives that are considered important both as a means to break the so-called intergenerational cycle of poverty, as well as to contribute to the financial independence of the beneficiaries and their families.

Studies of BF highlight its positive impact on central indicators of social development related to income and to fighting hunger and poverty (Lavinas, Cobo, and Veigas 2012), consumption of goods and services, education, health, and child mortality rates (Hanlon, Barrientos, and Hulme 2010; Soares, Ribas, and Osório 2010), family planning (Alves and Cavenaghi 2013), among others. These and other results have secured wide approval for the BF from international institutions and scholars, leading to the claim that this program has initiated a new trend in social protection in Latin America and should be held up as an example for other developing countries (Barrientos 2011, 2013; Hanlon, Barrientos, and Hulme 2010). Despite the predominance of women in this and other similar programs, many studies discuss CCTs without mentioning this specificity or showing concern for a gender perspective.

Indeed, *Bolsa Família* has functioned well as an emergency measure against poverty in Brazil and has worked in that capacity as a model for other countries. International recognition of the policy was evidenced in the creation of World Without Poverty (WWP) in 2013, an initiative of the United Nations, the World Bank, and the Brazilian Government created to systematize knowledge and provide information internationally on Brazil's approach to poverty reduction. However, from a gender and race perspective, there are a number of issues that make it less attractive as a policy model. This chapter will focus on said issues.

Women, especially black women, are the main recipients of social programs like BF. In 2014, women made up 93% of the BF's primary beneficiaries. They were also the heads of households of 88% of families enrolled in the *Cadastro Único* (Single Registry), which is the main database for access to any social program – 68% of them were headed by black women (ONU Mulheres 2016). When one speaks of poverty and access to social programs in Brazil, one is mainly talking about the experiences of black women. The predominance of women as beneficiaries of BF follows from an official recommendation based on a traditional understanding of gender roles that reinforces a division of labor by gender by relying on a particular view of women as good mothers (Molyneux 2006). According to this perspective, women are naturally responsible and committed to the best interests of their children, employing the resources at their disposal in ways that effectively ensure their families' well-being, which results in more efficient government spending. The deliberate focus on women (or mothers), based on this instrumental perspective, pays little or no attention to women's interests and gender relations and has been criticized by feminists who consider the adverse consequences of such a view for women themselves. These criticisms form the basis of the arguments presented in this chapter.

The policies analysed in this chapter are mainly those from the time of the PT government. After that period, since mid-2016, we have seen more than anything a dismantling of these policies that I indicate throughout the chapter. Recent changes in BF (discussed in the intruduction of this book) have weakened it as a project designed to fight poverty and at the same time have increased the costs of participating in this program for women. However, I will signal locate, and explain, inasmuch as possible, recent changes, and their implications, to the various dimensions of the program I explore.

The main objective of this chapter is to analyze BF and related policies aimed at promoting the financial independence and the human development of program beneficiaries and their dependents, from a gender perspective, which also includes consideration of issues of race and other intersectional matters. It intends to point out limitations in these projects due to the failure to incorporate such a perspective into their planning, implementation, and evaluation. The chapter also offers a discussion of possible initiatives that could make this program more oriented towards fostering gender justice.

The analysis is grounded on the capability approach to poverty and feminist theories of justice. Starting from the discussion of the concept of poverty as a lack of capability, the chapter considers to what extent CCTs, in particular BF, the focus of this study, promote human development. The work then develops a theoretical framework based on feminist perspectives on the concept of justice that will guide the analysis. The chapter proceeds to an analysis of *Bolsa Família* that reflects on its perspectives and political leanings, in order to discuss its limitations and consider alternatives based on a gender perspective. The final part summarizes the main issues addressed in the chapter and ends with concluding remarks.

Data analyzed and discussions raised stem from secondary study materials on the subject, such as chapters of academic books and journal articles, research and government reports, and lectures and seminars, among other sources. The data are also based on primary sources from interviews I conducted in February 2019 with women living in the poorest area of the *sertão* or hinterlands of Bahia for an earlier research project at the Federal University of Bahia, which intends to consider the impacts on women of recent changes to *Bolsa Família*. The study also draws on my own personal experience with this program. Between 2011 and 2014, I worked for the Federal Government as an advisor to the Executive Secretariat of the Ministry of Social Development and Fight Against Hunger, where I also coordinated its Gender and Women's Policy Committee. My experience as a member of the managerial body of the ministry that devised and implemented the BF program, as well as my work as a scholar and coordinator of a committee that challenged the limits of the existing policies for failing to include a gender perspective and proposed initiatives in this sense, enabled me to develop a specific view on that policy that informs my reading of it and the analysis I present in this chapter.

## Human Development for Whom?

Poverty is a contentious concept that encompasses objective categories related to access to tangible resources, especially income, and broader ones associated with cultural and political matters. The most traditional and narrowly defined interpretation of poverty associates it with lack of income or limited access to material means and opportunities. In this perspective, poverty is usually accessed based on considerations of poverty lines. Consistently, the notion of social development is closely tied to the idea of economic growth and stability, and social policy designs follow income generation initiatives. This conception informed much of the development work carried out during the 1960s and 1970s in different parts of the world and still stands today.

The works of Amartya Sen and Marta Nussbaum helped expand the concept of poverty beyond material means, offering conceptual support for shaping CCT policy frameworks. Concepts they developed or redefined, such as capability, functioning, and human capital, are broadly employed in academic, governmental, and multilateral circles. Amartya Sen's notion of poverty as lack of capability, or "the ability to do something" (Sen 2009) has particularly inspired the construction of a social development framework guided by the notion of the centrality of developing human capital. According to the capability approach, people's quality of life cannot be evaluated solely in terms of their access to material goods, but also, and particularly, in light of their potential to develop a certain functioning – that is, those things they are capable of doing or being in life, such as having a healthy body, educating themselves, having self-respect, participating in community life, etc. (Sen 1999). Sen (1979, 1999) considers that people differ in their abilities to turn resources into valuable "functionings." A physically disabled person, for example, needs different resources from her able-bodied peers in order to have similar capabilities. Thus, considerations of poverty based only on what people have, with disregard for what they might be able to do with it, are limited.

The capability approach attaches particular significance to the ability of people to build the kind of lives they have reason to value (Sen 1999; Nussbaum 2011). Poverty is seen as resulting mainly from constraints that impair people's freedom to choose and their capacity for action, which in order to be overcome require initiatives capable of fostering the development of such potentials. From this interpretation, Sen and Nussbaum put forward their idea about the centrality of initiatives meant to develop human capital, not as a means to an end (to improve material well-being), but as an achievement in itself, important for self-realization and development.

As I will discuss in greater breadth later in this chapter, although the capability approach has its inadequacies,[3] the idea of the interrelationship between welfare and capacity for action and self-realization that it champions has offered theoretical substance to broaden the concept of poverty and informed the rationale of initiatives aimed at fighting it. The concept of Human Development (HD), which Sen refers to as "the process of expanding the real freedoms that people enjoy" (Sen 1999, 3) and which the United Nations similarly defines as "the process of enlarging people's choices" (UNDP 1997, 15),[4] takes an important position in and is a center piece of the poverty reduction narrative of contemporary CCT programs such as BF.

Conditional cash transfer programs in Latin America began as isolated municipal and state projects developed by left-wing administrations during the 1990s and later were replicated and expanded upon by national governments (Lavinas

2013; Sánchez-Ancochea and Mattei 2011). Both at the local and national levels, these policies aimed at combating income poverty while concomitantly creating conditions to promote the economic autonomy of its recipients through human development initiatives (Bichir 2010). From the HD perspective advanced in CCTs, social inequalities limit opportunities for the improvement of knowledge and skills of members of the low-income groups, requiring them to access resources such as literacy, education, and basic skills, to be able to participate fully in society, and to be integrated into the labor market in a more qualified way. This dynamic, by contrast, would help to promote economic development that would serve as a safeguard against poverty in a "virtuous cycle."

According to Armando Barrientos, the idea of promoting social development through human development is what effectively distinguishes current CCT programs (which he calls "Human Development Income Transfers") from previous ones (Barrientos 2013). HD is underscored in the official texts and documents which supported the institution of BF, being presented as a center piece to long-term poverty reduction and breaking the so-called "circle of poverty" between generations. HD is operationalized through initiatives that help enhance individuals' overall skills, level of formal education, access to health programs, and so on (MDS 2014). *Plano Brasil Sem Miséria* (PBSM) (the Brazil Without Extreme Poverty Plan) further operationalizes these human development strategies through different actions, which will be discussed below.

## Plan *Brasil Sem Miséria* and the Human Development Project

In 2011, then-President Dilma Rousseff created the Brazil Without Extreme Poverty Plan, an ambitious project that included federal government initiatives integrated with those at the state and municipal levels, whose main objective was to eradicate extreme poverty through social assistance benefits and human development policies. Income benefits essentially consisted in conditional cash transfers by BF and the *Benefício de Prestação Continuada* (BPC) (Continuous Cash Benefit). Human development policies were operationalized in two main ways: increasing access to public education and health services, which would be driven by compliance with conditionalities, and fostering greater access to employment through urban and rural productive inclusion policies (Costa 2013; Falcão 2013). These HD strategies were aimed at two different audiences: children and adults.

First, the child-oriented HD project is based on the widespread perception in the social development environment that childhood is a time for shaping adulthood. As Esping-Andersen argues, the classic social policy literature states that "the early years of childhood are fundamental to shaping people's lives… [Thus], a social investment strategy focused on children must be the centerpiece of any social inclusion policy" (Esping-Andersen 2002, 30). In BF, the focus on children is considered a means to break a persistent cycle of intergenerational poverty. The program seeks to achieve this by imposing conditionalities on families to remain in the program: regulating school enrollment for children aged 6–15 years old and maintaining their attendance in classes at a rate of at least 85% and ensuring that youths aged 16–17 years old have school attendance rates of at least 75%, and that children under the age of seven are regularly seen at health clinics where they will receive vaccinations, health care, and medical check-ups. The Ministry responsible for the income transfer (formerly the Ministry of Social Development and Fight Against Hunger and currently the Ministry of Citizenship) monitors compliance with these conditionalities through regular reports, received from the ministries of Education and Health, that are collected through specific information systems (discussed in Chapter 2).[5] Requiring the conditionalities establishes a relationship of co-responsibility between the government and families – the agreement is arguably between the government and the women heads of household – whereby mothers are encouraged to continue doing what they have always done, but in a way that is regulated and monitored by the State.

Compliance with conditionalities becomes a particularly difficult task given the increasingly dismantling of public services in Brazil. Lena Lavinas's study (2013) demonstrates that under the Workers' Party governments there was greater growth of investments in income transfer programs than in public services. Romulo Paes-Sousa, who served as Executive Secretary of the MDS for a long period of time under the government of Dilma Rousseff, argues along the same lines that limited investment in public services has been one of the main obstacles to eradicating poverty in Brazil, and highlights as the main cause the social protection model of which the PBSM was part, "which prioritizes benefit offers over public services" (Paes-Sousa 2013). This characteristic of social protection proves contradictory in a program that supposedly aims to advance human development. Things have taken a turn for the worse since Rousseff was impeached as there have been significant cuts in spending to education, health, and social services, among other public policies.

Requiring compliance with conditionalities in a situation of low investment in public services places extra pressure and an overwhelming workload on these women, especially since their routines are already troublesome due to material scarcity. In addition to these women being overworked, time-use research with BF recipients reveals nuances that are difficult to measure but that capture the psychological stress they endure worrying about meeting program conditionalities. The pressure on beneficiaries and the stress generated by the fear of losing the benefit causes much of their day to be spent worrying about their responsibilities and supporting their families (Carloto 2016; see also Chapter 6 in this book).

If under the Workers' Party government conditions were already difficult for women, due to the very nature of the program, which did not include a gender equality dimension in its design, these conditions have only worsened under the last two administrations of Michel Temer and Jair Messias Bolsonaro. Whereas before the focus was on expansion of the program and the creation of alternative policies to potentiate the fight against poverty, the focus now is its reduction. Reduction in the number of recipients would only be positive in a situation where poverty was diminishing, which is far from the case. The number of people in extreme poverty has been growing since 2015, inverting the descending trend of former years. In November 2019, data from IBGE showed that between 2015 and 2019, 4.5 million additional people have fallen into extreme poverty (Nery 2019). Recent increases in unemployment rates, cuts in public spending, and lack of adjustments to the *Bolsa Família* grant are contributing factors. Since women are the ones who tend to be in charge of their families' welfare these cuts in the program have impinged particularly on them.

Moreover, changes in BF's guidelines have driven to an increase in what women pay to participate in the program. In February 2019, initiating a study on the effects of changes to the program, I traveled throughout the *sertão* (hinterlands) of Bahia, which is one of the poorest and driest regions of Brazil where, speaking with women about their recent experiences with *Bolsa Família* and other social programs, women reported a growing anxiety and insecurity over the fear of losing the benefit. Constant demands for updates to BF's database (the *Cadastro Único*), in an attempt to curb fraud, have made the costs of remaining in the program too high, discouraging women, particularly the most vulnerable among them, from remaining in the program.

Sônia,[6] who gets just over BRL60 a month (less than US$15 dollars), reported that for three consecutive months she had to pay BRL35 in transportation to go from the *quilombo* (a Brazilian settlement of runaway slaves of African origin, usually located far from major cities) where she lived to the county headquarters, a distance of almost 100 km to travel on an unpaved road, to try to resolve issues they found with her entitlement:

> Things have changed since that guy (what's his name?[7]) became president. They keep on finding issues with your benefit. Now they cut the benefit for no apparent reason. You have to block it to receive maternity pay otherwise they cancel it. I know to do that, but many women don't know or are unaware of the rules and find it difficult to deal with the bureaucracy. They may go months without receiving the benefit. That is, when it is not canceled altogether.

When BF is blocked or canceled, these women and their families are placed in a situation of great vulnerability since, while in other places BF may be a complement to other sources of income, in this region people have few employment options, with most families surviving on BF alone. The drought that is a hallmark of the region, which destroys the crops and kills the farm animals people depend on for nutrition, raises uncertainty about investing time and resources in domestic agricultural and livestock activities. In this context, in places where poverty predominates and the majority of people are BF recipients, support networks of family and friends are hardly an option for material aid. Solange, another BF recipient who lived in this same *quilombo*, said:

> Here everyone is poor, and with the cuts to BF, there are already many people going back to scavenging at the dump for a living. It's been six years of drought. Everything that is planted dies. Every time it rains, everyone goes to the fields to plant seeds, then the drought hits and everything that sprouted dies. Whenever it rains a little, we try planting again. If it rained here now, you would see everyone going to the fields. No one is lazy here. We are always planting seeds, but we harvest little. And here there is no other option for work; farming is all there is.

So far I have sought to substantiate my argument that, by requiring compliance with conditionalities, the HD project that focused on benefiting children increases women's workloads and generates psychological distress for them, disregarding women's well-being and putting into check the interpretation of CCTs as policies that favor HD. Below, I will discuss more specifically the HD project that is focused on the adult population, in order to consider how the lack of a gender perspective in initiatives aimed at achieving this aim further complicates the claim that CCTs are projects that advance HD.

In addition to children's development, PBSM contained initiatives aimed at promoting the social inclusion of adults, by providing opportunities that could lead to their financial independency from the State. They included: vocational training for urban and rural populations through the *Programa Nacional de Acesso ao Ensino Técnico e Emprego* (Pronatec) (National Program for Access to Technical Education and Employment); supporting the expansion of small businesses through access to the program *Micro Empreendedor Individual* (MEI) (Individual Micro Entrepreneur); through the provision of microcredit; direct purchase of food from rural farmers; technical assistance, among other initiatives.[8, 9]

These PBSM actions involved dimensions that were considered central for productive inclusion, but in addition to limitations related to the design of these initiatives, they were planned and implemented without regard for women's specific needs and interests. Thus, they tended to produce different outcomes for men and women. This section will focus on an analysis of vocational training, as this is where the shortcomings resulting from the absence of a gender perspective become particularly evident.[10]

Pronatec was the Federal Government's main vocational training program and the backbone of the productive inclusion strategy of PBSM. A well-trained workforce is certainly in growing demand by national and multinational companies. As such, vocational training aimed to meet two objectives simultaneously: to help beneficiaries foster their financial independence and to encourage economic growth.[11] Participation in vocational training courses was encouraged through resources made available to students such as: financial aid for food, transportation, teaching materials, etc. Child-care provisions, however, were not offered.

MDS did not provide effective data disaggregated by gender about these vocational training courses that could assist in adjusting policy from a perspective focused on gender. The data provided proved ineffective for such a purpose. For example, an official figure widely reported for years was that women made up 66% of persons pre-registered for Pronatec. This percentage refered to women who were both pre-registered in the courses and who belonged to the *Cadastro Único* database.[12] However, the data did not specify what percentage of them actually registered, participated, and completed the courses. Of these, how many were actually BF recipients? What courses were most in demand by these women? Did the training effectively contribute to their inclusion in the labor market? Considering the impact of the gender division of labor, it is to be assumed that women faced more challenges than did men to complete these courses, and that those who were BF recipients faced even greater challenges because they needed to perform a large number of tasks to ensure their survival and that of their family members, and also had to comply with the conditionalities required by the program. Another limitation is that these courses required applicants to have at least middle school education, which excluded most BF recipients since, according to Camargo, Curralero, and Licio (2013), overall 69% of them did not possess that level of education. In the northeast, where more than 50% of all BF recipients live, 20.3% of beneficiaries aged 25 years and older were illiterate (Camargo, Curralero, and Licio 2013; see also Chapter 2 in this book for data on how BF is distributed across regions in Brazil). The lack of disaggregated data, however, made it difficult to critically analyze and plan new Pronatec initiatives.

The instrumentalization of women, and lack of concern for issues and relations of gender in CCTs, presents itself as a contradiction of a policy that is purported to be aimed at advancing human development. If, as argued by Sen and Nussbaum and reaffirmed by the United Nations, HD refers to developing people's freedoms or increasing their capacity to develop fully in agreement with their personal abilities and choices, power is thus a central concept that must be taken into account. Accordingly, advancing HD requires initiatives that both promote such freedoms and counteract obstacles to them. Thus, HD cannot be realized through a political design that does not concern itself promoting alternatives for women's human development and in order to promote children's HD it reproduces traditional gender roles that have adverse consequences for the development of women's capabilities and freedom of choice.

Designing effective cash transfer policies that advance human development is no trivial task. However, the realization of such a project is facilitated if social inequalities are understood in their specificities and taken into account in planning such policies. This implies considering the multiple positions of people in different social structures and the relational dynamics that emerge from them. The capability approach is important because it expands the concept of poverty beyond the idea of a lack of income. However, insofar as it focuses on people's ability to develop their potential and prosper, it is limited to addressing the ways in which institutions and structures create and reproduce social inequalities (Du Toit 2004). The aim of considering inequalities in light of structural issues is best achieved by drawing from feminist theories of justice.

In the following section, I present a discussion of theories of justice in order to offer substance for analysis of the BF program from a gender perspective. The intention is not to propose a completely formed theoretical framework based on one or more theories of justice capable of assessing injustices based on universal indicators. Instead, in line with feminist interpretations that reject traditional theories of justice for their questionable universality, the present work intends to articulate core concepts and ideas from feminist perspectives on justice that assist in the task of analyzing conditional cash transfer programs in general and, more specifically, the BF program.

## Theories of Justice and Gender Justice

Traditional theories of justice are known for their distributivist content and universalist claims. They contain different notions of what counts as a distributive element but share the idea that justice concerns material distribution. John Rawls's *A Theory of Justice* (1971) is considered a model text from the perspective of justice as redistribution. Rawls considers injustices as originating from economic inequalities and presents arguments in favor of a liberal social State that promotes justice through universal social rights policies.[13] In this view, if all people had capital, goods, and opportunities in the same proportion, that would constitute a situation of social justice.

Feminists have criticized this interpretation of justice for its restriction to the distributive universe. Iris Marion Young (1990) argues that in this model, there is a neglect of structural and relational categories that would be central to interpreting injustices. People are "externally related to the goods they possess and the only relation to one another... that matters is a comparison of the amount of goods they possess" (Young 1990, 18). In other words, it presupposes structures and assumes "a social atomism inasmuch as there is no internal relation among persons in society relevant to considerations of justice" (Young 1990, 18). In this circumscribed notion of justice, there is no consideration of broader structural factors that generate injustice, such as: the capitalist system that constructs social inequalities through an international structure of exploitation and division of labor; institutional sexism and racism which perpetuate discrimination against women and black people through economic, social, and political structures resulting in their unequal inclusion in and influence over fundamental structures of decision making; gender norms which contribute to women being held accountable for household chores and responsibilities; a cultural structure which more easily subjects women and black people to violence and death due to prejudice. Susan Moller Okin (1989) underscores the limits of Rawls's perspective for failing to systematically consider, as he does in relation to other social institutions, the elements and changes needed to foster justice in the family. For Okin, it is essential to consider the gender dynamics within the family to understand the (in)justice produced in the public spheres.

The challenge of the supposed dichotomy between the public and the private spheres of social life has marked the history of the feminist movement. Okin (1989) effectively articulates this debate through her concept of "Cycles of Vulnerability," where she states that the (in)justice constituted in the family and in the public sphere of work and politics are interrelated and feed back into one another. The gender division of labor in the family restricts opportunities and shapes the conditions of women's inclusion in paid employment and political activities, which in turn reinforces their vulnerabilities and bargaining power in the family. Okin's analysis is based on the situation of women in Western countries, but Young argues that in countries of the Global South where social inequalities are greater, the "mutual reinforcement of vulnerability in the home and in wage work is even more pronounced" (Young 2009, 231). This perspective is also put forward by local authors who present detailed analysis relating the division of labor and responsibilities in the family to asymmetries in participation and decision-making power between women and men in politics and economics (Biroli 2016; Bruschini 2006; Bruschini and Ricoldi 2009). The interrelationship between these two spheres implies that building gender justice requires considering and acting on the power dynamics between men and women and the division of labor by gender in both the public and private spheres.

Some feminists warn that this debate may neglect differences between women of different social and racial backgrounds. They argue that differences of class and race should be considered central in this discussion, as they reveal distinct experiences of inequality and exploitation among women (Saffioti 2013). For upper and middle-class women, there is the option of subcontracting other women (usually black or immigrant women) to assist them with the tasks normally assigned to their gender, making the former more likely to advance in the world of labor and politics.[14] Thus building gender justice entails considering differences between women from different social and racial groups. But even if there are significant differences in the amount of work and care in which different groups of women may engage, responsibility for such activities (either by directly carrying them out or by contracting others to do so) is usually assigned to them irrespective of social class or racial background. In the context of the discussions presented here, which focus on poor and black women recipients of BF, that is an issue of even greater relevance.

Distribution is a central dimension of the concept of justice. Particularly in a historical period marked by great social inequalities and poverty, such as the present one, in which the promise of a multiplier effect of economic growth is an increasingly distant and discredited project, thinking in distributive terms is essential for a project that aims to build justice. Proper distribution, however, requires redistribution, implying in structural changes such as higher taxation on profit and inheritance, progressive income taxes, land reform, and investment in universal public policies such as health, education, and housing that can ensure the full development of people's capabilities and their active participation in society. While *sensu stricto* CCT programs cannot be thought of as a redistributive policy, they are now presented as the main policy for dealing with the consequences of a national economic development project based on concentration of income. While not ideal, such programs are a welcome contribution to the fight against poverty. However, issues of distribution need to be considered in light of other forms of injustice arising from non-material relations, such as racism and sexism, which result from and in structural inequalities and are key in thinking of a more inclusive social development project that is more effective in building social justice.

The obliteration of multiple forms of relationships and power structures in assessments of inequality is not restricted to distributive theories of justice; it is quite common among mainstream social theories in general. Public policy theories, for example, which most directly influence academic interpretations in this area as well as government and state policies, are known for their focus on labor issues, as feminists have long pointed out. Ann Shola Orloff (1993), for example, argues that Gosta Esping-Andersen's perspective on "power resources" is based on a generic view of the citizen as male, working-class, and autonomous (free from family obligations and ties), thus proving ineffective in explaining women's relationship to the State and in constructing alternatives for State action beyond issues of distribution. Like Orloff, other authors point to the gender biases of interpretations of these theories and propose distinct methods of observation and analysis that take into account the conditions and roles of women in society, enabling the construction of new models of social welfare (Daly and Lewis 2000; Sainsbury 1994). It is worth reiterating, as feminists (black feminists in particular) historically have, that approaches assumed to be universal and, as such, valid for all contexts and situations are shaped by a particular and restricted view of the social subject and process, being, therefore, limited to taking into account the diverse and specific experiences of women and of members of other discriminated and exploited social groups.

Opposite to the distributive and universalist approach to justice is a conception of it based on the idea of justice as recognition. Injustice is characterized here as a lack of recognition of the multiple forms of differences and identities, and as the inferiorization of members of certain social groups, which harms their life experiences and self-esteem. Authors who hold this view describe how people subjected to sexism, racism, and colonialism, for example, are psychologically affected by degrading stereotypes and attitudes that affect their self-esteem and possibilities for self-realization (Fanon 2008; Honneth 1995; Taylor 1994). The proposed projects to overcome obstacles and grievances impelled by non-recognition are distinct and may focus on public actions from the State, such as in

Taylor's project on respect and recognition (1994), or in the autonomous actions of subjects through processes of self-resignification and revaluation of identities, as proposed in Fanon's existentialist work (Fanon 2008). Common to these interpretations is the notion that justice requires appreciation and strengthening of group identity, leading to a process of increasing the self-esteem and self-realization of its members.

Some feminists consider a model of justice shaped by subjective and cultural aspects as limited and essentialist. Fraser argues that supporting the justice argument in the dimension of self-esteem and focusing on psychological aspects that limit the self-realization of people is similar to victim blaming and ends up adding "insult to injury." The negative aspects of non-recognition are not found in the manifestation of such psychological effects, but in the construction of differentiated statuses (Fraser 2003). This perspective focuses on factors external to people that suffer from aggravations resulting from lack of recognition that damage their self-esteem. In other words, the most important thing to consider are the structures that generate misrecognition.

Young (2008b) emphasizes the importance of cultural factors as a means of constructing injustices, however she also points to the limitations of perspectives that focus exclusively on this dimension. But in addition to her emphasis on structural aspects, she also explores issues endogenous to groups that suffer injustices in order to identify the limits of this perspective. She argues that the cultural model of justice tends to presuppose group homogeneity, essentializing identities and ignoring the differences between group members (Young 2008b). According to Young, this perspective assumes a similarity between group members that is not feasible to interpret the injustices produced by differences in gender, race, and (dis)ability, among others, which do not require differentiation, but inclusion based on difference. The identities and interests of people and groups would always be in motion in a process of constant reformation.

Young's (2008b) perspective, which she calls the "structural inequality approach," offers an intersectional reading of inequalities promoted by structures that do not champion differences, and by hierarchical relationships that promote privileges. Groups interact through social axes characterized by hierarchies and privileges on different fronts, which affect the living experience of their members generating injustices. Justice, in this perspective, requires taking into account the politics of difference, whereby there is recognition of the specific conditions that gave rise to injustices and the implementation of new agreements.

Although in some of her works, Fraser seems to dichotomize cultural and economic processes,[15] as pointed out by some feminist authors such as Young (2008a) and Phillips (2008),[16] in others her analysis takes on more integrative contours. If the latter approach is taken in such a way as to consider different dimensions of justice as directly interconnected and equally important, said perspective helps to systematize an analytical framework to consider situations of gender injustice in social policy designs such as that of CCTs. Fraser does this in the tripartite approach she develops, whereby she maintains that justice presupposes parity of participation, which "requires social arrangements that permit all (adult) members of society to interact with one another as peers" (Fraser 2003, 38). These arrangements would be based on economic, cultural, and political dimensions, which she calls: redistribution, recognition, and representation (Fraser 2005).[17] For her, although different spheres of justice are interrelated, this does not mean that acting on one of them will suffice to correct the injustices of the others since each instance of (economic, cultural, or political) injustice has a particular and immediate structural basis and requires distinct "remedies" (Fraser 1995).

Fraser argues that in order to overcome injustice it is necessary to build specific policies capable of acting on these different structures of inequalities. Policies implemented to correct one of these dimensions need to be assessed in relation to their impact on the others, otherwise they run the risk of worsening injustices (Fraser 1995, 2003, 2005). From this perspective, the effectiveness of government projects like income transfer programs cannot be properly assessed through a distributive dimension only, such as when considering how many people are above or below the poverty line, but also based on a cultural dimension and a political one.

Based on these multidimensional feminist perspectives on justice, I present in the next section an analysis of the *Bolsa Família* program focused on gender perspectives. I explore the limitations and possibilities of this program by looking at the economic, cultural, and political dimensions of justice, and I consider initiatives more inclusive of differences and that could favor building gender justice.

## Reflections on Gender Justice in the *Bolsa Família* Program: Beyond Redistribution

Most CCT programs opt to target women as recipients of the transfers. That tendency rests on an instrumental logic that regards women as the best stewards of resources provided by social policy programs. The view that women are more responsible for their families' best interests and as such would employ resources more reasonably is found in written documents, it is manifested in spaces of policymaking and policy management, and it often appears in speeches by public officials and authorities. Below, former President Dilma Rousseff, during a ceremony in Irecê, Bahia, marking the beginning of Women's month, expresses such a view:

> And, so, I want to refer here to family farming, to families of men and women farmers, and remind you that in both *Bolsa Família* and family farming we have looked to women with much care and with great affection. Because women are key when it comes to family. Everyone here knows that it is almost impossible for a mother to leave her child without food...she

> would go hungry herself to feed her child. That's why we prefer women to be the primary cardholding beneficiaries of the BF program. It is therefore important to increase the value and the amount of credit available to women so that they can have their Pronaf. Through Pronaf, a woman can find funding for her crafts, for example. She can sew; she can make sweets, that is, she can contribute to improving her family's income.
>
> *(Rousseff 2011)*

President Roussef's speech is an example of how official narratives on women in public policy tend to reinforce traditional gender roles and to reproduce the discourse of women's inferiority. The selfless attitude of women at the expense of their own needs and interests is reaffirmed by being praised, and as such there is a reinforcement of a misogynist culture that marks the life experience of women (and girls) as less important and as inferior to that of men, and that has consequences for both women's participation in the public sphere and the affirmation of their physical and psychological dignity.

In addition to speeches that essentialize traditional gender roles, official advertisements and publications spread the image of women as mothers, usually in pictures and videos of them together or holding children. Men, however, are portrayed as workers, driving tractors and working on public works or farming, or performing other productive activities traditionally associated with the male gender.

Bradshaw (2008) argues that the instrumental focus on women in CCT programs suggests that governments regard men's behavior towards their families as generally irresponsible, but prefer not to take that into account when designing public policies. As a result, the "deprivation suffered by women through their altruism is not problematized but explicitly reinforced as the social norm" (Bradshaw 2008, 195). A culture that assigns women responsibility for unpaid work caring for one's family, and that constructs gender inequalities in both the private and public spheres, rather than being destabilized, is actually encouraged. Meanwhile men's irresponsible behavior is entirely ignored. While benefiting from women's efforts, these programs reinforce and perpetuate gender inequalities.

Ministerial committees on gender equality,[18] which were created during President Lula's administration and which were expanded during the presidency of Dilma Rousseff, are openly critical of the instrumentalization of women in social policy programs. In the face of opposition and critiques, the tendency is for the reconfiguration of the official narrative. In spaces of public administration and authority it was common to hear that transferring the benefit to women would be a way for the State to recognize, through redistribution, the value of the work they would otherwise be doing for free. This transfer of a relatively small value for tasks as demanding as those carried out by recipients, particularly those in extreme poverty, is explained as a politics of recognition. However, recognition presupposes inclusion through the valorization of the social group and its members, and it requires the transformation of oppressive social norms and not the affirmation of differences that perpetuate gender injustices.

The deconstruction of traditional norms is favored when public officials such as social workers, health agents, and BF managers are convinced of the importance of such a task and are qualified to carry it out, which in turn is enhanced by vocational training. Otherwise, the tendency is that they will encourage women in the program to play the role of "the good mother." Capacity building in gender issues and relations is a current demand of federal committees promoting gender equality. In 2014, when 45,000 workers from the *Sistema Único de Assistência Social* (SUAS) (Single Social Assistance System) were going to be trained, the MDS Committee on Gender and Women's Policy planned specific initiatives for such a purpose and negotiated and agreed with the National Social Assistance Secretariat to include a gender perspective in all modules proposed in their educational program, and a specific one to discuss the central issues surrounding this theme. However, all of this content was eventually removed from the curriculum plan sent to the states and universities that would develop the courses. The strong influence of familism in Social Assistance in Brazil (Mioto 2006) makes it difficult to implement perspectives and initiatives aimed at building gender equity (see Chapter 2).

Considering the diversity of experiences and the intersectionality of forms of oppression, building more inclusive social and human development projects is fundamental in the context of CCT policies and public policy in general. This requires assessing the distinct realities lived by women and men and their experiences with public services and policymaking that takes said experiences into account. This necessitates, firstly, disaggregated data that can provide information that captures important aspects of women's experiences in light of the intersections of race, ethnicity, age, etc., and, secondly, assessment of the multiple impacts of social protection policies and services on women.

Studies show, for example, that unemployment levels are high among women receiving BF. Research by Lavinas, Cobo, and Veigas, based on a sample of women beneficiaries of BF, shows that among this population the average unemployment rate is 34%, which reaches 50.6% among women between the ages of 16 to 24 years. These rates are well above the average unemployment rate (of 8%) in metropolitan cities at that time (Lavinas, Cobo, and Veigas 2012). These findings are reinforced by other studies in the area. Montali's study of the poorest 50% of the population shows large asymmetries between men and women regarding their unemployment rates, wages, and working conditions.[19] The differences are greater between female heads of household and single mothers (Montali 2014), particularly when they are black (Mariano and Carloto 2013; IPEA et al. 2011). Among employed female heads of household, only 33% were in stable employment situations. The percentage of men in the same situation was 60% (Montali 2014). Therefore, policy analyses of BF need to take into account data such as these in order to: ascertain to what extent policies ancillary to those focused on income transfer models aimed at creating economic empowerment alternatives through productive inclusion are actually working; identify constraints; and put forward new policy initiatives.

Historically, feminists have emphasized the importance of paid work for women's autonomy. However, for women BF recipients, performing paid activities may not be a viable option given the scarcity of employment opportunities, or they may find themselves forced to accept employment under conditions that do not favor empowerment. Research by Lavinas, Cobo, and Veigas (2012) maintains that women living in extreme poverty and accessing BF do not consider paid work as a means of promoting their autonomy. This is not surprising if we take into account their busy and exhausting routines struggling to make a living through informal, underpaid, and often low status jobs, while taking responsibility for family tasks and care and, on top of that, complying with BF conditionalities.

In the *sertão*, or hinterlands in the countryside of northeastern Brazil, a region with the highest percentage of BF beneficiaries, there are few options for paid employment, but some of the available opportunities consist in extremely exploitative and strenuous jobs. Jussara, a young black woman with whom we spoke when on a study tour in February 2019, received less than BRL50 (reais) a week (less than $12) for the work she performed five days a week, working 12-hour days harvesting sisal palm. Like her co-workers, she sleeps in a country camp on makeshift straw beds, wakes up at 4 o'clock in the morning, has restricted access to water that does not allow her to bathe daily, and must provide her own meals (Sacchet and Spatuzzi 2019).

This example of the kind of jobs available to some women in poverty allows us to contextualize their working conditions and struggle for survival. Given the unequal division of labor in the family, insufficient and inefficient public services, and the fact that poor women cannot afford private care services, unsafe, underpaid, and low status paid work increases the burden of responsibilities placed on women without necessarily granting them more freedom of choice and autonomy. Such an observation does not intend to deny the importance of employment as a source of income for these women; rather, as black feminists have long claimed, it seeks to identify the limit of an economic based discourse about women's autonomy and empowerment that fails to take into account the often-harsh reality of the experiences with paid work for some women, especially black women. It also involves evaluating the quality of labor policies in the country that allow the existence and proliferation of activities analogous to slave labor, such as those experienced by Jussara.

Inclusion in the labor market is constrained and at the same time defined by work dynamics and responsibilities in the domestic sphere. In addition to unequal workloads between men and women in the domestic sphere in Brazil, recorded by many time-use studies, the identification of certain activities as feminine and others as masculine predisposes women to jobs that reproduce their roles in the family, which tend to be underpaid, informal, and of lower status. Black women predominate in these types of occupations, showing that, in addition to gender, race is an important marker in the structuring of social inequalities. Public policies interested in promoting women's inclusion in the labor market need to consider the "cycles of vulnerability" that settle and feed back between the private and public spheres. Such policies should create services and initiatives that address the specific needs of women and that, at the same time, seek to deconstruct them in light of their being gendered activities.

For women in BF, mostly black, who cannot afford to pay for care services or for help with household chores and responsibilities, public services are essential to foster their participation in the labor market. Based on the sample of BF beneficiaries interviewed by Lavinas, Cobo, and Veigas (2012), 90.3% considered the lack of access to services such as day care centers to be the main factor hindering their search for paid work. Other studies on this topic point to similar results (Bruschini and Ricoldi 2009; Mariano and Souza 2015; Montali 2014; Sorj 2014; Sorj, Fontes, and Machado 2007).

Through the *Plano Brazil Sem Miséria* the MDS implemented in 2012 two initiatives which, although not planned for women's autonomy, had elements that contributed to it. One of them, within the jurisdiction of a plan called *Brasil Carinhoso* (Loving Brazil), aimed to increase local day care and preschool offerings for BF beneficiaries, through financial incentives from the Federal Government.[20] The other initiative, called *Mais Educação* (More Education), was a program in partnership with the Ministry of Education, aimed at expanding full-time education to geographic regions where most residents were recipients of BF. Both of these initiatives are welcomed from a perspective aimed at fostering women's autonomy. However, they were not designed with women's interests in mind, but as a means of reducing poverty among children through access to better education and care. Thus, as is usually the case, they tended to produce unexpected and unwanted results for women. For example, because day care centers and preschools are considered educational activities, it was common for local governments to discontinue these services during holiday periods as they understood they should be guided by the same rules as schools and, as such, follow the same schedule of activities. That is, although women could benefit from these policies, because gender was not a constitutive part of their planning processes, their needs and interests were compromised in the process. This is an example of how the absence of a gender perspective can undermine the outcome of a policy that could otherwise work to promote women's autonomy. These policies, which were underinvested and consequently limited in scope from the outset, became even more restricted with the spending cuts in education and public services in general seen recently in the country as a consequence of parliamentary reforms (see the introduction for further information).

Some authors have attributed a number of positive outcomes to *Bolsa Família* because it allows women access to cash. They claim that it has elevated women to a new degree of autonomy and empowerment, giving them greater power to interfere with family decisions, and has helped increase their status in the community, even affording them opportunities to leave abusive relationships (Soares and Silva 2010; Rego and Pinzani 2013). This positive outlook on BF is sometimes expressed about other CCTs as well; however, other scholars have challenged such praise observing that the value of the cash transfer is insufficient to generate such empowerment. Some of these studies contend that, rather than empowering women, CCTs and their related conditionalities trap women in a situation of dependence on the State without real options of viable ways out (Tabbush 2010; Bradshaw and Viquez 2008). Molyneux (2006) considers that even if women in CCTs may acquire a certain level of financial autonomy, this would not translate into empowerment, which is a complex process that requires more than just access to a small amount of money. This view is similar to that of other authors for whom BF may improve the status of women among their families but ultimately prove ineffective in more broadly promoting women's autonomy and empowerment (Lavinas, Cobo, and Veigas 2012; Mariano and Carloto 2009, 2013).

The discussion on empowerment within the context of CCT can lead to different conclusions, depending on the interpretation of this concept (not always made explicit), that sometimes contribute little to advance the debate. From a racial and gender justice perspective, I think it is rather useful to consider the extent to which access to the benefit promotes more effective changes in the lives of these women, helping improve their ability for action to change oppressive and exploitative relationships and structures, or just facilitates the performance of their traditional role in the family and community. While it might be argued that achieving the second is not a trivial matter for women in poverty, this is not the most effective way to promote lasting changes in their lives. Thinking in terms of empowerment requires considering issues of power relations and structural inequalities.

Considering BF through the lens of gender justice also implies taking cultural issues into account, analyzing how they affect the experiences of women in the program. Some research reports on the psychological stress that results from the humiliation that BF recipients often suffer when interacting with school officials, health professionals, municipal public managers, and social workers (Carloto 2016; Marins 2014; see also chapter 8 in this book). They recount situations of hostility and disrespect and how these women feel inadequate in their role as mothers. Situations in which professionals, who should understand this policy as a right, frame the benefit as a handout offered to complacent people who "take advantage" of the State. Failing to acknowledge people in a situation of poverty as deserving respect, people who as citizens in a situation of need have the right to social assistance, contributes to spreading a negative and prejudiced image of BF recipients, adding grievance to their material needs. In this sense, justice requires initiatives to combat prejudice in order to stop the humiliation suffered by the beneficiaries.

Despite some changes in perception, it is still quite common for BF recipients to be publicly represented (in the media, right-wing protests/demonstrations, everyday conversations, etc.) as lazy, opportunistic, irresponsible, and even privileged. Women are the main victims of this process of non-recognition. Although research shows that the average number of children of beneficiaries is no higher than that of non-beneficiary families in the same socioeconomic group (Alves and Cavenaghi 2013), women in the former are accused of procreating to increase the amount of the subsidy. The role of social protection and promotion played by this program is ignored when it is referred to as the "Vote-buying Grant" (*Bolsa Voto*), "The Laziness Grant" (*Bolsa Preguiça*), and other nicknames popularly given to the program that spread prejudices and stereotypes about program recipients and their dependents. Considering that 93% of the primary beneficiaries are women and that most of them are black, these narratives lead to a gendered and racialized notion of the "undeserving poor."

The lack of recognition of rights to social protection and social assistance programs is not restricted to some public service professionals or to the average conservative public, as discussed above, but may be a view held by beneficiaries themselves. According to Rego and Pinzani (2013), 75% of the BF recipients they interviewed considered this program to be a government handout or a gift from President Lula, who implemented the policy. Rego, at the "Gender and *Bolsa Família*" Seminar held in Brasilia in 2013, organized by the MDS Committee on Gender and Women's Policy, reported that some women interviewed by her commented jokingly that President "Lula was their new husband" (Rego and Pinzani 2013). In other words, the stipend is framed either as handouts from the State or as a gift from a male provider. This suggests that addressing the cultural dimensions and impacts of the program is important in the fight against poverty.

Viewing the benefit as a handout may be associated not only with conservative ideologies but also with misinformation about rights, especially when it comes to program participants. Among BF recipients, either lower levels of formal education or illiteracy are common and make it harder for them to gain access to information. There are no participatory initiatives promoted by the program whereby BF recipients and members of the government and the public administration can communicate, discuss this and other policy initiatives, and establish means of social control and accountability. Social participation leads to a more informed understanding of the role of the State and notions of individual and collective rights. Citizens that are aware of these issues can, in turn, more easily counter the prejudice of the conservative public, as well as demand their rights assertively and with dignity before public managers and authorities.

Thus, social participation may counter a trend towards bias and promote knowledge about rights. Participatory initiatives could adopt different formats, such as specific spaces for women or mixed-gender communication groups. These spaces could encompass discussions about issues related to the program and beyond, including issues of gender, family, care, violence, work, or whatever topic participants deemed important, contributing to promoting new perceptions of rights and relationships. This is not to suggest that participation in these groups should be a new conditionality, as this would put extra pressure on already overburdened women. These initiatives would have to constitute voluntary participation processes, which could be encouraged and supported by public administrations.

As feminist theories of justice highlight, building gender justice requires paying particular attention to issues of power. Brazil's notorious asymmetry of power between men and women in different spheres is evidenced in studies about the low presence and influence of women in politics and economics, as well as about women's time-use and gender-based domestic violence. In the context of this analysis, I circumscribe the issue of power to two interrelated dimensions: a) women's ability to pursue their goals without being held back by others and to ensure they enjoy dignity and freedom; b) their ability to participate in economic, social, and political processes on equal terms with men.

First, combating gender-based violence is a key factor in strengthening women's independence and capacity for action. Thus, it should be a central issue when designing and monitoring any policy that targets women. However, this is not the case with BF, as there is no official assessment on the impact of this program on gender-based domestic violence. Brazil has one of the most internationally recognized gender-based violence laws (the Maria da Penha Law), but it is still among the countries with the worst rates in this type of violence, ranking fifth in the world in feminicide (Gustafson 2019). The effectiveness of this law depends on public investment in services aimed at preventing and meeting the demands of female victims. It also requires commitment and allocation of resources by local and state governments, which are not always observed. The national plan *Mulher Viver sem Violência* (Woman Living Without Violence), created in 2014 during the Dilma Rousseff administration, was agreed on by all states and implemented in just three. The plan brings together the main assistance services offered to women victims of gender-based violence under one roof, namely the *Casa da Mulher Brasileira* (CMB) (Brazilian Women's House), the main social facility of this service. However, by the end of 2019 the number of CMBs (just three) had not increased, and those in place operated inadequately and with a scarcity of resources. To make matters worse, in 2020, the federal government announced that there would be no new investments in this program.

Second, women's ability to participate in politics is influenced not only by material conditions, but also by institutional rules and objective conditions, such as time and energy available for engaging in such activities. With 15% of women in parliamentary positions in the Lower House, Brazil, together with Paraguay, ranks last among Latin American countries in terms of women's presence in these positions. Some of the key factors that explain this limited presence include: an electoral system that favors campaign individualization; lack of a proper ceiling for campaign spending; and an ineffective electoral justice that fails to penalize parties that do not abide by rules aimed at increasing the number of women elected. Said rules entail quotas for female candidacies (a minimum of 30%) and for the distribution of public funds (in direct proportion to the percentage of female candidates) (Sacchet 2008, 2018; Sacchet and Speck 2012). Political participation is key for building capability. Yet, it requires time and energy, which are in deficit among women overburdened by housework and family responsibility, as time-use studies on the Brazilian case confirm (see Chapter 2). A CCT program that, on the one hand, requires women to comply with conditionalities and, on the other hand, does not concern itself with providing conditions for women to participate in processes that could help improve their skills, consciousness, and capabilities, does not favor women's political participation and personal autonomy.

CCTs are important State policies as they provide a safety net against financial insecurities. In cases of material destitution, the State must ensure a standard of living that enables people to avoid the physical and psychological stress that this situation entails. But they could be significantly improved upon. The fight against poverty requires effective and inclusive economic, cultural, and political development initiatives designed to promote the economic inclusion of people in need in general, and of women in particular, and human development projects that promote women's capacity building beyond occupations associated with traditional gender norms. This means, among other things, that policies such as productive inclusion are designed to meet the needs of women (from different races, ethnicities, ages, abilities, etc.). Pronatec, for example, would need to encourage and present conditions for women to be trained to perform vocations beyond those identified as adequate for women. Existing initiatives of intermediation for work should be expanded and effectively conducted through services such as the *Sistema Nacional de Emprego* (SINE) (National Employment System) or other initiatives that do not privilege men or practice gender discrimination.[21] Considering the high levels of illiteracy or low levels of basic formal education among BF recipients, vocational courses tailored to this demographic are needed, otherwise the most at-risk beneficiaries will be excluded. Perhaps these projects could be combined with educational initiatives aimed at helping improve reading and writing skills.[22]

The initiatives presented require the improvement and expansion of universal policies in areas such as health and education, as well as the creation of specific ones aimed at taking into account women's needs and interests and, at the same time, stopping the mischaracterization of some policies (such as parental leave) as women's policies. In order to function as inclusive processes, these policies must be planned, implemented, and evaluated intersectionally, so that existing differences among women are taken into consideration. These initiatives will only be viable through structural reforms that lead to expansion rather than reduction of State and public services, as recently seen in Brazil.

Finally, institutional agents that promote gender equality within the state are central to the implementation of women's rights and gender policies and to the transversalization, intersection, and coordination of these policies, fighting prejudices in political processes. Most federal ministries have internal committees to address gender issues and women's policies. They communicate and coordinate actions between the ministries. These committees have limited power insofar as they do not command resources or have their own organizational structures. As they effectively act as advocacy spaces, they depend on public officials being receptive to their ideas and showing "goodwill." However, as a rule, feminist ideas and recommendations in policymaking spaces such as the MDS (now Ministry of Citizenship) are seen as immaterial and secondary to the "concreteness" of hunger and material destitution. In this silencing of the gender perspective, and through a gaze that claims to be neutral and universal, but is in fact biased, governmental structures contribute to reinforcing and perpetuating the adversities women face and the hierarchical power relations in which they are inserted and thereby failing to promote more inclusive political processes that would be effective in the fight against poverty and extreme poverty.

## Conclusions

This chapter has considered the BF program from a gender perspective employing in its analysis the capability approach and feminist theories of justice. First, by exposing a broader concept of poverty sustained by the work on capability of Amartya Sen and Martha Nussbaum, this study has questioned the premise that the BF program is a policy that fosters human development. In this perspective, building capabilities or creating possibilities for HD is considered essential to lift people out of poverty. However, this ideal is jeopardized by the lack of initiatives in this program that could favor the participation of women in education, and vocational trainings and by the requisite that they comply with conditionalities, which overburden them and generate worries and anxiety, despite being in a situation with little and/or precarious access to public services. Under these conditions, women lack the means to develop their own human capital. Thus, there is an inconsistency between the focus on HD of *Bolsa Família* – and indeed of most CCTs – and their actual practices related to the instrumentalization of women in these programs. The absence of a gender perspective becomes a hindrance to advancing HD and limits the construction of a more sustainable and effective social development project.

Second, feminist theories of justice go further than capability approaches by offering an analytical model that considers social inequalities beyond issues of redistribution through analyses that take into account the multidimensionality and interconnectedness of different forms of injustice. Social injustices are considered to be constituted by material, cultural, and political processes built on discriminatory and hierarchical relationships and exploitative structures.

An analysis of BF's gender dimension from the perspective of feminist theories of justice have allowed this chapter to pursue a number of objectives: to point out the cultural, political, and economic limitations of CCT programs; to propose specific initiatives in these areas while considering their integrated character; and to develop and present arguments in favor of a more holistic model of anti-poverty policy, one that takes gender inequalities into account and is more effective at combating poverty and advancing human development.

The data and arguments presented throughout this chapter show that combating poverty presupposes initiatives far beyond distributive policies. Poverty is more than material need and is experienced differently according to the multiple positions of the person or group in the social structure. In addition to the lack of material goods, living in poverty is a complex experience, with cultural, social, and political facets, based on relationships and structures that generate inequalities and subalternities between people. Understanding the multiple processes that generate inequality is, therefore, essential for the development of more effective public policies to fight poverty.

## Notes

1 I would like to thank the Beatrice Bain Research Group (BBRG), at the Gender and Women´s Studies Department, of the University of California Berkeley, where this project started and was partly conducted. I would like to say a special thanks to my colleagues at BBRG for their feedback on earlier versions of this work and to Gillian Edgelow for her support always. A special thanks also goes to the Postgraduate Program in Interdisciplinary Studies on Women, Gender and Feminism, of the Federal University of Bahia.
2 For a more detailed contextualization of the political and economic elements that gave rise to these programs, see Chapter 2 of this book.
3 The capability approach has been criticized for several reasons, which are beyond the scope of this article. See Fabre and Miller (2003) and Phillips (2001) for critiques.
4 Based on Sen's approach, the United Nations defines human development as "the process of broadening people's choices"... which enables them to "live a long and healthy life, educate themselves, and enjoy a decent standard of living," and "political freedom, other guaranteed human rights, and various elements of self-respect" (UNDP 1997).
5 Some conditionalities apply to women directly, referring specifically to women's reproductive health, and involve regular gynecological check-ups for women aged 14–44 years, whereby they receive guidance about their maternal and reproductive health and prenatal / post-natal check-ups with health professionals. Conditionalities related to women's health are not monitored.
6 To ensure the anonymity of our respondents, all of the names used here are fictitious.
7 She was referring to Michel Temer.
8 For further details on this subject, see: Rocha, Sacchet, and Favilla (2014).
9 All of these BSM actions, planned as policies complementary to BF, were abandoned by the current government, restricting the program essentially to cash transfers.
10 For a discussion on credit and the problems resulting from the financialization of the economy, see Lavinas 2017.
11 Productive inclusion initiatives were offered to BF recipients as well as a broader audience of people who are not as poor and are enrolled in the *Cadastro Único* (Single Registry). The Single Registry collects data from families whose income is less than a total of three minimum wages, or up to an average of half a minimum wage per family member. For a detailed discussion of how the Single Registry collects data, particularly in relation to minority communities see, Direito and Lício (2014), and chapter 2 in this book.
12 See chapter 2 for information on how *Cadastro Único* works.
13 Universal principles of justice would result from a particular method of abstraction of rights, which he calls the "original position," which would ensure impartiality. Rawls

considers that his conception of justice can offer "a model by which the distributive aspects of the basic structure of society can be judged" (Rawls 1971, 9).

14 In Brazil, there are in fact substantial differences between white and black women regarding the inclusion of women in the labor market in terms of wages / salaries. For more, see the second chapter in this book.

15 See Fraser (1995, 2003).

16 Fraser herself explains that these are analytical distinctions constructed for heuristic purposes only (Fraser 1995, 70).

17 For an explanation of what each one of these dimensions entails, see Fraser (2005).

18 During President Dilma Rousseff's government, most ministries established internal gender committees, which aimed to implement a gender perspective in different policies and to act transversally on the policy initiatives of other ministries and governmental or intersectoral agencies. Few of these committees remain. They are usually coordinated directly with the agency most specifically responsible for policies focused on thinking about women and gender policy, namely the Secretariat of Policies for Women. At the MDS, this work was carried out by the Committee on Gender and Women's Policy.

19 Overall (without disaggregating data by social class), women earn 74% of what men earn, but black women earn only 40% of the salary earned by white men (IBGE 2015).

20 MDS paid around 50% more per child enrolled in day care centers if they were children of BF beneficiaries.

21 I have already visited SINEs that had job openings only for bakers and bricklayers but that only accepted applications from men to fill such positions.

22 *Mulheres Mil* (Thousands Women), an initiative that, unlike Pronatec, focuses on educating women by enhancing their knowledge, has always been a project limited in scope because it has not received the proper attention and financial incentive.

## References

Alves, José Eustáquio Dinis and Suzana Cavenaghi. 2013. "O Programa Bolsa Família e as Taxas de Fecundidade no Brasil." In *Programa Bolsa Família: Uma Década de Inclusão e Cidadania*, edited by Tereza Campello and Marcelo. C. Neri, 233–246. Brasília: IPEA.

Barrientos, Armando. 2011. "Social Protection and Poverty." *International Journal of Social Welfare* 20, no. 3: 240–249.

Barrientos, Armando. 2013. "Human development income transfers in the longer term." Working Paper, no. 116. Brasília: International Policy Center for Inclusive Growth.

Bichir, Renata Mirambola. 2010. "O Bolsa Família na Berlinda? Os desafios atuais dos programas de transferência de renda." *Novos Estudos-CEBRAP* 87: 115–129. https://doi.org/10.1590/S0101-33002010000200007.

Biroli, Flávia. 2016. "Divisão Sexual do Trabalho e Democracia." *Dados-Revista de Ciências Sociais* 59, no. 3: 719–754. https://doi.org/10.1590/00115258201690.

Bradshaw, Sarah and Ana Quirós Víquez. 2008. "Women Beneficiaries or Women Bearing the Cost? A Gendered Analysis of the Red de Protección Social in Nicaragua." *Development and Change* 39, no. 5: 823–844.

Bradshaw, Sarah. 2008. "From Structural Adjustment to Social Adjustment A Gendered Analysis of Conditional Cash Transfer Programmes in Mexico and Nicaragua." *Global Social Policy* 8, n. 2: 188–207. https://doi.org/10.1177/1468018108090638.

Bruschini, Maria Cristina Aranha and Arlene Martinez Ricoldi. 2009. "Family and Work: Hard Reconciliation for Low-income Working Mothers." *Cadernos de Pesquisa* 39, no. 136: 93–123.

Bruschini, Maria Cristina Aranha. 2006. "Trabalho Doméstico: Inatividade Econômica ou Trabalho Não-remunerado?" *Revista Brasileira de Estudos Populacionais* 23, no. 2: 331–353. https://doi.org/10.1590/S0102-30982006000200009.

Camargo, Camila F., Claudia Regina Baddini Curralero, Elaine Cristina Licio, and Joana Mostafa. 2013. "Perfil Socioeconômico dos Beneficiários do Bolsa Família: o que o cadastro único revela?" In *Programa Bolsa Família: Uma Década de Inclusão e Cidadania*, edited by Tereza Campello and Marcelo. C. Neri, 31–32. Brasília: IPEA.

Carloto, Cássia. 2016. *As Condicionalidades do Programa Bolsa Família e o Uso do Tempo das Mulheres no Trabalho Doméstico Familiar*. Relatório de Pesquisa apresentado ao CNPQ (research paper presented to the funding institution, CNPQ).

Costa, Patricia Vieira da. 2013. "Um outro Brasil é Possível". In *O fim da Miséria é só um começo. Plano Brasil Sem Miséria: 2 anos*, edited by MDS (Ministério do Desenvolvimento Social e Combate à Fome), 4–5. Brasília: MDS.

Daly, Mary and Jane Lewis. 2000. "The concept of social care and the analysis of contemporary welfare states." *The British Journal of Sociology* 51, no. 2: 281–298. https://doi.org/10.1111/j.1468-4446.2000.00281.x.

Direito, Denise and Elaine Cristina Licio. 2014. "A Experiência Brasileira de Cadastramento Diferenciado de Grupos Populacionais Tradicionais e Específicos." Work presented in Congreso Internacional del CLAD sobre la Reforma de Estado y de la Administracion Pública, Ecuador.

Draibe, Sonia. 1993. "As políticas sociais e o neoliberalismo." *Revista USP* 17: 86–101.

Du Toit, Alexander 2004. "'Social Exclusion' Discourse and Chronic Poverty: A South African Case Study." *Development and Change* 35, no. 5: 987–1010.

Esping-Andersen, Gøsta. 1990. *The Three Worlds of Welfare Capitalism*. Princeton: Princeton University Press.

Esping-Andersen, Gøsta. 2002. "A Child-Centered Social Investment Strategy." In *Why We Need a New Welfare State*, edited by Gøsta Esping-Andersen, 26–67. New York: Oxford University Press. doi:10.1093/0199256438.001.0001.

Fabre, Cécile and David Miller. 2003. "Justice and Culture: Rawls, Sen, and O'Neill." *Political Studies Review* 1, no. 1: 4–17. https://doi.org/10.1111/1478-9299.00002.

Falcão, Tiago. 2013. "É possível crescer incluindo". In *O fim da Miséria é só um começo. Plano Brasil Sem Miséria: 2 anos*, edited by MDS (Ministério do Desenvolvimento Social e Combate à Fome), 20–22. Brasília: MDS.

Fanon, Frantz. 2008. *Black Skin, White Masks*. New York: Grove Press.

Fraser, Nancy. 1995. "From Redistribution to Recognition? Dilemmas of Justice in a 'Post-Socialist Age.'" *New Left Review* 212: 68–94.

Fraser, Nancy. 2003. "Social Justice in the Age of Identity Politics: Redistribution, Recognition, and Participation." In *Redistribution or Recognition? A Political-philosophical Exchange*, edited by Nancy Fraser and Axel Honneth, 7–109. USA: Verso.

Fraser, Nancy. 2005. "Mapping the Feminist Imagination". *Constellation* 12, no. 3: 395–307.

Gustafson, Jessica. 2019. "Brasil caminha para liderar ranking mundial da violência contra mulher." *Catarinas*, January 28, 2019. https://catarinas.info/brasil-caminha-para-liderar-ranking-mundial-da-violencia-contra-mulher/.

Hanlon, Joseph, Armando Barrientos, and David Hulme. 2010. *Just Give Money to the Poor: The Development Revolution from the Global South*. Sterling, VA, USA: Kumarian Press.

Honneth, Axel. 1995. *The Fragmented World of the Social: Essays in Social and Political Philosophy*. Edited by C. W. Wright. New York: State University of New York Press.

IBGE (Instituto Brasileiro de Geografia e Economia). 2015. *Síntese de Indicadores Sociais: Uma Análise das Condições de Vida de população brasileira: 2015*. Rio de Janeiro: IBGE.

IPEA (Instituto de Pesquisa e Economia Aplicada) et al. 2011. *Retratos das Desigualdades de Gênero e Raça*. Fourth edition. Brasília: IPEA.

Lavinas, Lena, Barbara Cobo, and Alinne Veiga. 2012. "Bolsa Família: impacto das transferências de renda sobre a autonomia das mulheres pobres e as relações de gênero." *Revista Latinoamericana de Población* 6, no. 10: 31–56.

Lavinas, Lena. 2013. "21st Century Welfare." *New Left Review*84: 5–40.

Lavinas, Lena. 2017. *The Takeover of Social Policy by Financialization: The Brazilian Paradox*. New York: Palgrave Macmillan.

Mariano, Silvana and Cássia Carloto. 2009. "Gênero e Combate à Pobreza: Programa Bolsa Família." *Revista Estudos Feministas* 17, no. 3: 901–908. https://doi.org/10.1590/S0104-026X2009000300018.

Mariano, Silvana and Cássia Carloto. 2013. "Aspectos diferenciais de inserção de mulheres negras no Programa Bolsa Família." *Sociedade e Estado* 28, no. 2: 393–417.

Mariano, Silvana and Márcio Ferreira de Souza. 2015. "Conciliação e tensões entre trabalho e família para mulheres titulares do Programa Bolsa Família." *Revista Brasileira de Ciência Política* 18: 147–177. https://doi.org/10.1590/0103-335220151806.

Marins, Mani Tebet Azevedo de. 2014. "Repertórios morais e estratégias individuais de beneficiários e cadastradores do Bolsa Família." *Sociologia & Antropologia* 4, no 2:543–562.

Mioto, Regina CéliaTamaso. 2006. "Novas propostas e velhos princípios: a assistência às famílias no contexto de programas de orientação e apoio sociofamiliar." In *Política social, família e juventude: uma questão de direitos*, edited by Mione Apolinário Sales, Maurício Castro de Matos, and Maria Cristina Leal, 43–60. Second edition. São Paulo: Cortez.

Molyneux, Maxine. 2006. "Mothers at the Service of the New Poverty Agenda: Progresa/Oportunidades, Mexico's Conditional Transfer Programme." *Social Policy and Administration* 40, no. 4, 425–449. https://doi.org/10.1111/j.1467-9515.2006.00497.x.

Montali, Lidia. 2014. "Família Trabalho e Desigualdades no Início do Século XXI." *Revista Brasileira de Sociologia-RBS* 2, no. 4: 109–134. http://dx.doi.org/10.20336/rbs.79.

Nery, Carmen. 2019. "Extreme poverty affects 13.5 million persons and hits highest level in seven years". *Summary of Social Indicators, IBGE*. November 6, 2019. https://agenciadenoticias.ibge.gov.br/en/agencia-news/2184-news-agency/news/25895-extreme-poverty-affects-13-5-million-persons-and-hits-highest-level-in-seven-years.

Nussbaum, Martha. 2011. *Creating Capabilities*. Cambridge, Massachussets: Harvard University Press.

Okin, Susan Moller. 1989. *Justice, Gender, and the Family*. New York: Basic Books.

ONU Mulheres. 2016. *Mais igualdade para as mulheres brasileiras: caminhos de transformação econômica e social*. Brasília: ONU Mulheres.

Orloff, Ann Shola. 1993. "Gender and the Social Rights of Citizenship: The Comparative Analysis of Gender Relations and the Welfare State." *American Sociological Review* 58, no. 3: 303–328.

Paes-Sousa, Rômulo. 2013. "New Strategy for Poverty Eradication in Brazil: The Emergence of the Brasil Sem Miséria Plan." *One pager* 214.

Phillips, Anne. 2001. "Feminism and Liberalism Revisited: Has Martha Nussbaum Got It Right?" *Constellations* 8, no. 2: 249–266.

Phillips, Anne. 2008. "From Inequality to Differences: A Severe Case of Displacement?" In *Adding Insult to Injury: Nancy Fraser Debates her Critics*, edited by Kevin Olson, 112–125. London: Verso.

Rawls, John. 1971. *A Theory of Justice*. Boston: Harvard University Press.

Rego, Walquíria Gertrudes Domingues Leão and Alessandro Pinzani. 2013. "Liberdade, Dinheiro e Autonomia: O Caso do Programa Bolsa Família." In *Programa Bolsa Família: Uma Década de Inclusão e Cidadania*, edited by Tereza Campello and Marcelo. C. Neri, 359–366. Brasília: IPEA.

Rego, Walquíria Gertrudes Domingues Leão. 2013. "Resultados de Pesquisa sobre o Bolsa Família." Lecture at the Seminar Mulheres e Bolsa Família, Brasilia, March 8.

Rocha, Marcelo Cardona, Teresa Sacchet, and Kátia Favilla. 2014. "Programa Bolsa Família: Perspectivas a Partir do Olhar de Gênero e da Diversidade Sociocultural de Povos e Comunidades Tradicionais." In *Avaliação de Políticas Públicas: Reflexões acadêmicas sobre o desenvolvimento social e o combate à Fome*, edited by MDS (Ministério do Desenvolvimento Social e Combate à Fome), vol. 1, 82–93. Brasília: MDS.

Rousseff, Dilma. 2011. "Discurso da Presidenta da República, Dilma Rousseff, durante cerimônia de início do Mês da Mulher: Trabalho e Cidadania." Irecê, Brasil, March 1 2011. http://www.biblioteca.presidencia.gov.br/discursos/discursos-da-presidenta/iscurso-da-presidenta-da-republica-dilma-rousseff-durante-cerimonia-de-inicio-do-mes-da-mulher-trabalho-e-cidadania.

Sacchet, Teresa. 2008. "Beyond Numbers: The Impact of Gender Quotas in Latin America." *International Feminist Journal of Politics* 10, no. 3: 369–386. https://doi.org/10.1080/14616740802185700.

Sacchet, Teresa and Bruno Wilhelm Speck. 2012. "Financiamento Eleitoral, Representação Política e Gênero: uma análise das eleições de 2006". *Opinião Pública* 18, no. 1: 177–197. https://doi.org/10.1590/S0104-62762012000100009.

Sacchet, Teresa. 2018. "*Why gender quotas don't work in Brazil? The role of the electoral system and political finance*." Colombia Internacional 95: 25–54. https://doi.org/10.7440/colombiaint95.2018.02.

Sacchet, Teresa and Julia Spatuzzi Felmanas. 2019. "As Sertanejas são, antes de tudo, fortes: Pobreza, trabalho, e políticas sociais no Sertão Baiano." *Le Monde Diplomatique, Brasil*. July 2, 2019. https://diplomatique.org.br/as-sertanejas-sao-antes-de-tudo-fortes/. Saffioti, Heleieth. (2013) *A Mulher na Sociedade de Classes: Mito e Realidade*. Third edition. São Paulo: Expressão Popular.

Sainsbury, Diane. 1994. *Gendering Welfare States*. London: Sage.

Sánchez-Ancochea Diego and Lauro Mattei. 2011. "Bolsa Família, Poverty, and Inequality: Political and Economic Effects in the Short and Long Run." *Global Social Policy* 11, no. 2–3: 299–318. https://doi.org/10.1177/1468018111421297.

Sen, Amartya. 1979. *Equality of What? The Tanner Lecture on Human Values*. Stanford: Stanford University.

Sen, Amartya. 1999. *Development as Freedom*. Oxford: Oxford University Press.

Sen, Amartya. 2009. *The idea of Justice*. Cambridge, Massachusetts: The Belknap Press of Harvard University Press.

Soares, F. V. and E. Silva. 2010. *Conditional Cash Transfer Programmes and Gender Vulnerabilities in Latin America: Case Studies from Brazil, Chile, and Colombia*. London: Overseas Development Institute.

Soares, Fabio Veras, Rafael Peres Ribas, and Rafael Osório. 2010. "Evaluating the Impact of Brazil's Bolsa Família: Cash Transfer Programs in Comparative Perspective." *Latin American Research Review* 45, no. 2:173–190. doi:10.1353/lar.0.0088.

Sorj, Bila, Adriana Fontes, and Danielle Carusi Machado. 2007. "Reconciling work and family." *Cadernos de Pesquisa* 37, no. 132: 573–594.

Sorj, Bila. 2014. "Socialização do cuidado e desigualdades sociais." *Tempo Social* 26, no. 1: 123–128.

Tabbush, Constanza. 2010. "Latin American Women's Protection after Adjustment: A Feminist Critique of Conditional Cash Transfers in Chile and Argentina." *Oxford Development Studies* 38, no. 4: 437–459. https://doi.org/10.1080/13600818.2010.525327.

Taylor, Charles. 1994. "The Politics of Recognition." In *Multiculturalism: Examining the Politics of Recognition*, edited by A. Gutman, 25–73. Princeton: Princeton University Press.

UNDP (United Nation Development Programme). 1997. *Human Development Report 1997*. New York, NY.: Oxford University Press.

Young, Iris Marion. 1990. *Justice and the Politics of Difference*. New Jersey: Princeton University Press.

Young, Iris Marion. 2008a. "Structural Injustice and the Politics of Difference." In *Contemporary Debates in Political Philosophy*, edited by T. Christiano, and J. Christman, 362–383. New Jersey: Blackwell Publishing Ltd. doi:10.1002/9781444310399.

Young, Iris Marion. 2008b. "Unruly Categories: A Critique of Nancy Fraser's Dual Systems Theory." In *Adding Insult to Injury: Nancy Fraser Debates her Critics*, edited by Kevin Olson, 89–106. London: Verso.

Young, Iris Marion. 2009. "The Gendered Cycle of Vulnerability in the Less Developed World." In *Toward a Humanist Justice: The Political Philosophy of Susan Moller Okin* edited by D. Satz and R. Reich, 223–238. New York: Oxford University Press.

# 4

# THE *BOLSA FAMÍLIA* PROGRAM IN BAHIA

## Intersections of Class, Gender, Race, and Generation

*Josimara Delgado and Márcia Tavares*

### Introduction

The development of the *Bolsa Família* (BF) program over the years exposes important aspects of inequalities and social and political contradictions in Brazil. While the program has an important impact on the reduction of poverty, cash transfer policies are put forward as a monetized and targeted social protection strategy, and part of a process of dismantling public policy provisions that are fundamental for the working class, such as health and social security. The strategy to prioritize funds, and monetary benefits, is also questioned due to the centrality that it places on the family, not in the sense of its protection, but of making responsible, and electing it as the "natural" source of social protection.

More recently, since the impacts experienced in the country by social and political counter-reforms, social assistance policy has been severely affected, breaking up the Unified Social Assistance System. There has been a cut in benefits that has resulted in the penalization of large sections of the Brazilian working class, precisely at the time it is affected by the processes resulting from productive restructuring, which has made the labor market in the country even more exclusionary.

In this chapter, we reflect on these aspects of BF, presenting and discussing two axes that we have developed in our studies and research. The first axis is related to our theoretical searches that bring together, on the one hand, readings on contemporary social policies based on Marxist criticism and, on the other, feminist debates, predominantly with a materialist and anti-capitalist base, guided by the intersectionality between class, race, gender, and generation. From this theoretical path, we will discuss how the design of social protection, and social assistance policy in particular, integrates the contemporary strategies of capital, to guarantee the accumulation process. This is achieved through the exploitation of labor and the expropriation of workers' rights, especially gendered and racialized social groups, such as black women who form the majority of the social base of *Bolsa Família* program beneficiaries.

We argue that, in Brazil, black women have faced greater difficulties in entering the formal labor market, and accessing the status of social security beneficiaries over generations, on account of structural and institutional mechanisms, such as racism and the gender division of labor, which contribute towards making invisible their specific trajectories and demands for social protection. Therefore, we propose a discussion on social assistance policy, and cash transfer programs in particular, based on a feminist critique. We indicate how these social protection strategies restore ways of oppressing poor women and, to a large extent, do not contribute towards the critical and emancipating combat of this situation of poverty, and also take into account the inequalities and oppressions of gender and race.

The *Bolsa Família* program beneficiaries are families who live in poverty and extreme poverty.[1] The program recommends that the recipient is preferably a woman who is committed to fulfilling the conditionalities related to the tasks of childcare and maintaining family order. In addition, they are encouraged to work and become entrepreneurs in the subsistence and service sectors, such as the production and sale of handicrafts and food, and giving manicures. The benefit awarded to women becomes a gender trap, since a percentage of them are the main economic providers in the family group and, as the program's point of contact, they must be responsible, often exclusively, for the care and social protection of the family.

The second axis we refer to revolves around the specific characteristics of Salvador, and the northeast, through data analysis that enables us to reconstruct a more concrete social terrain, formed of historical determinations that are displayed in numbers and narrated trajectories. We present data on the sociodemographic condition of Salvador, collected from Inter-Union Department of Statistics and Socio-economic Studies (DIEESE) and Brazilian Institute of Geography and Statistics (IBGE) documents, and institutional monitoring and evaluation reports. We also discuss research data produced within the Interdisciplinary Studies on Women, Gender and Feminism Program (PPGNEIM) and Study Group on Social Inequalities, Public Policies and Social Services (DSPPSS) at the Federal University of Bahia (UFBA). The empirical material of this research is based on narratives and interviews held with female BF beneficiaries in Salvador.

The data and reflections that arose from the research with the users' accounts contributed towards establishing the proposed debate, by retrieving social storylines, built in specific times and spaces, and within which we can understand how class, race, gender, and generation produce real experiences of oppression, exploitation, and resistance. The stories reconstruct a dense social fabric in which we see violence reproduced among generations of poor black women, with a gender content, labor exploitation, appropriation of their time in care-related tasks, and the formation of solidarity and mutual assistance networks. Similarly, the accounts enable possible tendencies, advances, and challenges to be identified, for the program to be established and effective as a mechanism to promote social rights and to tackle poverty.

The *Bolsa Família* program, adopting a familistic perspective, disregards the extent to which the intersection of gender and race make black women susceptible to vulnerable situations, which prevents them from escaping poverty and exclusion. Therefore, a gender reading from an intersectional approach is fundamental to reveal both the limits of *Bolsa Família*, and the need for its formulation and establishment as a universal, non-targeted program.

In addition to this introduction, this chapter is made up of another three sections. One is about social protection, and the contemporary crisis, in which we seek to provide some historical and theoretical foundations, to understand the crisis and its structural connection with the contemporary movement of capital, characterized by the financialization of the economy, and its effects on social protection. We also show the role of social assistance and cash transfers in managing poverty, and the reproduction of the more subordinate and precarious social groups in this context, including female cash transfer beneficiaries. Also, as part of this debate, we seek to understand the effects of the capitalist crisis in Brazil, retrieving some historical tendencies from our social protection system, and highlighting specific forms of reproduction, through action of the state and its institutionality, and race and gender inequalities. In the next part of this chapter, we present and discuss quantitative and qualitative research data. Lastly, in the third section, we bring together the analyses put forward in the chapter to tie up the different axes discussed, to highlight their specific contribution, and to identify other possibilities for discussion from these texts.

## Social Protection and the Contemporary Crisis: Historical Social Assistance Possibilities

As mentioned above, the theoretical-methodological approach of this chapter assumes the retrieval of some debates on social protection in the context of the capitalist crisis, with an emphasis on the role of cash transfer policies. To this end, we start with literature that is based on the foundations of the Marxist tradition, to understand the BF program in the debate on structural racism, and from feminist perspectives. Together, these approaches allow a critical analysis of the technical and economic-based nature with which public policies have been handled in the narratives and practices of contemporary neoliberal governments, which overlook the links between social policies and the development of capitalism, with its multiple exploitation and oppression mechanisms, above all with a class, racial, and gender content.

We start the proposed discussion by retrieving the topic of public social protection in contemporary times, from the remission of the structural crisis of capitalism, evident since the 1970s, and experienced in the entire capitalist world.[2] According to Mészáros (2011, 11), this is an "endemic, cumulative, chronic and permanent" crisis, in which "the capital system, with its unlimited expansion, converts into an uncontrollable and deeply destructive procedure." It is a deep and extensive recession that has affected the entire capitalist economy, with a significant decline in profits. With a capitalist base, this crisis includes economic, political and ecological dimensions, and is generalized through the "brutally predatory form of capitalism that we experience today: globalized, financialized and neoliberal" (Arruzza, Bhattacharya, and Fraser 2019, 45).

The emphasis in times of crisis is on the direct submission of social rights to the economic, political, social, and cultural strategies adopted by capital, both for it to be reproduced, and to recreate the social conditions required for its growth and accumulation. In practice, this has taken place through dismantling public social protection systems, as a group of rights guaranteed by the state through public funds. Policies and services suffer from deep-rooted precariousness and dissolution, and their purpose becomes the optimization of capital.

Pierre Dardot and Christian Laval (2016) put forward some fundamental aspects of this framework, which we turn to due to their relevance for an analysis of social assistance. For the authors, the neoliberal issues and dominant rationality of this system are guided specifically by the market vision of flexible labor, and the policy of reinsertion into the job market. According to them, there is a focus on the struggle against poverty, which occurs through solidarity with the excluded but in a way that does not create dependence, and it is always conditional upon personal effort and work (Dardot and Laval 2016).

The focus on combating poverty as the option for public social protection has been a way of passing on the costs to the employed, since public social policies are financed by income tax, and not by altering the concentration of income. With regards to this "functionality of poverty," and policies that focus on the most deprived, Paugam and Duvoux (2008), analyzing the French financial situation after 20 years of integration policies through a minimum income, show how this initiative has contributed towards keeping specific groups in lasting poverty, whilst also making them more productive, by training them to execute more precarious jobs. Thus, they make a relation between the precariousness of labor and social assistance, insofar as this has operated as an activation policy for the labor market, contributing towards the reproduction of the material and symbolic conditions required to perform more demeaning market activities.

In Brazilian context, Silva (2010) highlight that information and data from various studies enable us to consider that the nature and level of the impact of BF on the beneficiary families is limited to meeting immediate needs, without enabling more far-reaching changes in these families' living standards. While the state focuses its actions on the family, the process of individualization (or establishing "capabilities" or "autonomy") is encouraged, through which the individual is responsible for escaping their situation of social precarity, "responsibly" fulfilling the policy's requirements. In the contemporary debate on the role of the state in economic and social development, various analytical instruments (capability, empowerment, governance, and human and social capital) emerge as a form of activating this new form of citizenship, based on the values of cooperation (Marins 2018).

Many analyses have been carried out to clarify the connection of cash transfers with monetization and activation processes for the labor market, highlighting the impacts on the economy and the assisted population. For example, Gisele Souza da Silva (2012) researched the transfer of part of the resources allocated to cash transfer programs to "paying agents" (Silva 2012, 222); in other words, banking and financial institutions. In the case of BF, this is *Caixa Econômica Federal*. Payment to the bank is linked to the number of beneficiary families. According to the author, "between 2006 and 2010 almost BRL 1.7 billion was transferred for this purpose, which means a large amount of resources from public funds for the direct remuneration of interest-bearing capital" (Silva 2012, 228).

Another dimension of this circuit of monetization and financialization is the fact that few resources are allocated to transfer programs, and the values of the benefits are minimal, which characterizes this strategy as comparatively cheap in relation to universal policies. Despite the impact of extreme poverty on their condition, for the population this assistance does not provide them with a new way to be integrated into society. If we compare the value of the benefit with the value of the income derived from labor, a minimum salary and retirement, its residual nature is clear. As the Inter-Union Department of Statistics and Socio-Economic Studies demonstrated, in 2017, the average value of BF was approximately 2.5 times less than the amount required to buy a commodity bundle in the capital of São Paulo, at an estimated price of BRL 435.00 (DIEESE 2017b) or approximately USD 138.00 during the period considered. The value of the minimum montly salary at the time was BRL 937.00 reais, which is equivalent to USD 299.36.

In this chapter we highlight the meaning of social assistance and cash transfers in the context of a crisis of capital. We aim with this to understand who the female social assistance beneficiaries are, from the point of view of a hegemonic logic that establishes contemporary social dynamics. Those beneficiaries are part of the more subordinate and precarious social groups in society, since they are responsible for the social reproduction of very poor groups, in a poor way; in other words, without public resources and with a meagre income: low cost social reproduction (Falquet 2013), understood as one of the perverse outcomes of the gender division of labor[3] in contemporary times. While these women perform this role, part of the groups to which they belong, made up of temporary workers, or those without any productive activities, are the target of mass imprisonment policies (Alexander 2018), or victims of institutional violence and extermination processes by the state (Almeida 2018). From this more distant and abstract point of view, the "destructive procedures" of the system are observed, in the sense that the destruction and reversal of standards of sociability and citizenship that were once possible within the logic of capital are now destroyed, increasing the levels of inequality, and penalizing the social groups that are historically those whose bodies and stories have been most exploited, expropriated, and made invisible.

In our research, these issues are considered in an interlocution with data on female *Bolsa Família* beneficiaries in Salvador, which returns us to a more concrete field of the real world, in which the history of labor and social protection in Brazil is a fundamental element. It is in this concrete field that the reach and limits of *Bolsa Família* for Brazilian women and those from Bahia, in particular, can be more clearly illustrated. In Brazil, the effects of the crisis are felt within a social fabric already characterized by a complex and deep-rooted system of inequalities reproduced through state action and its institutionality. One of our next objectives in this chapter is to discuss some of the traits of this social fabric, how the intersections between gender, class, and race are formed in the configuration of inequalities, and the answers given by the state, in terms of social protection.

## Social Assistance and Cash Transfer Policies in Brazil

For Latin America, and especially Brazil, for at least 20 years this way of conducting the crisis of capitalism has resulted in the submission of domestic economic and social policy guidelines to the financial demands of international institutions, such as the World Bank, which are interested in creating conditions to commoditize social life in the country, facilitating the exploitation of natural resources, and essential sectors of the economy. This process has reinforced the historical traits in Brazilian social formation, such as the exploitation of labor, unemployment, the concentration of income, gender division of labor, and racism. One of the preferred strategies to establish this social (un)protection model was to strengthen one of the historical traits of social protection in Brazil, which is its pronounced familistic nature (Mioto, Campos, and Carloto 2015).

Brazil has not achieved a standard of protection in the molds possible in the Fordist-Keynesian context. Unemployment is constant in the labor market (Santos 2008), not only in the more recessive periods. Similarly, for many decades, the social protection model has been limited to the logic of social insurance and a model of citizenship, necessarily associated with the formal insertion of workers into the labor market, and centered on the right to retirement and a pension (Santos 1979).

From 1930, the Brazilian state established a standard of responses to social issues, in which the urban working class was recognized at the public level, granting social rights directly linked to production and social security contributions. Similarly, in the state narrative the working family – considered a nuclear family organized around a providing father, a mother who is a carer and the moral domestic guardian, and children – is held up as a moral unit, and cell, in which the state is established.

However, this strategy did not guarantee universal protection, since it let significant segments of workers – those who were not formally part of the labor market, performing activities without a formal contract, in part-time activities, and domestic work – fall by the wayside. These are quite common working conditions in Brazil. Within these groups of workers, we highlight rural workers, who were not included in any welfare policy until the 1960s. This exclusion was also determined by race and gender, with a strong presence of women and the black population among the unprotected workers.

Despite its limitations, this was a strategy that was institutionalized in Brazil through state action, in the sense of forming the idea of a nation guided by work and dignifying the image of the worker, silencing the inequalities that were reproduced and enhanced in this agreement (Colbari 1995). Here we consider regional differences in Brazil, the asymmetries of gender and race, and rural and urban inequalities. From a political-ideological point of view, this strategy was only achieved by adapting the various cultural, religious, and racial traditions present in the lives of Brazilian workers to the logic of urban-industrial work, and national unity – a process characterized by exercising power permeated by racism and sexism (Colbari 1995; Almeida 2018).

This intervention model, and the inherent notion of family, standardize specific universal situations and social practices, replete with inequalities and violence. Therefore, the first point to highlight is the gender inequalities reproduced under this state intervention model. The citizenship agreement led by the state in Brazil has a strong familistic matrix, establishing a family model in which women's time and work are appropriated, without remuneration, to reproduce the workforce. This agreement ideologically constructs, and reproduces, the image conceived of the role attributed to women, which is symbolically represented as an important place to maintain domestic morality and social order.

This discussion has been held in the field of feminist theories, following criticism of the welfare state (Pateman 2000; Fraser 2016). This critique calls into question the naturalization of the duties of caring as female attributes. Tronto (1997) claims that caring is an activity guided by gender, both within the market and the private sphere. The jobs carried out by women are generally those involving care. According to the author, this is because femininity is constructed as the antithesis of masculinity, which is reflected in the traditional gender roles for women and men. Thus, while "men care about, women take care of" the family (Tronto 1997, 199). Consequently, the traditional care role re-establishes the configuration of the division of the world between male (production/public) and female (reproduction/private).

Mota (2015) draws attention to the fact that the hegemonic model of family organization highlights an ideal of care (in which other models should fit), which in addition to creating a distinction between people (of different genders, sexes, classes, and race), establishes a distinction between families. While female practice is exercised within the private domain, care produces privileges for men, insofar as they are exempted from this responsibility, while it generates oppression for women and overloads them.

Patriarchal and capitalist domination form two sides of the same way of producing and reproducing life and a specific social order. Although female oppression preceded the advent of capitalism, it takes and highlights the contradictions present in societies based on private property, in order to favor capitalist accumulation – whether related to gender, race, ethnic, religious, and nationality distinctions, or any other criterion (Andrade 2015). This is an arrangement that contributes towards the reproduction of poverty, the exploitation of women, misogyny, and income inequalities, since women still remain responsible for reproduction and unpaid labor; they are devoted to taking care of the home, their children, the sick, the elderly, and their spouses. Essentially, men and women's responsibilities within their families are guided by gender relations, legitimized by patriarchal order (Silva and Tavares 2015).

Interpreted from a gender perspective, this familistic perspective of Brazilian social policy emerges as a mechanism that has had important repercussions on the way that women, especially the poorest, have been treated by national social protection systems. The regulated citizenship model, focusing on the formal worker's family, makes invisible the work and needs of women and their demands within the sphere of reproducing social life. Obviously, this is a fact that has made it difficult for women to remain in the labor market and continue to access to labor rights, particularly retirement. Women's lives, both in past and current generations, are more affected by periods of interrupted work activities due to the demands of caring, which has led to a reduction in female contributions and a subsequent delay in their retirement (Saboia 2006).

In terms of long-lasting processes in Brazilian society, the weight of this condition has rested on the women who had unequal access to the productive domain, with lower salaries and insecure jobs. This is a heavily racialized group. Consider, for example, the case of domestic labor in Brazil, and its relation with the exploitation of these women. Historically dedicated to subsistence labor, it is black women who carry out the most precarious jobs, and head the households with lower incomes (Carneiro 2011; Biroli 2018). Thus, with their trajectories, they unveil the gender and racial division of labor (Hirata and Kergoat 2007; Almeida 2018) as effective processes in the formation of the working class and the world of work in Brazil (Bairros 1995).

According to the Gender Statistics Study: Social indicators of women in Brazil (IBGE 2018a), in 2016, the number of hours that women dedicated to taking care of people and/or domestic chores was 73% more than men (18.1 hours as opposed to 10.5 hours). When breaking down the data by region, the greatest inequality in the distribution of hours for these activities is concentrated in the northeast region, where this figure is approximately 80% more hours than men, equivalent to 19 hours per week. The division by color or race demonstrates that black or brown women are those most engaged in the care of people and/or domestic chores, forming a total of 18.6 hours per week in 2016, while there is little variation for men, when the variation of color, race, or area of residency are examined.

Also, according to the IBGE study, a spatial breakdown reaffirms regional inequalities, identifying a higher concentration of women who work part-time in the north and northeast regions. Another aggravating factor of gender inequality is highlighted with a breakdown of the indicator by color or race, where the 2016 data illustrates that 31.3% of black or brown women held part-time jobs, compared to 25% of white women. The proportion of black or brown[4] men was 16%, while only 11.9% of white men held part-time jobs.

It is important to highlight that, through practices and discourse that reproduce the asymmetries of gender and race, poor women who do not have access to formal jobs have been occupying an important part of the group of workers who are placed outside regulated citizenship standards. This group has counted, and counts on, social protection by means of social assistance, which, for many decades has remained connected to assistentialism and philanthropy and, therefore, is characterized by a lack of planning and financing, and actions that focus on the poorest groups – a clear method of maintaining poverty and social needs as an element of political bargaining. The liberal concept of labor is that a worker should provide for their family with the sale of their workforce and, therefore, with their salary (Boschetti 2016), while justifying that those who are "unfit" are assisted through charity (Mota 2010; Boschetti 2016), establishing a practical and symbolic relationship between women, poverty, unproductive work, and philanthropy.

Since the drafting of the 1988 Federal Constitution, social protection in Brazil has been deflected by establishing a social security system through contributions, in the case of social security policy, and non-contributory contributions, as in health and social assistance policies. The implementation of this system was an undeniable achievement by workers, and an advance for Brazilian society. However, this historic gain was overshadowed by the logic established, with the neoliberal offensive in Brazil, which resulted in the subordination of Brazilian social security to the "recommendations" of international institutions (World Bank and IMF, etc.) and their financial and fiscal constraints.

Therefore, Brazilian society was not able to enjoy the impacts of fully-developed, universal social security, and the introduction of the structures required to guarantee that right. Security policies in Brazil did not form an "unified protection mechanism," but rather a "contradictory unit" (Mota 2010, 133), provided by the commodification and privatization of welfare and health policies, and advances in social assistance, as the main social protection mechanism, whose flagship is cash transfer programs.

As we discussed in the first part of this chapter, despite its importance in tackling the absolute poverty of high percentages of workers, the cash transfer strategy in Brazil has been largely established to the detriment of public investments in fundamental policies for the working class, such as health and welfare. Within social assistance, as we mentioned in the previous section, it is a low-cost policy for the state, and the service structure set out in the Unified Social Assistance System has also been dismantled. This is in a context in which the increase in poverty and relative over-population, due to structural unemployment and precarious jobs, means that the population requiring a social assistance policy is growing rapidly. In this process of exploitation and expropriation, black women become the base for a large workforce available for the more precarious and insecure jobs, mainly in sectors in which this type of labor, such as domestic labor, care, and subsistence work, have traditionally predominated.

With this debate, we consider that some socio-historic foundations are laid, for us to think about what the social protection model, centered on cash transfers, represents for the beneficiaries. Therefore, the first issue to be mentioned is that in this context of crisis, international institutions and agencies, governments and investigators appoint women as the "agents" who perform an important role in the "development process." From then on, social policies have gradually focused on women, highlighting the need to "increase the human" or "social capital" of poor women/mothers, taking an ambiguous stance, oscillating between promoting their productive role (which involves more training to secure better jobs, and to improve the family's economic situation), or strengthening their reproductive role: the return to the home and the community (which means more training for them to be better mothers, controlling the birth rate, involvement in community life and the state makes access to resources possible if a male figure is absent).

Care is awarded a moral significance that limits women/mothers, whose bodies, as Grisci (1995) highlights, are placed at the service of reproducing gender relations and machinized so that they adjust to fulfilling their legitimized duty, gender-related responsibilities, and perfection of the child they are raising. Thus, the women who are the recipients of cash transfer programs, such as *Bolsa Família* are caught in a gender trap, since remaining on the program entails fulfilling the conditionalities, which involves a work overload, and an increase in social time, but also results in shame and blame if they are not able to satisfactorily fulfil these *requirements*. This is seen as an inability, and personal *failure*, in addition to carrying the *stigma* of being "dependent" on state "help," in which the mandatory proof of poverty deprives them of their dignity as citizens (Pereira and Stein 2010).

Luana Passos de Souza (2015) argues that adoption of the discourse on the "feminization of poverty" by governments and international institutions was parallel to a higher inclusion of poor women in direct cash transfer programs. Being a recipient is based on the assumption of a greater responsibility, of fulfilling the conditionalities, but also on their capacity to be a mother, and allocating the resources for the family's well-being. Therefore, these programs do not focus on their productive inclusion and upward mobility, and do nothing to contribute towards eliminating the asymmetry in the gender and race relations that characterizes these workers' life trajectories, and those of preceding and successive generations.

In effect, plans prepared in 2015 to subsidize the Action Plan that forms Basic Integrated Planning to tackle violence against women in Bahia reveals that in the Southern Lowlands Territory,[5] for example, the majority of women are *Bolsa Família* program beneficiaries, and there are very few training courses available that do not reproduce the gender stereotypes associated with females. Therefore, they predominantly focus on care, and do not burden the municipalities because they are cheap, such as, receptionist, manicurist, cooking, making snacks, cleaning/filleting fish to sell, and making lingerie, among others, resulting in insecure jobs with low pay that make little contribution towards their autonomy and empowerment (Vanin 2016). It is observed that the activities are cumulative, alongside domestic chores, social reproduction of the family, and replenishment of the workforce, which are traditional roles carried out by women-mothers-carers, while the state is exempt from the responsibility of guaranteeing social protection to families. It establishes a new form of oppression-exploitation of women, and their capacity (Delgado and Tavares 2012).

In BF fieldwork, conducted in the DSPPSS research group and PPGNEIM, one of the central focuses is on the use of interviews with beneficiaries, which is the basis for empirical material. In this work, we give priority to learning about the most expressive people in this program: black women. The research shows there is an inter-generational reproduction of poverty in the beneficiaries' families, involving preceding and successive generations, with a strong presence of black women heading the households (Mariano, Tavares, and Delgado 2018).

Positioning ourselves in this empirical universe – the city of Salvador, Bahia, in the Brazilian northeast – we deal with a reality that expresses the serious regional inequalities in the country, demonstrated in numbers and trajectories which, in different ways, register the various faces of poverty, in their clear relations with the structures that promote injustice in relations between classes, races, and genders.

We have argued here that an important element in understanding BF is understanding poverty, which is the program focus as part of broader relations that cut across society and politics in Brazil. Particularly important for this study has been relating the debate on poverty to the structural inequalities of society and, especially, to the reality of unemployment and precarious work. According to the benchmark adopted, the profile of social assistance users is characterized by a high number of unemployed people, who are capable of working, and at the age to work, but are not able to access the formal market and or paid employment.

According to the Inter-Union Department of Statistics and Socio-Economic Studies (DIEESE 2018) Employment and Unemployment Research, the annual unemployment rate in the state capital is 24.9% of the economically active population, the highest since 2003. Between 2017 and 2018, approximately 23,000 formal jobs were lost, while the number of those without formal employment grew by 19,000, and also the number of self-employed workers by 14,000 (DIEESE 2018). In 2018, for the second consecutive year, there was a quantitative increase in jobs for women from the Metropolitan Region of Salvador, while the number and unemployment rate for women also increased, with the former reaching the highest level of the historical series, which started in 1997, and the latter, achieving the highest percentage since 2003.We see how this situation is reflected in the *Bolsa Família* figures. According to the *Bolsa Família* program Unified Register Social Information Report, published by the Ministry of Citizenship, in April 2019, the state of Bahia had 3,029,880 families registered on the Unified Register, with 1,846,806 of these families being BF beneficiaries, approximately 29.9%. Each family receives an average sum of BRL 185.65 per month. In the state capital, Salvador, there were 173,658 families benefiting from BF, approximately 13.8% of the total population of the municipality, including 49,089 families who, without the program, would be living in extreme poverty (Brazil 2019).

In the northeast, and Bahia, BF addresses the reality of the extreme precarity of workers, the majority of whom are black, and whose families have been excluded from better jobs, and access to goods and services for generations. The Social Indicators Summary, which provides an overview of the Brazilian population's living conditions (IBGE 2018a), demonstrates that, in 2017, the northeast had the highest concentration of those living poverty – 44.8% of the country, which corresponds to 25.5 million people. The document takes the criteria adopted by the World Bank as a parameter, which classifies as poor those with a daily income of under USD 5.50, or BRL 406.00 per month, by purchasing power parity.

According to this parameter, in the same year, the proportion of people resident in Salvador below the poverty line corresponded to almost half of that found in the state as a whole: two in every ten inhabitants (corresponding to 715,000 people). The document also identified that between 2014 and 2017, in the northeast region the unemployment rate rose from 8.5% to 14.7%. In 2017, the proportion of workers engaged in informal jobs reached 56.2%. In relation to the average monthly per capita household income, the lowest average recorded in the country was in the northeast (BRL 984.00), where almost half the population (49.9%), had an average monthly per capita household income of half a minimum salary.

The data shows that this poverty is gender and color-related. Célia Regina Sganzerla and Eva Borges (2014), who investigated who and where the deprived people of Bahia are, identified that among the people registered on the Single Registry as being legally responsible for the family, 93.5% are female, while only 6.5% are male. In relation to the age range, the majority are between the ages of 25 and 34, which, together with the 16 to 24 age group, corresponds to more than 40% of those legally responsible, meaning that the person legally responsible for BF in Bahia according to government recommendations, is not only female, she is also young.

In turn, Souza and Couto (2015), outlining the profile of BF beneficiaries in Bahia based on the 2010 demographic census, identified that the majority of beneficiaries are brown (75.6%), followed by black people (12.8%).[6] White people corresponded to only 10.7% of beneficiaries. According to the G1 Bahia journal (2019), Continuous National Household Sample Survey (PNAD *Contínua*) data released by IBGE in 2018, reveals that one in every five people who lived in Bahia self-declared as black, which corresponded to 3,389,881 Bahian people, or 22.9% of the state's population. The survey also showed that Bahia had the second largest black population in the country in absolute numbers (the state of São Paulo was in first place) and remained the only state in the country in which black people formed a more expressive segment in the general population than those self-declared as white, approximately 18.1% of the population of Bahia. On the other hand, if we take the Black Movement's[7] classification, and add together the number of people who self-declared as black and brown, we identify that, in 2018, 11,994 million people in Bahia were black, which is approximately 81.1% of the population.

This general data signals the importance of BF in the reality of Bahia, considering that the state has a significant territorial reach, and the territories are extremely poor. Therefore, we should put forward some reflections based on this study, the focus of which has been the program's specific characteristics, and the information available from an intersectional perspective.

Speaking of the trajectory of black women who are *Bolsa Família* beneficiaries, is seeing how the first ties forged between mothers and daughters, for different generations of black women on the outskirts of Salvador, were central to reproducing a relationship generally linked to a domestic impoverished center. The livelihoods of these families are guaranteed through a combination of low salaries from insecure jobs, an unsteady income from informal activities, and carrying out several types of unpaid jobs, such as domestic services and care.

This empirical material has enabled us to think about the family – above all, the one that is the object of intervention and regulation within the field of public policies, which is the working class family – from a point of view that considers, from the categories of gender, race, and age, the diversity of their concrete arrangements, and the invisibility of certain subjects, in the eyes of the state and its policies. In this case, we refer, in particular, to black women and the families formed by these women. This approach provides us with the bases to denaturalize the idea of a "family in a vulnerable situation," present in the Brazilian state's actions and discourses, and social policies in distinct contexts throughout history, perceiving it as an idea permeated by sexism and racism and effective ideologies in the world of work in Brazil.

In Deise Souza Santos' research (Santos 2018), the empirical base is the life stories of six black, adult women, with precarious socio-occupational in the job market, and recipients of *Bolsa Família*, all resident in the same neighborhood in the outskirts of Salvador. In the discussion presented here, we will refer to the stories of three women, among those interviewed by Santos (2018), a selection that enables a given social characteristic to be reconstructed. There are three black, adult women, the heads of households made up by them, their children, and/or grandchildren. Dandara is 37, completed high school, is divorced and the mother of a 11-year-old daughter, and 21-year-old son, from different relationships. She is the daughter of a domestic worker, who was also a single mother of two children. She now lives with her 60-year-old mother and her children. Dandara has never held a formal job, having performed the roles of nanny and salesperson; her *Bolsa Família* benefit has been suspended, since she has been unable to fulfil some of the conditionalities. Akotirene is 55, studied until the fourth year of basic education, but did not complete this; she is single, the mother of five children, and has 13 grandchildren; she lives with one son and a grandson; she is the daughter of a laundress who has passed away. She has worked for only six years in official employment, with her work booklet signed and, today, in addition to BF, she sells grilled corn. Iracema is 60, studied until the fourth year of basic education, is single, and the mother of five children from two different relationships; she lives with two children and her sister. She has worked as a domestic worker, daily cleaner, and salesperson, but never formally. She currently sells cosmetics.

Santos (2018) begins her study by drawing attention to the fact that, amongst black, working women, the existence of a female head of the house is a recurrent feature.[8] A partner abandoning the family home, and separation caused by domestic violence, affects the lives of the interviewees and their mothers. The author highlights how in the narratives work appears as an element that supports the objective conditions in which relationships with their sons and daughters, partners, and community networks were constructed, and with complex scenarios, characterized by oppressive matrices, connected to gender relations and the family. The stories reveal the conditions in which real women engage in motherhood. These conditions are strongly characterized by the universe of work, and hierarchized and unequal relations between the sexes, especially with regards to the distribution of the responsibilities of caring for children. The three interviewees have similar experiences as mothers and daughters: they all had to deal with the absence of a male figure. The generational dimension of motherhood is demonstrated in its interlace with class, race, and gender, as Akotirene reported:

> Well, what happened during my childhood? Work, because my father went to Rio, and my mother stayed here in Salvador. We were very young when he left. My mother earned money by washing clothes. I had to help her: We were at the fountain on Mondays, Tuesdays and Wednesdays; she did the ironing on Thursdays and Fridays! [iron that used hot coals] (…) My mother and I battled on! (…) On Thursdays and Fridays, she used a charcoal iron, as we didn't have electricity; on Saturdays, we left in the morning, walking from here to Ribeira. Me with a little bundle on my head. How old was I?

> Seven! My mother had three or four bundles on her head, one on top of the other and I had two, that I could manage; I carried what I could. And so, that is how it was, you know?!
>
> *(Santos 2018, 87)*

A mutual support network between mothers and daughters is seen here, constructed in the domestic space, which enabled the conciliation of family and productive life, both for the newer and older generations.

There are several issues to analyze on this topic that illustrate the women's relationship with work, the domestic space, and motherhood. An initial approach enables us to rediscover an old debate in Brazilian socio-anthropology, which points to the family as a value, and important code for the material and symbolic reproduction of the worker and their family. Cynthia Sarti (1996) highlights the specific nature of the working family model, as of a moral value, centered on the principle of reciprocity, where the family and kinship predominate over individuals. Simoni Guedes' research (1998) shows that the "help" category is fundamental within the universe of urban workers, as a way of defining family relationships, and links to a relative.

We cannot fail to notice the presence of family solidarity, the need to "help at home," since the central code of the exchanges contains a naturalization of child labor as part of socialization, seen as necessary, and the only form possible for poor women. Thus, the interviewees' accounts are a record of how badly paid, and informal work, has been formed historically in Brazil, as a female activity, and for black women in particular. This it is social architecture, in which this socialization for work was not publicly questioned, that makes invisible the social problems characterized by unequal conditions. This naturalization, in the case of paid domestic labor, also played a fundamental role for white women from the elites and middle class to enter the labor market. But, above all, the narratives show how both in the past and present extremely precarious work situations are only possible because a family structure is maintained, so that the household income is always complemented by subsistence activities carried out by younger and older women.

This is an important issue that indicates the need to introduce the questions of race and class when the subject is female labor, considered from a feminist perspective. It is noted in these accounts that, for black women for various generations, their insertion into the world of work is something that happened at a young age. This work was/is a space, where their labor power was exploited, and a concrete experience of racist and sexist stigmas and oppressions. In these conditions, it is interesting to note how they may interpret the domestic space (the home) as a space to experience a warm welcome and solidarity, especially in relationships with other women.

Thus, the story of Iracema, now aged 60, provides another dimension to the issue. She shows how "working outside the home" emerged as a possibility to escape the oppression of an extremely violent father who prevented her, her siblings, and her mother, from working and studying. In addition, at home, Iracema was responsible for domestic chores, and looking after her younger siblings, including a sister with disabilities. It shows how family ties, and the connection with the domestic space are formed, in a real environment of dominated women, as the feminist movement and gender debates have reported.

However, as Iracema's story also illustrates, leaving home for the labor market does not release black women from the dictates of the sexual and racial division of labor. In this context, work does not take on the meaning of emancipation, and constructing a career but rather of alienation and distress and, therefore, once again, the possibility of counting on the family, or re-establishing family arrangements, emerge as an important support and source of dignity.

For Iracema, who left her parents' house at the age of 19, already a single mother of two children, she started to experience a precarious and informal job as a domestic worker: "I went to the depths of other people's kitchens to work." Once more, what gave the hard work that Iracema found "in the depths of the kitchens" meaning was the possibility of counting on her mother, and rebuilding a new domestic base for her and her children. Initially, when Iracema without her children`s father decided to leave her parents' house where she had lived with her spouse, the children stayed with her mother, so that she could go to work. Some time later, working and with her own home, Iracema brought her mother and children to live with her, removing her from the cycle of domestic violence in which she had lived for decades.

In Asenate Franco's doctoral research (2018),[9] with female rural workers in Bahia who had experienced/experience situations of domestic and family violence, we observed that they were all *Bolsa Família* program beneficiaries, and they correspond to the socio-economic profile presented above. They had entered the labor force at an early age as children (some from the age of three), were forced to stop studying, whether because they were not able to balance it with family farming activities, taking care of younger siblings, or due to fatigue, and is reflected in learning difficulties, or even the lack of schools in the rural communities where they live. As adults, with a low level of education, or illiterate, they engage in family farming activities or work with their spouses and children as land tenants, while taking part-time informal, menial jobs without any labor rights. They carry out a series of parallel activities on an income that guarantees the family group's subsistence: making and selling snacks, a widow's pension, midwife, domestic worker, daily cleaner, and helping relatives, among others.

We highlight that on account of the activities these women carry out in the countryside, generally concentrated in family farming, their work is not recognized and is often classified as "help." Consequently, they do not receive any remuneration, as Zacimba, aged 51, considers when justifying to Franco (2018) the lack of payment for cultivating the land with her spouse, who refused to provide basic family needs apart from food. Thus, Zacimba provided services on farms to meet other needs, besides relying on support from relatives and "help" from her children, who started to work in the fields from the age of five: "All of my children here, they got their first teeth in the fields, helping" (Franco 2018, 126), but, she explains that, unlike her, they worked and studied.

Another way of complementing the family income, for those who live in the context of poverty and extreme poverty, is the resource that the *Bolsa Família* program passes on, but for this benefit to be received on a monthly basis the recipients must comply with some conditions, such as proving that their children attend school. On the other hand, contrary to Brazilian legislation,[10] parents continue to consider child labor – working in the fields or at home – as "help," seeing it as a learning and training process for new generations to work in the family production unit.

The narratives of the women interviewed by Franco (2018) also enable us to infer that the benefit guaranteed their survival, as Luíza confirms – "I live from *Bolsa Família* [just BRL 87.00]" (Franco 2018, 250) – added to a daughter's financial assistance, which is shown to be recurrent among the families, in which grandmothers, mothers, and daughters create a network of intergenerational solidarity and support each other. From an older generation, she clarifies: "There was no *Bolsa Família* at that time, [...] when the food I had in my house ran out, and so that my children didn't go hungry, I had to go to my grandmother's house ..." (Franco 2018, 265).

However, in the rural setting, neither the solidarity network between the women, or receipt of the benefit, have been able to break up asymmetrical gender relations and the violent situations they have faced, whether by exploiting their labor, disguised as "help," or in marital relations. Hostages of a patriarchal cultural that reinforces and naturalizes gender inequality, these women are entrapped, by the socialization process, learning to suppress suffering, and living with a *continuum* of violence in their lives, anchored in the belief that a man is the backbone of the house, without whom the family/home collapses. In other words, if receipt of *Bolsa Família* guarantees an improvement in the material conditions in which these women survive, on the subjective level, the benefit is more like "help," for which they feel grateful, but it does not produce effective changes in their daily struggle for survival. Their personal statements suggest reflections on the intergenerational reproduction of poverty, and lack of mobility, with regards to their occupational situation, which in turn hinders autonomy and effective changes in their lives.

In effect, exploring some of the data collected in Salvador in 2018, as part of a broader investigation carried out in some of the Brazilian state capitals among BF beneficiaries coordinated by a team at the State University of Londrina, we can identify, as members of the team responsible for the work in Salvador, some aspects we consider pertinent for reflection. The empirical material of the research is made up of 33 interviews; 23 of them are from black (black and brown) women. With regard to their civil status, 16 women are single, and live in households made up of them and their children. The majority of the women did not marry the father of their children, or they have separated from him. The group of interviewees is made up of women aged between 23 and 62, with a significant concentration aged between 35 and 50, with 12 of them in this age range; seven women are under 35, and five are older, aged between 58 and 62. Although they are at distinct moments of their family and reproductive life, from the point of view of job placement all the women are unemployed and/or working informally.

The interviewees' paid work trajectories illustrate the difficulty of entering the formal market, even as freelancers. The possibility of having formal work was only presented to three interviewees, two of them older, aged 56 and 61, and the other 34. The others, although they had executed various paid activities throughout their lives, and in some cases since childhood, have never worked formally. They have remained in informal jobs, working as cleaners, carers, manicurists, and food and drink sellers. Notable is the age they started working: 16 of them related that they had started carrying out a paid activity in the labor market before the age of 18, and ten of them before the age of 14.

The age of starting activities in the labor market has a bearing on the educational trajectory, and is specified according to race and gender. In 2016, PNAD showed that 39.6% of Brazilian workers started working before the age of 14. For those workers who had no education, or had not completed basic education, the percentage rose to 62.1 (IBGE 2017). This is also the case with the interviewees. However, unlike the older generations who, although in the labor market at a very young age, with more stability, and the ability to access social security benefits, these workers seem to represent a new generational group for which the right to work and its emancipatory dimensions are being denied. The Brazilian worker's contributory capacity is currently low due to their precarious position in the labor market and structural unemployment. This is the reality of BF beneficiaries. Research indicates that for the group of people aged over 55, approximately 10 million "either do not have income from retirement or a pension, or are involved in economic activities that do not provide them with social security coverage. In other words, they are excluded from labor and social security guarantees to deal with old age" (DIEESE 2017a, 13).

Motherhood is put forward as one of the reasons women drop out of education and formal work. Therefore, in general, returning to work and study emerges as a future project that they nurture, although on a dreamlike level:

> I have a plan, because you have a child and you have to have someone to look after them; you have to pay someone; I have to live near my mother; that sort of thing; that is all to do with working. So, I am still getting organized.
>
> *(Márcia)*

> I intend to. I always think about studying, going back to studying, which is very important. I think that is how we look at things … it has to be like that, having the conditions, having studied at a faculty and studying more…
>
> *(Renata)*

Many explain the main obstacle to putting this project into action is childcare, since the public service structure is precarious and deficient. There is also an inequality in the division of domestic chores, with their execution still mainly being a woman`s responsibility:

> Ah, I would like to because … I want…, I don't have the courage to go back to studying again. Ah, I don't know, the routine… taking care of the house and my son; when I get home at night, it is the time for you to stop, and rest a little, and then you have to go to school, and added to that, there is no school nearby; all the schools are far away.
>
> *(Lúcia)*

Despite this, it is interesting to note that, when comparing their lives and those of their mothers, the vast majority of interviewees put forward the differences, evaluating their maternal trajectory as having been more unfortunate, due to hunger, violence, and premature labor:

> My mother's was much more difficult, so I can't compare it. My mother did not have a childhood and went to work at a young age. My mother, from what she says, has worked since the age of 9; her mother put her to work at the age of 9.
>
> *(Andréia)*

> My mother's is more, is much different. My mother was beaten a lot. I have never been beaten by a man. My mother almost died from being beaten.
>
> *(Antônia)*

Analyzing these narratives, from the viewpoint of several generations, we see that the beneficiaries' family trajectory represents a certain continuity, generated by poverty, precarious working and housing conditions, a lack of social protection, the continuity of the gender division of labor, and the predominance of a female head in the home, which means an accumulation of activities and responsibilities for women. On the other hand, as they also observe, for this generation there are gains with regards to the ability to choose a partner, and fewer violent situations, which does not necessarily mean a male absence in their lives; it could be fathers of other children, brothers, and relatives who are part of their sociability network (Hita 2014) which they can rely on, but also protection and social assistance to which they have access and can consult when they feel threatened, which was impossible for the generation of older women.

## Final Considerations

This chapter has shown that historically BF has prioritized women for receipt of the benefit. The centrality occupied by females in the program has produced a series of debates, studies, and research on the link between BF and gender relations. However, in the state of Bahia, it is observed that BF presents specific characteristics, in which gender relations and the forms of family organization, intersected with the dimensions of class, race, generation, and territory, produce trajectories and experiences that had not been considered when formulating and implementing the program.

As we have observed, the state of Bahia and its municipalities form a space characterized by poverty, a significant female presence, and the existence of people who are predominantly black (black and brown). This framework confirms the urgency of including a connection with the dimensions of class, gender, and race/ethnicity, among others, in the content of any public policies, to produce more equal and effective actions. The state should incorporate this focus in the formulation, planning, execution, and monitoring of policies, plans, and social programs, to avoid strengthening inequalities and asymmetries of class, gender, and race which fuel disparities, practices of institutional racism, and various types of negligence.

The role attributed to the vast majority of BF beneficiaries as women-mothers-carers homogenizes and standardizes women, often without respecting their choices and voices, indicating that, at times, the conditionalities ignore the daily routine of women, their challenges and limits, disregarding lives already devoid of so many possibilities.

Certainly, we are aware that being a program recipient guarantees women a small amount of purchasing power that helps them to meet the family group's basic needs, and assists in improving their living conditions. However, this does not grant them financial autonomy, since it is dependent on fulfilling these conditionalities and the benefit is suspended if they are not fulfilled. Therefore, meeting these requirements is an obligation that affects their position in the labor market, spurring them to take on part-time, badly-paid, and intermittent labor activities, which allow them to reconcile domestic chores, care for the family group, and survival strategies.

At a personal level, the term "benefit" suggests its status as a bonus, or a favor granted, which makes it difficult for women to understand the program and social assistance as a public policy to which they have a right. Thus, the program negates its power of agency, and constitutes citizenship regulated under new molds, granting recipients relative autonomy.

Furthermore, any possible impact on the daily lives of women only becomes feasible via intersectoriality; in other words, by connecting social assistance/BF with other policies and their respective programs, such as work, housing, health, and education. In addition, both the formulation of program actions and their operationalization, monitoring, and evaluation should pay attention to the synchronized movement that produces situations of oppression (of gender, race, class, and age/generation) experienced by women, otherwise it will continue to perpetuate inequalities and prejudices.

For the time being, BF may succeed in mitigating poverty, and contribute towards improving the material conditions of families' lives. However, by endorsing stereotypes that link women to the provision of the family group's care and well-being, it contributes towards preserving patriarchal and racist structures that, in Bahia, expose them to different expressions of violence, whether in the domestic, institutional, or social sphere. Therefore, it is not an effective mechanism to promote social rights and to tackle poverty.

## Notes

1 There is an income limit to assign the families at these two levels, which permits the inclusion of people on the program with an income per person of up to BRL 89.00 per month (living in extreme poverty); and families with an income per person of between BRL 89.01 and BRL 178.00 per month (living in poverty), provided they have children or adolescents aged up to 17 as family members (for more information on this see Chapter 2).

2 Without straying from the proposal of this chapter, whose axis is the analysis of a real and concrete situation, and not a more in-depth epistemological debate on our theoretical choices, a brief methodological note is appropriate at this point. At this time of reflection, we work with a more abstract level of knowledge, in which the phenomena are considered as general laws, such as historical tendencies. For us, the debate on social protection in contemporary times is enriched when discussed at this level, since it is only in this way that we can access the fundamental dimensions of the issue; in other words, some of the logic of this system that, despite existing at a real and concrete level of relations, is not immediately explained, requires a more generalized and abstract approach. The reference to this level of explanation in this text is combined, further on in the chapter, with an analysis of more specific ways through which the general tendencies of capitalism have been established in specific times and spaces. This is how we will approach the specific characteristics of the crisis and social protection in Brazil, and this is the path we have adopted, to think about the specific historical ways that racism, chauvinism, and sexism have gained strength in the capitalist crisis processes, both around the world and in the Brazilian context. Therefore, we seek to identify the more universal historical tendencies, capturing them in their concrete forms of expression, which implies working with contradictory dynamics, always characterized by the real and daily reproduction of deep levels of inequality and social and human diversity. We should also mention in this rapid digression, that this theoretical-methodological selection aims to situate the debate within a perspective that shies away from a dogmatic reading of capitalist laws, unable to approach diversity and specific historical characteristics, but we also seek to distance ourselves from proposals that are quite common in current times, which, in an attempt to understand the real dimensions of social life, completely rule out any reference to totalizing historical processes, and universalized tendencies, remaining only at the most phenomenological and descriptive level of differences.

3 For materialistic feminists, the cluster of forms of exploitation, domination, and appropriation that women experience, despite their important expression in the ideological field, have a material basis – the gender division of labor (Falquet 2013; Guillaumin 2014; Kergoat 2012) – a practice that is socially constructed around the idea that, due to biological elements, there are male and female activities, and the establishment of a hierarchy between these two types of labor, awarding superiority to male

attributes, considered productive, and disqualifying, and making socially invisible, the field of social reproduction, commercial labor and care, naturally attributed to women (Hirata and Kergoat 2007). In this approach, it is important to consider, when we think of the various historical forms of gender division of labor, the ever present connection between the two ways of using the female workforce, exploiting and appropriating women's time and bodies (Kergoat 2016; Guillaumin 1994 ).

4 IBGE uses the term *pardo* (brown) to classify individuals who have a mixture of black or indigenous origins with any other color or race and self-declaration as being of a brown ethnicity. The brown population joins together people who self-identify as: *mulata, cabocla, cafuza,* or *mameluca.* The institute also includes individuals who self-declare as being a mixture of black with a person of another color or ethnicity in this segment of the population (TODAPOLITICA 2019).

5 Bahia occupies a 567,295 km area and has 417 municipalities, currently distributed among 27 Territories of Identity (TI), including the Southern Lowlands Territory, which joins together 15 municipalities, and forms the state of Bahia planning and public policy management unit. The above-mentioned report is the result of a contract signed between the State of Bahia Department of Policies for Women (SPM/BA) and the Federal University of Bahia (UFBA) in 2013 executed by the Center for Interdisciplinary Studies on Women (NEIM/UFBA) researchers.

6 In its research, IBGE adopts a self-declaration criterion to classify the population by color and race, providing five groups: white (individuals who declare they are white), brown (those who declare they are brown), black (those who declare they are black), yellow (those who declare they are yellow, of oriental origin), and indigenous (person who declares they are indigenous or Indian) (A GAZETA 2008).

7 The historian, Mozart Linhares da Silva, in an interview with IHU On-Line (Silva 2015), reflects on the Brazilian state's biopolitical practice focused on the extinction of black people, and he explains that: "What the proselytism of a racial mixture proposes is their disappearance. This is the meaning of Brazilian eugenics. (…) Mixed race is a transitory category, just as 'brown' in the censuses, is a category that announces racial undecidability, or rather, the deracialization of black subjects." Continuing, he considers the Black Movement's redefinition of the race category and argues that: "It makes sense that the confirmation of blackness involves the denial of being of a mixed race as a possible identity. For the Black Movement, 'black and brown' should not be divided into two categories, as IBGE does in the censuses, and, instead, should consider the addition of black and brown, as black" (Silva 2015).

8 For example, on matriarchal families in Salvador, Bahia, see Hita (2014).

9 The subjects of the study were 20 rural working women, who took part in an outreach project, and socio-educational activities, directed by the researcher in six rural communities in Governador Mangabeira and Muritiba, towns in the countryside of Bahia. This contributed towards forming relationships of trust, sharing their life stories with the author.

10 For example, see article 7, item XXXIII of the Federal Constitution, the Child and Adolescent Statute regulations (Law 8.069/1990) and Decree No. 6.481/2008, which regulates articles 3, subparagraph "d", and 4 of International Labour Organization (ILO) Convention No. 182, which addresses the prohibition of the worst forms of child labor, and suggests immediate action for its elimination.

## References

A GAZETA. 2018. "Preto ou negro? IBGE Explica Classificação de Cor e Raça em Pesquisas." *A Gazeta,*November 21. https://www.gazetaonline.com.br/noticias/cidades/2018/11/preto-ou-negro-ibge-explica-classificacao-de-cor-e-raca-em-pesquisas-1014156744.html.

Akotirene, Carla. 2018. *O que é Interseccionalidade*. Colection Feminismos Plurais, edited by Djamila Ribeiro. Belo Horizonte: Letramento.

Alexander, Michelle. 2018. *A Nova Segregação: Racismo e Encarceramento em Massa*. São Paulo: Boitempo, 2018.

Almeida, Sîlvio Luiz de. 2018. *O que é Racismo Estrutural?* Colection Feminismos Plurais, edited by Djamila Ribeiro. Belo Horizonte: Letramento.

Amaral, Marisa Silva and Marcelo Dias Carcanholo. 2009. "A Superexploração do Trabalho em Economias Periféricas Dependentes." *Revista Katálysis* 12, no. 2: 216–225. http://dx.doi.org/10.1590/S1414-49802009000200011.

Andrade, Joana El-Jaick. 2015. "O Feminismo Marxista e a Demanda pela Socialização do Trabalho Doméstico e do Cuidado com as Crianças." *Revista Brasileira de Ciência Política* 18: 265–300. https://doi.org/10.1590/0103-335220151810.

Anzorena, Claudia. 2010. "'Mujeres': Destinatarias Privilegiadas de los Planes Sociales de Inicios del Siglo XXI - Reflexiones desde una Perspectiva Crítica de Género." *Revista Estudos Feministas* 18, no. 3: 725–746. http://dx.doi.org/10.1590/S0104-026X2010000300006.

Arruzza, Cinzia, Tithi Bhattacharya, and Nancy Fraser. 2019. *Feminismo para os 99%: um Manifesto*. São Paulo: Boitempo.

Bairros, Luíza. 1995. "Nossos Feminismos Revisitados." *Revista Estudos Feministas* 3, no 2: 458–463.

Bartholo, Letícia, Luana Passos, and Natália Fontoura. 2017. *Bolsa Família, Autonomia Feminina e Equidade de Gênero: o que indicam as Pesquisas Nacionais?* Texto de Discussão 2331. Brasília: Ipea.

Biroli, Flávia. 2018. *Gênero e Desigualdades: Limites da Democracia no Brasil*. São Paulo: Boitempo.

Boschetti, Ivanete. 2016. *Assistência Social e Trabalho no Capitalismo*. São Paulo: Cortez.

Carneiro, Sueli. 2011. *Racismo, Sexismo e Desigualdade no Brasil*. São Paulo: Selo Negro.

Chesnais, François. 2011. "Mundialização: O Capital Financeiro no Comando." *Revista Outubro* 5, no. 2: 7–28.

Coggiola, Osvaldo. 2013. "Programas Sociais Compensatórios: A Experiência Brasileira." *Revista Praia Vermelha: Estudos de Política e Teoria Social* 23, no. 1: 69–116.

Colbari, Antônia. 1995. *Ética do Trabalho*. São Paulo: Letras e Letras.

Crenshaw, Kimberlé. 2012. "A Intersecionalidade na Discriminação de Raça e Gênero." *Cruzamento: Raça e Gênero* 1: 7–16.

Dardot, Pierre and Christian Laval. 2016. *A Nova Razão do Mundo: Ensaio Sobre a Sociedade Neoliberal*. São Paulo: Boitempo.

Delgado, Josimara and Márcia Santana Tavares. 2012. "(Trans)versalidades de Gênero e Geração nas Políticas Sociais: O Lugar de Mulheres e Idosos." *Caderno Espaço Feminino* 25, no. 2: 79–97.

DIEESE (Departamento Intersindical de Estatística e Estudos Socioeconômicos). 2017a. *A Reforma da Previdência e a Desproteção dos Idosos*. Nota Técnica 174. São Paulo. DIEESE.

DIEESE (Departamento Intersindical de Estatística e Estudos Socioeconômicos). 2017b. *Nota à imprensa. Custo da Cesta Básica Sobe em 20 Capitais*. São Paulo. DIEESE.

DIEESE (Departamento Intersindical de Estatística e Estudos Socioeconômicos). 2018. *Mercado de Trabalho na Região Metropolitana de Salvador*. Pesquisa de Emprego e Desemprego. Salvador. DIEESE.

Falquet, Jules. 2013. "O capitalismo financeiro não liberta as mulheres: análises feministas materialistas e imbricacionistas." *Crítica Marxista* 36: 9–25.

Franco, Maria AsenateConceição. 2018. "Será o Homem a Cumeeira da Casa? Ou Sou Dona do Meu Próprio Nariz? Violência Contra Mulheres Rurais na Bahia." PhD dissertation, Universidade Federal da Bahia.

Fraser, Nancy. 2016. "O feminismo, o Capitalismo e a Astúcia da História." *Revista Outubro* 26: 31–56.

G1 BA. 2019. "Participação de pretos ou pardos entre os mais ricos chega a 73,5% na BA, diz IBGE; índice é o maior do país" 2019. *G1 Bahia*, November 6, 2019. https://g1.globo.com/ba/bahia/noticia/2019/11/06/participacao-de-pretos-ou-pardos-entre-os-mais-ricos-chega-a-735percent-na-ba-diz-ibge-indice-e-o-maior-do-pais.ghtml.

Grisci, Carmem Lígia Iochins. 1995. "Mulher-Mãe." *Psicologia: Ciência e Profissão* 15, no. 1–3: 12–17. https://doi.org/10.1590/S1414-98931995000100003.

Guedes, Simoni Lahud. 1998. "Redes de Parentesco e Consideração entre Trabalhadores Urbanos: Tecendo Relações a partir de Quintais." *Caderno CRH* 29: 189–208.

Guillaumin, Colette. 1994. "Enquanto Tivermos Mulheres para nos Darem Filhos: A Respeito da Raça e do Sexo." *Revista Estudos Feministas* 2, número especial: 228–233. https://doi.org/10.1590/%25x.

Guillaumin, Colette. 2014. "Prática do poder e ideia de natureza." In *O patriarcado desvendado: teorias de três feministas materialistas: Colette Guillaumin, Paola Tabet, Nicole- Claude Mathieu*, edited by Maira Abreu, Maria Betânia Ávila, Verônica Ferreira, and Jules Falquet, 27–99. Recife: SOS Corpo.

Hirata, Helena, and Danielle Kergoat. 2007. "Novas Configurações da Divisão Sexual do Trabalho." *Cadernos de Pesquisa* 37, no. 13: 595–609.

Hita, Maria Gabriela. 2014. *A Casa das Mulheres n'outro Terreiro: Famílias Matriarcais em Salvador*. Salvador: EDUFBA.

IBGE (Instituto Brasileiro de Geografia e Estatística). 2017. *Síntese dos Indicadores Sociais 2017*. Brasília: IBGE.

IBGE (Instituto Brasileiro de Geografia e Estatística). 2018a. *Estatísticas de Gênero: Indicadores Sociais das Mulheres no Brasil*. Estudos e Pesquisas, Informação Demográfica e Socioeconômica no. 38. Rio de Janeiro: IBGE.

IBGE (Instituto Brasileiro de Geografia e Estatística). 2018b. *Síntese dos Indicadores Sociais 2018*. Brasília: IBGE.

Kergoat, Danièle. 2012. *Se battre, disent-elles*...Paris: La Dispute.

Kergoat, Danièle. 2016. "O cuidado e a imbricação das relações sociais". In: *Gênero e trabalho no Brasil e na França: perspectivas interseccionais*, edited by Alice Rangel de Paiva Abreu, Helena Hirata, and Maria Rosa Lombardi, 17–26. São Paulo: Boitempo.

Küchemann, Berlindes Astrid. 2010. "Mulheres, Estado e Cuidados: Tensões e desafios do Feminismo." Paper presented in International Seminar Fazendo Gênero 9, Florianópolis. http://www.fazendogenero.ufsc.br/9/resources/anais/1278114245_ARQUIVO_TextoASTRIDparaST12.pdf.

Mariano,Silvana and Cássia Carloto. 2013. "Aspectos Diferenciais da Inserção de Negras no Programa Bolsa Família." *Sociedade e Estado* 28, no. 2: 393–417.

Mariano, Silvana, Márcia Tavares, and Josimara Delgado. 2018. "(Entre) Visões de Pobreza sob Lentes de Gênero e Geração: As Percepções de Beneficiárias do Programa Bolsa Família em Salvador-BA." Paper presented in XX Encontro da Rede Feminista Norte e Nordeste de Estudos e Pesquisas sobre Mulheres e relações de gênero-REDOR (National Meeting). Salvador.

Marins, Mani Tebet Azevedo de. 2018. "O 'Feminino' como Gênero do Desenvolvimento." *Revista Estudos Feministas* 26, no. 1: 1–13. https://doi.org/10.1590/1806-9584.2018v26n1e00030.

MDS (Ministério do Desenvolvimento Social e Combate à Fome). n.d. "Relatório Bolsa Família e Cadastro Único – Salvador." http://www.mdsgov.br/bolsafamilia.

Mészáros, István 2011. *A Crise Estrutural do Capital.* São Paulo: Boitempo.

Meyer, Dagmar Estermann. 2000. "As Mamas como Constituintes da Maternidade: Uma História do Passado?" *Educação & Realidade* 25, no. 2: 117–133.

Mioto, Célia Tamaso, Marta Silva Campos, and Cássia Maria Carloto (Eds.). 2015. *Familismo, Direitos e Cidadania: Contradições da Política Social.* São Paulo: Cortez.

Mioto, Regina CéliaTamaso, MarthaSilva Campos, Telma CristianeSasso de Lima. 2006. "Quem Cobre as Insuficiências das Políticas Públicas? Contribuição ao Debate Sobre o Papel da Família na Provisão de Bem-Estar Social." *Revista Políticas Púbicas* 10, no. 1: 165–183.

Mioto, Regina CéliaTamaso. 2008. "Família e Políticas Sociais." In: *Política Social no Capitalismo: Tendências Contemporâneas*, edited by Elaine Boschetti, Silvana Mara Morais dos Santos, Regina Célia Tamaso Mioto and Elaine Behring, 130–148. São Paulo: Cortez.

Moreira, Nathalia Carvalho, Marco Aurélio Marques Ferreira, Alfonso Augusto Teixeira de FreitasCarvalho Lima, and Ivan Bec Ckagnazaroff. 2012. "Empoderamento das Mulheres Beneficiárias do Programa Bolsa Família na Percepção dos Agentes dos Centros de Referência de Assistência Social." *Revista de Administração Pública* 46, no. 2: 403–423. https://doi.org/10.1590/S0034-76122012000200004.

Mota, Ana Elizabete. 2010. "A Centralidade da Assistência Social na Seguridade Social Brasileira nos Anos 2000." In *O Mito da Assistência Social: Ensaios sobre Estado, Política e Sociedade*, 133–146. Second edition. São Paulo: Cortez.

Mota, Ana Elizabete. 2012. "Crise, Desenvolvimentismo e Tendências das Políticas Sociais no Brasil e na América Latina." *Configurações* 10: 29–41. https://doi.org/10.4000/configuracoes.1324.

Mota, Fernanda Ferreira. 2015. "Cuidado e Desigualdade de Gênero: Discussões Sobre uma Democracia Mais Justa." Worked presented in VIII Congreso Latinoamericano de Ciencia Política, Peru. http://files.pucp.edu.pe/sistema-ponencias/wp-content/uploads/2014/12/Cuidado-e-desigualdade-de-g%C3%AAnero_discuss%C3%B5es-sobre-uma-democracia-mais-justa-Fernanda-Ferreira-Mota1.pdf.

Pateman, Carole. 2000. "El Estado de Bienestar Patriarcal." *Contextos* 2, no. 5: n.p.

Paugam, Serge and Nicolas Duvoux. 2008. *La régulation des Pauvres.* Paris: PUF.

Pereira, Potyara Amazoneida P. 2008. *Política Social: Temas e Questões.* São Paulo: Cortez.

Pereira, Potyara Amazoneida P. 2009. "Do Estado Social ao Estado anti-social." 2009. In: *Política Social, Trabalho e Democracia em Questão*, edited by Potyara Amazoneida, Ivanete Boschetti, Rosa Helena Stein, and Sílvia Cristina Yanoullas, 209–234. Brasília: Universidade Federal de Brasília.

Pereira, Potyara Amazoneida P. 2012. "Utopias Desenvolvimentistas e Política Social no Brasil." *Serviço Social e Sociedade* 112: 729–753.

Pereira, Potyara Amazoneida P. and Rosa Helena Stein. 2010. "Política Social: Universalidade Versus Focalização. Um Olhar Sobre a América Latina." In: *Capitalismo em Crise, Política Social e Direitos*, edited by Ivanete Boschetti, Elaine Behring, Silvana Mara Santos, and Regina Miotto, 106–130. São Paulo: Cortez.

Saboia, Vivian Aranha. 2006. "As Desigualdades de Gênero na Previdência Social na França e no Brasil." *Cadernos CRH* 19, no. 46: 123–131. http://dx.doi.org/10.9771/ccrh.v19i46.18551.

Santos, Deise Sousa. 2018. "Políticas Sociais e Intersecções na Trajetória de Vida de Mulheres Negras: Estudos Sobre as Usuárias dos Serviços Socioassistenciais em um CRAS de Salvador." Master's dissertation, Universidade Federal da Bahia.

Santos, Josiane Soares. 2008. "Particularidades da 'Questão Social' no Capitalismo Brasileiro." PhD dissertation, Universidade Federal do Rio de Janeiro.

Santos, Wanderley Guilherme dos. 1979. *Cidadania e Justiça*. Rio de Janeiro: Campus.

Sardenbergg, Cecília M. B. 2015. "Caleidoscópios de Gênero: Gênero e Interseccionalidades na Dinâmica das Relações Sociais." *Mediações* 20, no. 2: 56–96.

Sarti, Cynthia Andersen. 1996. *A Família como Espelho: Um Estudo Sobre a Moral dos Pobres*. São Paulo: Cortez.

Sganzerla, Célia Regina and Eva Borges. "Quem São e Onde Estão os Pobres da Bahia. 2014." *Bahia Análise e Dados* 24, no. 4: 657–670.

Silva, Maria Ozanira da Silva. 2010. "Avaliação de políticas e programas sociais: aspectos conceituais e metodológicos." In: *Avaliação de políticas e programas sociais: teoria e prática*, edited by Maria Ozanira da Silva e Silva, 37–96. São Paulo: Veras.

Silva, Ermildes Lima da and Márcia Santana Tavares. 2015. "Desconstruindo Armadilhas de Gênero: Reflexões Sobre Família e Cuidado na Política de Assistência Social." *Revista Feminismos* 3, no. 2–3: 78–90.

Silva, Giselle Souza da. 2012. *Transferência de Renda e Monetarização das Políticas Sociais: Estratégia de Captura do Fundo Público pelo Capital Portador de Juros. In: Financeirização, Fundo Público e Política Social*, edited by Sara Granemann, Evilasio Salvador, Ivanete Boschetti and Elaine Behring, 219–240. São Paulo: Cortez.

Silva, Mozart Linhares da. "O cromatismo que nega o negro. Entrevista especial com Mozart Linhares da Silva." *Instituto Humanista Unisinos*, September 20, 2015. http://www.ihu.unisinos.br/entrevistas/546948-o-cromatismo-que-nega-o-negro-entrevista-especial-com-mozart-linhares-da-silva-.

Souza, Luana Passos de. 2015. "Bolsa Família: Socializando Cuidados e Mudando as Relações de Gênero?" Master's Dissertation, Universidade Federal Fluminense.

Souza, Thais Andreia Araújo de and Ana Cristina Lima Couto. 2015. "Programa Bolsa Família: Características e Perfil da Pobreza entre os Beneficiários nos Estados do Paraná e Bahia." *Informe Gepec* 19, no. 2: 41–56.

TODAPOLÍTICA. n.d. "*A População Parda no Brasil.*" https://www.todapolitica.com/pardo/.

Tronto, Joan. 1997. "Mulheres e Cuidados: O Que as Feministas Podem Aprender Sobre a Moralidade a partir Disso?" In: *Gênero, Corpo, Conhecimento*, edited by Alison M. Jaggar, and Susan R. Bordo, 186–203. Rio de Janeiro: Rosa dos Tempos.

Vanin, Iole. 2016. *Relatório do diagnóstico do Plano Integral Básico SPM* (Research Report) Salvador: SPM/UFBA.

# 5

# THE *BOLSA FAMÍLIA* PROGRAM

## Reflections on Its Role in Social Protection and Gender Relations in Brazil

*Luana Passos, Simone Wajnman, and Fábio Waltenberg*

### Introduction

Commemorating 15 years of existence, the *Bolsa Família* Program (PBF) (Family Grant Program) has become one of the main components of Brazilian social protection policy. Internationally, it is among the most successful experiences with conditional cash transfer programs (CCT). Innovative and of a hybrid nature since its inception, Brazil's CCT program has been perfected over time, taking into account the recommendations of the specialized literature and the needs of the concrete reality in which the program is inserted. *Bolsa Família* (BF) (Family Grant) has served different functions, especially that of reducing poverty as a "final safety net" (Barr 2012). A vast national and international academic literature attests to the diverse benefits of the *Bolsa Família* Program, such as increasing school attendance and lowering children's retention at school, reducing child mortality, and increasing the proportion of children vaccinated at the correct age.

As undeniable as *Bolsa Família*'s success may be – at least in terms of its main purpose – one cannot ignore the possibility that its indirect impact may distance it from the aim of its founding principle of promoting a more equitable society. It is in this scenario of unintended effects that the debate and the controversies about *Bolsa Família* and gender issues emerge. The literature points to many indications that the program is based on traditional gender roles, like a large part of CCT programs. This chapter contributes with reflections and a quantitative study on this subject. Specifically, we investigate the extent to which the participation of women in the *Bolsa Família* Program affects relevant indicators in the debate about the sexual division of labor, namely participation in the labor force, employment, formal or informal work, housework and care, and time use.

We argue that Brazilian social protection, as a whole, is incomplete insofar as it does not offer all of the benefits found in more advanced welfare states: for structural reasons, Brazil's welfare state is not developed sufficiently to eliminate the various manifestations of poverty; moreover, the other pillar of the welfare state, that of the provision of public services, has neither the scope nor the desired quality. It is in this context of a "welfare state under construction" that *Bolsa Família* – its limits and potential – is discussed and a theoretical framework is presented that relates the concepts of gender roles, the sexual division of labor, and an incomplete and unequal female revolution in order to support an investigation of the implications of the program for gender, which is a controversial issue in the literature.

With recent data from the *Continuous National Household Sample Survey* (PNAD Contínua),[1] a survey conducted periodically by the *Instituto Brasileiro de Geografia e Estatística* (IBGE) (Brazilian Institute of Geography and Statistics), the quantitative exercise uses the methodology propensity score matching to define treatment and control groups. We estimate how participation in the program affects a number of labor market and household time-use outcomes. The results lead us to conclude not only that the program does indeed improve the lives of women, but also that it does not promote a marked female autonomy.

## The *Bolsa Família* Program and its Role in Brazilian Social Protection

Within complex welfare states composed of various forms of social protection, the following four categories of individuals are eligible for cash payments:[2]

i Elderly people who do not receive social security because they have not contributed enough over the course of their professional lives;
ii Elderly people who contributed and receive social security benefits the values of which are too low and insufficient to get them out of poverty;
iii Individuals of working age who do not contribute to social security and who do not earn enough income to get out of poverty (e.g., housewives or low-paid informal employees);
iv Individuals of working age who have contributed to social security and are therefore protected against certain specific social risks (e.g., eligible for maternity leave, unemployment benefits, etc.) but who do not earn sufficient income to get out of poverty – for example because they have low-paying jobs and large families (especially with children and elderly dependents).

There are not enough economic incentives for private institutions to protect people in an economically viable way against the social risks mentioned in points (i–iv) above, nor can private charity handle all this, so it is up to the state.

Subject to different ideological framing, the extent and the degree of generosity of the CCTs are issues on which a consensus will never be reached. More so than say Social Democrats, Egalitarians will be in favor of greater benefits and of those benefits being granted to more people. Social Democrats are less draconian than Libertarians, whose radical fringes will generally be opposed to any kind of assistance measure. But ideology is not the only source of divergence. Concrete evidence of the positive and negative effects of each social assistance policy, from a perspective that grants prominence to efficiency and empirical evidence, is also important. Income transfers could contribute to increasing workers' health and ability to work, for example, with positive impacts on their productivity, but at what budgetary cost and with what disincentivizing effects on the labor market?

Above all, the populations of developing countries will be subject to the four difficulties associated with the groups listed above (i–iv), to a greater or lesser extent according to the fraction of the population covered by social security (e.g., with formal versus informal labor contracts) and the generosity of social security benefits (e.g. how generously unemployment insurance is in terms of eligibility for benefits, the duration of the provision of those benefits, and their value). But the degree of exposure to hardship will also depend on: the wages paid to the lowest paid workers (are there many working poor?); demographic characteristics (do families have many children and/or senior dependents?); and the structure of the provision of public services, for example: are there options for free or subsidized day care centers, schools, and health care – among so many other factors.

To meet the needs of the four groups and the various social risks to which they are subjected, the most developed welfare states have implemented different types of income transfer benefits, including:

a Earmarked benefits, such as housing allowances or subsidies, food stamps, and the like, to help households with specific difficulties;
b Child benefits, generally universal, to assist families during child rearing, whose job opportunities are potentially affected by the responsibilities to care for children, especially when there are no free or affordable day care or preschool options;
c Tax credits, aimed at complementing income, granted to low-paid workers in the formal sector; provided by the government, the benefit ends up working as a subsidy to low-paid jobs;[3]
d Non-contributory assistance benefits, paid to impoverished seniors;
e Assistance benefits paid both to adults who are of working age but who are unfit to work, and to those in poverty;
f Assistance benefits paid to adults of working age who are fit to work and impoverished, regardless of whether they are employed or unemployed; this modality of intervention is understood as the final safety net.

Cases (d) and (e) find significant equivalents in Brazil in both the *Benefício de Prestação Continuada* (BPC) (Continuous Cash Benefit) – a non-contributory benefit intended for poor adults who are unable to work due to disability as well as for poor senior citizens – and the *Previdência Rural* – a semi-contributory benefit, aimed at assisting impoverished seniors. In the national context, such benefits are of reasonable value (equivalent to a minimum wage) and include a significant number of people. Type (c) is exemplified by the *Abono Salarial,* a complementary wage, resembling a tax credit, that in Brazil is paid by the government only to a subset of low-paid, formally-employed workers.

In Brazil, the housing policy has historically been incipient and has not treaded the path of granting benefits aimed at paying tenants' rent, but rather through aid in the acquisition of property (*Banco Nacional da Habitação; Minha Casa Minha Vida,* etc.). There were, at the turn of the century, earmarked benefits, such as food and gas allowances; however, such policies are no longer extant. Type (a) benefits, therefore, are not an important component of social protection provided by the federal government. Nor does there exist any benefit explicitly recognized as a child benefit; type (b) in the classification used here has never been created in the Brazilian case.

Despite the budgetary importance of some of these benefits or programs, such as the BPC, *Previdência Rural, Abono Salarial,* and *Minha Casa, Minha Vida* – whose budget is waning at the present moment – or even the contributory social security benefits that ensure a minimum income for unemployed workers and the elderly, Brazilian social protection as a whole is incomplete insofar as it does not offer all of the benefits found in more advanced welfare states. Nor are social protection policies sufficient to eliminate poverty in its various manifestations, for structural reasons, such as the sheer numbers of poor and extremely poor individuals, the large proportion of workers employed informally, the low values of most benefits, or the low pay obtained in jobs at the base of the wage pyramid. Also, because the other pillar of the welfare state, the provision of public services such as education, health care, and personal care, in general, has neither the scope nor the desired quality, forcing families, even poor ones, to seek out some of these services in the private market, which Esping-Andersen (1990) refers to as insufficient de-commodification.

The *Bolsa Família* program fulfills function (f) above. It is the final safety net granted to working age adults who are able to work, but who are poor or extremely impoverished, whether they are employed or not. But the program is not limited to this as it also acts as a child benefit restricted to the poor (not universal) and has absorbed many earmarked benefits that existed before. It is a very important benefit, because it plays a role analogous to the final safety net in the most advanced social protection systems, as well as presenting several shortcomings rooted in the functioning of a capitalist society, labor markets, and the limitations of the Brazilian welfare state. It also has many limitations, in part because it is unable to meet all of the expectations / responsibilities that rest on its shoulders simultaneously – including those resulting from changes in the scope of gender relations – and in facing the typical dilemmas of any targeted social assistance scheme in any country in the world.

There are three classic criteria for assessing redistribution programs (Barr 2012):

- i The value of the benefit must be sufficient to meet the objective of ensuring a decent life for the beneficiary;
- ii Its cost must be adequate, including expenditures related to paying the benefit itself, but also administrative costs;
- iii It must be effectively targeted, benefiting all those, and only those, who should be beneficiaries.

The interaction of these criteria is not simple, and inevitably leads to dilemmas. If increasing the benefit is optimal from the point of view of the first criterion, it by definition affects the second, and puts pressure on the third – the higher the benefit value, the greater the incentive for more people to seek it out, increasing the need for regulating or monitoring the program and the costs associated with it, including expenses arising from unduly including beneficiaries in the program. In addition to this, there are also issues of political economy: value increases can provoke resentment in those who do not receive the benefit because they believe (however mistakenly) that they work to finance other people's benefits, a belief which in the long run can erode the working, middle, and affluent classes' support of welfare programs that include among their beneficiaries adults fit to work.

In order to implement a targeted cash transfer policy, the most intuitive approach is the so-called "classical targeting" or "ideal solution" (Besley and Kanbur 1993), which seeks to provide the benefit to those able to demonstrate that their incomes fall below a certain threshold. Such accurate information about who is or is not poor should facilitate targeting in a relatively precise way. But differentiating the poor from the non-poor, at a low cost, is no simple task, especially in a job market as informal as Brazil's. Striking a rigid boundary between eligibility and ineligibility based on income can also produce side effects, including the so-called "poverty trap" (lack of incentive to cross the line and lose the benefit) and stigma (a psychological burden akin to shame often endured by those who receive benefits).

An alternative is indicator targeting, which requires the definition of variables correlated with poverty, not manipulated by the individual at low cost, and easily observable by the program managers. Examples of indicators include: the presence of children or seniors at home; the number of dependents in the home; the region in which the family lives; ethnicity, etc. Examples of such benefits are: child benefits, affirmative action, and regionalized benefits. No indicator will be perfectly correlated with poverty, but some may have a high correlation. The advantages are minimizing income verification costs and side effects associated with classic targeting. The most obvious disadvantage is the possible targeting failures (inclusion of the non-poor, exclusion of the poor).

There is also a third modality: self-targeting (or "ordeal mechanisms," to use Gruber's (2013) terminology). Examples of a monetary version are the tax credits already mentioned that require the beneficiary to be employed and to pass an income test, since only those who can prove they receive remuneration below a certain threshold are eligible for the benefit. The advantage is that it is possible to minimize the problems associated with classical targeting. But the risk of targeting failures remains, such as excluding those who, for legitimate reasons, cannot meet the eligibility conditions (e.g., because they have to take care of a dependent). And it can also foster a large number of "working poor."[4]

Ingeniously, perhaps benefitting from the accumulated experience in the design and implementation of social assistance policies in other countries, the *Bolsa Família* Program has combined characteristics of the first two types of targeting, as it tests in a very rough way the per capita household income (as in the classical targeting) and offers additional benefits to families with children (as in targeting by indicators). In addition, it incorporated a conditionality logic aligned with the third type of targeting, requiring consistent and sustained school attendance of children, regular medical examinations of pregnant women, etc.

Such conditionalities assume characteristics of care. The feminist literature on the *Bolsa Família* program focuses its criticism precisely on this assumption, as the conditionalities overwhelmingly attribute to women almost sole responsibility over children/dependents, thus reinforcing gender stereotypes. The critical aspect of *Bolsa Família*'s role in promoting female autonomy is that the program fights poverty by means of women, who are the ones responsible for complying with conditionalities (Gomes 2011; Carloto 2012; Santos 2014) and for effectively managing a very small amount of money received by the family (Lavinas, Cobo, and Veiga 2012; Lavinas 2014). The analytical work in this chapter rests precisely on this dimension: gender issues.

Finally, it should be noted that the program has some pioneering features insofar as it includes:

- a "guaranteed return," which affords families who voluntarily leave the program the option of being readmitted without going through the entire selection cycle application process again;
- b the "permanence rule," which ensures families will remain in the program, even if their per capita income surpasses the program's eligibility threshold during a biennium.

These elements are in line with recommendations from a certain international literature, such as Barr (2012), but are not yet widespread internationally. Paiva et al. (2014) argue that the program's "guaranteed return" and "permanence rule" policies represent a strengthening of the role of the *Bolsa Família* Program as a component of the Brazilian social protection system, by alleviating families' fear of no longer being entitled to the benefit if they successfully pursue and secure job opportunities that may actually be quite unstable or precarious.

Regarding the criteria for evaluating a targeted policy, there is no doubt that the value of the *Bolsa Família* benefit is insufficient to meet the more ambitious goal of ensuring a decent life for beneficiary families, given that the average benefit is far from the minimum wage – considered the lower income threshold to meet a family's basic needs. For example, in 2018, the average *Bolsa Família* benefit was BRL189 (approximately $52 USD), while the minimum wage was set at BRL954 (approximately $261 USD).[5] In 2018, the program met its goal of alleviating the poverty endured by beneficiaries in over 14 million households. Given the complexity of the program, administrated by federal and municipal agencies, program administration costs are not precisely calculable; however, estimates indicate that they are not high. The total cost of the program to the state, including disbursements with benefits and administrative costs would be around 0.4–0.5% of the Gross Domestic Product (GDP) in 2018. It does suffer from some inclusion errors (anecdotal cases are exploited in the media) and exclusion errors (on which incidentally the empirical strategy of this chapter is based). But the efficacy and precision of the program's targeting is considered reasonable when compared to other income transfer programs, with over 90% of beneficiaries being among the poorest 40% (Silva et al. 2018).

In any case, the program is not immune to the dilemmas of targeted income transfer policies; it has resided, and will permanently reside, under the influence of vectors acting in the opposite direction: it is impossible to meet the first objective without affecting the second and third. It runs the risk of leading to poverty traps, possibly expressed in their subtlest form as informality traps – and also causing resentment in non-beneficiaries.

In short, the *Bolsa Família* program serves multiple purposes in an incomplete welfare state of a middle-income country marked by social inequality and informality in the labor market: it is Brazil's final safety net, as well as the country's take on a *child benefit* (targeting only the poor). Moreover, it has assumed the role of distributing earmarked benefits that existed before in other policies / programs. Ingeniously designed, this hybrid program combines classical targeting with a strategy based on indicators. If, on the one hand, it is rigorous in imposing conditionalities, on the other, it generously offers policies such as "guaranteed return" and the "permanence rule" (both being important, fair, and smart). But it carries in its DNA the dilemmas and contradictions inherent to targeted policies, and no reform can solve them all.

This is the context we should have in mind when carrying out the analysis proposed in this chapter, which is to evaluate the performance of the *Bolsa Família* program under the scrutiny of a perspective critical of gender disparities and inequities.

## Gender Roles in the Public and Private Spheres and Economic Differentials

*Bolsa Família* has been criticized for reinforcing traditional gender roles, instrumentalizing women in the fight against poverty (Gomes 2011; Carloto and Mariano 2010; Carloto 2012; Lavinas, Cobo, and Veiga 2012; Lavinas 2014; Santos 2014). Identifying women as responsible for managing the child benefit, making them guarantors of school attendance and of the health of their children, in a way naturalizes the traditional role of caregiver assigned to women, relieving men of their responsibilities in raising children. Contemplating the limitations and potential of the *Bolsa Família* program in Brazil's system of social protection (section 2), this section discusses this gender-based assignment of roles in the context of what is called the incomplete gender revolution – as described in Esping-Andersen (2009), Esping-Andersen and Billari (2015), as well as in England (2010), among others. Brazil is in such a stage in this process, and this chapter considers the specificities of *Bolsa Família* beneficiaries in this scenario.

The traditional sexual division of labor associates men with a greater responsibility for paid work and women with a commitment to reproductive activities. Thus men assume the role of external providers by securing resources to support the household; women, on the other hand, assume responsibility for the direct domestic provision of care and services that promote the welfare of their family members. Since care and other domestic activities have been performed for centuries by women with little or very low exchange value, domestic production has come to be associated with the absence of economic value (Folbre 2002; Melo and Thomé 2018). Although essential to all stages of human life, these activities do not, in principle, require investment in formal education or prior training, which would legitimize their devaluation.

This specialization of gender roles was appropriate in a context of high fertility rates, as it was necessary to divide adults into the roles of providing resources and caring for their offspring. However, throughout the industrialization process, women gradually joined the labor market, initially to supplement family income, but progressively creating their own spaces with greater investments in education and pursuing professional careers (Goldin 2006; Goldin and Katz 2002). In this way, women have entered the productive sphere and at the same time have limited their reproductive role by reducing the number of children they have and increasing access to alternative goods and services to cover part of the household chores. However, women's entrance into the labor market has not corresponded to a redistribution of domestic work between women and men (England 2010; Guedes and Araújo 2011; Bandeira and Melo 2013; Hirata 2015).

The *incomplete gender revolution theory* is a framework increasingly used to explain the impasses generated by asymmetry in the distribution of gender roles, connecting family changes with the economic roles of individuals (Esping-Andersen 2009; Esping-Andersen and Billari 2015; England 2010; Goldsheider, Bernhardt, and

Lappergard 2015; Ruggles 2015; Cherlin 2016). It comprehensively analyzes gender roles in economic, social, and political activities and the division of domestic work, which impacts not only on women's participation in the labor market and in society, but also on the behaviors of families, marriages, and fertility. The term gender revolution is adopted to refer to changes in gender relations in the public and private spheres, encompassing different aspects of society's adaptation to the redefinition of women's roles. In short, the revolution would take place in two parts: in the first one, the influx of women into the labor market would have destabilized the traditional male-breadwinner / female-homemaker model. As a result of this reduction in specialization – which places a greater value on traditional family arrangements – divorce and cohabitation have become more common, families have become more diverse, and birth rates have declined. In the second part of the revolution, which may be unfolding in some societies today, forms of more egalitarian partnerships are beginning to develop, in which men increasingly engage in domestic chores (Goldsheider, Bernhardt, and Lappergard 2015). Thus, partnerships would become more stable than those based on an imbalance whereby women bear most of the burden of domestic activities and family care while also accounting for a significant portion of financial responsibilities.

Based on evidence of the first part of this gender revolution, with change being restricted to the role of women, research in Family Demography has almost unanimously predicted the continued decline of marriages (in number and length) and fertility. However, recent evidences shows that some societies have responded to the conflicts generated by the asymmetry of men and women's respective roles through the development of more egalitarian partnerships, which leads to the expectation that the transition from the first to the second part of the gender revolution shall reverse trends in the decline of families. Esping-Andersen and Billari (2015) propose a theoretical model in which, through the diffusion of more equal gender norms, partnerships gradually become more egalitarian and a new equilibrium of marital and family relations emerges. The rate of diffusion of the process should vary from country to country. This process would reverse the tendency that low fertility and widespread divorce are the hallmarks of family life. Additionally, in this model, equilibrium also implies higher female participation rates, since women are able to better perform their economic activities when they divide household chores equally with their family members.

Other authors are much more cautious about this optimistic view, as the division of labor is still far from being considered egalitarian, indicating that the second part of this gender revolution may be stalled (England 2010; Cherlin 2016; Ruggles 2015). Goldsheider, Bernhardt, and Lappergard (2015) argue that in some countries this process is progressing so slowly that it will probably take many decades to complete. In addition to the major differences between countries, there may also be large disparities between social groups, so that very disparate patterns of behavior might be unfolding within countries, with more egalitarian relations becoming a privilege among the rich and well-educated (Cherlin 2016).

Brazil has certainly stalled in the first phase of the so-called gender revolution, and if there is any indication of progress towards the second part of the transition, the signals are strongly concentrated among the rich and educated. Overall, women still have greater difficulty accessing the labor market than do men, both in terms of the quantity and quality of jobs they can reach. But the biggest obstacles to women's access to the labor market are in the domestic sphere, where the traditional division of labor has evolved little (Araujo and Scalon 2006; Guiginski and Wajnman 2016; Biroli 2018; Jesus 2018).

The so-called female maternity penalty and marriage penalty are the price women pay in the labor market for being heavily committed to care and domestic activities (Waldfogel 1997; Budig and England 2001; Anderson, Binder, and Krause 2003; among others). Symmetrically, the benefits men receive for these services and care are identified as the male marriage and paternity premium (Hersch and Stratton 2000; Killewald and Gough 2013; Adler and Oner 2013; among others). Studies in Brazil that quantify the share of the gender pay gap using the combination of female penalty and male premium, despite being incipient, are based on clear evidence (Guiginski and Wajnman 2016; Souza 2016; Madalozzo and Blofield 2017). Empirical findings also reveal a maternity penalty and paternity premium in the likelihood of mothers and fathers being economically active. In other words, having children reduces the likelihood that Brazilian women will enter and remain in the labor force and, conversely, favors men's economic participation (Costa 2007; Guimarães and Santos 2010; Guiginski and Wajnman 2016; Passos 2018).

An essential feature of the Brazilian case, as well as those of many other less developed countries, is the ease of outsourcing part of the domestic work. Poorer women, mostly black and low-educated, are available to do housework for others at a very low price, freeing, to some extent, the most educated women to pursue and develop their own careers in what is referred to in theory as the delegation model. Significant changes are taking place in the paid domestic labor market, as younger women tend to have more access to formal education, thus rejecting this type of occupation. In addition, better regulation of the rights of domestic workers (housemaids, babysitters, etc.) is making these services more expensive (Guerra and Wajnman 2016). However, the existence of a strong domestic outsourcing culture in Brazil adds an important dimension of inequality in terms of the labor market conditions faced by women and the possibilities open to them for more egalitarian partnerships. While a large part of wealthy families resolve their gender conflicts by hiring other women to do housework, poorer families most often cannot afford such help. The result is that women in these families are penalized in their insertion in the labor market while remaining accountable for domestic work.

In an unpublished work, Jesus (2018) estimates the age profiles of production, consumption, and transfers of unpaid domestic work and shows that, as in the various countries for which these profiles were estimated, in Brazil women are the net donors/providers of domestic work (family care and housework in general) and services from adolescence to old age, and men are the net beneficiaries of this domestic work throughout their lives. Breaking down transfers by per capita household income groups for the year 2013 shows that the poorest women begin to take on responsibilities related to housework and care of other household members from the age of 13 years and only become purely recipients at close to 80 years old. Among the richest women, the onset of the donor phase occurs much later, around 28 years of age, which coincides with the average age at maternity. In addition, the average amount of net hours transferred by women is significantly higher among the poorest individuals: for them the average is four hours per day, while among the richest it is no more than 1.5 hours per day.[6] For men, who are net receivers of domestic care activities performed by women throughout their lives, social class and income level matter very little. The differences between the per capita household income deciles are minimal. In adulthood, when the greatest productive and reproductive demands coincide, men are, without distinction according to income level, recipients of transfers of domestic work performed by women. This evidence reinforces the argument that the maternity penalty is heavily concentrated among the poorest women, those who cannot afford "substitutes" for their domestic work and to whom society as a whole does not provide comprehensive public care services for children and other dependents (Budig and Hodges 2014).

It should be borne in mind that the *Bolsa Família* Program specifically focuses on the families hardest hit by the contradictions inherent in an incomplete gender revolution. The program impacts on families that need to generate an income from as many adults as possible – often relying on children as well – but this is where the division of domestic work is more asymmetrical and harmful to women. Therefore, it is fair to say that public policies aimed at these families should be concerned with not reinforcing an asymmetry unfavorable to women. However, it also makes sense to argue that the *Bolsa Família* Program reduces the maternity penalty for poorer women by linking a benefit to family care work, which would have a redistributive connotation.

It is true that the *Bolsa Família* Program relies on the traditional division of gender roles. But their goal is not to reinforce these roles, but to take advantage of them by guiding women's use of resources. Placing responsibility over such matters of family exclusively on women, "naturalizes" the role of women as caregivers, at the same time that it raises the low value usually associated with such care activities by attributing a monetary value / income to this function. By placing importance on caring for children's health and education as a way out of poverty and matching a conditional financial resource to this end, the program reinforces the crucial importance of care activities.

It should be emphasized that if the program supports and naturalizes the female role in care, it may also to some extent displace men from the only domestic task commonly associated with their gender: management of the family's financial resources. Qualitative research on the *Bolsa Família* Program indicates that there is a feeling on the part of the beneficiaries that they are contributing to the household budget as program beneficiaries. They also reported feeling benefited by the widening of their range of choices for the home, without depending on the approval of their partners (Bartholo, Passos, and Fontoura 2017).

Thus, the effects of the *Bolsa Família* Program on the gender dimension and the sexual division of labor are controversial. Quantitative research tends to identify a certain worsening of women's lives, due to the reinforcement of the asymmetrical sexual division of labor. However, when the beneficiaries themselves are given a voice in ethnographic research, focus groups, and semi-structured interviews, their views about their "empowerment," citizenship, and the state's recognition of their existence emerge. This research contributes to the empirical literature on the subject, without losing sight of the nuances pointed out by qualitative studies on what may be a favorable, negative, or even contradictory effect of the *Bolsa Família* Program on women's lives.

## Methodology

### *Data Source*

We employ as our data source the PNAD *Contínua*, conducted by the IBGE throughout Brazil, covering urban and rural areas up until 2017. This data source was chosen for at least three reasons, namely because: it is the most up-to-date basis for identifying persons who receive income from social assistance programs, such as *Bolsa Família*; it presents a wide range of information on personal and household characteristics representative of the entire population; the information is timely and of a high quality.

Table 5.1 contains information about the characteristics of women, 18 to 60 years of age – both beneficiaries and non-beneficiaries of the *Bolsa Família* Program – who are poor, that is, who live on a monthly per capita household income less than or equal to BRL170.00 (approximately US$47). There are significant differences between these groups, which corroborates the need to use a matching technique in order to be able to collate comparable groups.

**TABLE 5.1** Beneficiaries and non-beneficiaries of *Bolsa Família*, according to select characteristics

| *Variables* | *Beneficiary women* | *Poor non-beneficiary women* |
|---|---|---|
| Share of labor force (%) | 37.68 | 20.20 |
| Share of those employed (%) | 64.12 | 43.95 |
| Share of those employed in the formal sector (%) | 1.97 | 3.38 |
| Share of those who provide care in a general way (%) | 65.69 | 46.31 |
| Share of caregivers of children aged 0–5 years (%) | 38.61 | 26.32 |

**TABLE 5.1** (*Cont.*)

| *Variables* | *Beneficiary women* | *Poor non-beneficiary women* |
|---|---|---|
| Share of caregivers of aged 6–14 years (%) | 40.29 | 22.93 |
| Hours of paid work (in weekly hours) | 24.20 | 28.33 |
| Hours of unpaid care (in weekly hours) | 26.60 | 22.41 |
| Years of completed formal education | 6.68 | 8.87 |
| Share of women who are heads of household (%) | 47.90 | 35.54 |
| Share of those who identify as Black (%) | 81.66 | 70.48 |
| Share of households with children (aged 0–14 years) (%) | 81.18 | 59.65 |
| Share of households with elderly dependents (aged 70 years and over) (%) | 0.29 | 1.36 |
| Proportion of urban residents (%) | 54.43 | 76.80 |
| Proportion of residents in the most affluent regions (%) | 17.84 | 45.00 |
| Average monthly income from main job (in BRL) | 257.58 | 532.01 |

Source: own elaboration based on PNAD Contínua microdata, 2017.

## Empirical Strategy

The purpose of this research is to evaluate the effects of women's participation in a social protection program (namely, the *Bolsa Família* Program) on the sexual division of labor, taking as its proxy work performance (participation, employment, formalization, and work hours) and family dedication (availability for family care, hours dedicated to family care, and housework).

To estimate the impacts of the *Bolsa Família* Program on the gender dimension, the ideal way would be to evaluate the variables of interest (economic performance and care) in a situation in which the same person receives or does not receive the benefit. In other words, the best group for comparison with individuals in the treatment (beneficiaries of *Bolsa Família*) would be the same individuals but not in the treatment group (non-beneficiaries of *Bolsa Família*). Since in a given period a woman can either participate in the program or not, it is challenging to find a group that is counterfactual to the group in the treatment.

Among the various ways of performing a matching, this research opted for an approach based on propensity score, i.e., the probability of being part of the treatment group. Propensity score matching represents the comparison between a control group (non-*Bolsa Família* women) and a treatment group (*Bolsa Família* women), by estimating the average effect of the treatment on those included in it. In this procedure, the selection of program participants is established through a range of observable variables, so that when comparing the control group and the treatment, there is a great similarity regarding the observable variables, with potential differences in participation in the *Bolsa Família* Program.

Through a logistic regression, a group of characteristics is synthesized in a score, which represents the probability that an individual is a beneficiary of *Bolsa Família*. Then, an individual who is a *Bolsa Família* recipient is compared with a peer who is not, but who has a very close score.[7]

To define the propensity score, or the probability of inclusion in the BF program, the following probit model was estimated:

$$BF = \alpha + \sum \beta_i X_i + \varepsilon$$

where BF represents the dummy variable that indicates participation in the *Bolsa Família* Program, and $X_i$ the vector of observable characteristics: age; years of study; children in household aged 0–3 years; children in household aged 4–6 years; youths in household aged 7–14 years; dummy for those who self-reported identifying as Black; dummy for being a spouse; dummy for being the head of household; dummies for the five Brazilian macro-regions; dummies for urban area; per capita household income. The vector of observable characteristics follows, to the extent of the availability of variables in the database, the empirical impact studies of the area such as Passos and Waltenberg (2016); Tavares (2010); Cacciamali, Tatei, and Ferreira (2010); Duarte, Sampaio, and Sampaio (2009).

After pairing, the effects of the *Bolsa Família* Program on the variables of interest are estimated for each paired sample.

To measure the effect of the *Bolsa Família* Program on women's participation, employment, and formalization in the labor market, the following probit model was estimated:

$$y_1 = \alpha + \beta_1 BF + \sum \beta_i L_i + \varepsilon$$

where $y_1$: dummy representing participation (or employment or formalization) in the labor market; BF: dummy representing participation in the *Bolsa Família* Program; $L_i$: vector of observable characteristics: age; years of study; dummy for those who self-reported identifying as Black; dummy for head of household; dummy for children in household aged 0–3 years; dummy for children in household aged 4–6 years; dummy for youths in household aged 7–14 years; dummy for seniors in household aged 70 years and older; dummy for the five Brazilian macro-regions; dummy for urban area.

To measure the effect of the *Bolsa Família* Program on the overall care of children aged 0 to 5 years and youths aged 6 to 14 years, the following probit model was estimated:

$$y_2 = \alpha + \beta_1 BF + \sum \beta_i L_i + \varepsilon$$

where $y_2$: *dummy* representing participation in family care (general, children aged 0 to 5 years, youths aged 6 to 14 years); BF: *dummy* representing participation in the *Bolsa Família* Program; $L_i$: vector of observable characteristics: age; years of study; dummy for those who self-reported identifying as Black; dummy for head of household; dummy for work hours; dummy for children in household aged 0–3 years; dummy for children in household aged 4–6 years; dummy for youths in household aged 7–14 years; dummy for seniors aged 70 years and older; dummy for the five Brazilian macro-regions; dummy for urban area.

To measure the effect of the *Bolsa Família* Program on the family care and housework provided by women, the following ordinary least squares model was accessed:

$$y_3 = \alpha + \beta_1 \, BF + \sum \; \beta_i \, W_i + \varepsilon$$

where $y_3$: variable that represents the time dedicated to care and housework weekly; BF: dummy variable representing participation in the *Bolsa Família* Program; $W_i$: vector of observable characteristics: age; years of study; dummy for those who self-reported identifying as Black; dummy for head of household; dummy for work hours; dummy for children in household aged 0–3 years; for children in household aged 4–6 years; for youths in household aged 7–14 years; dummy for seniors aged 70 years and older; dummy for the five Brazilian macro-regions; dummy for urban area.

To estimate paid working hours, the problem of data censorship should be considered. This problem refers to the fact that the variable work hours is representative only of individuals who are employed in the labor market, therefore, a self-selected sample by those who decided to be economically active and were able to find a job. For Heckman (1979), a sample that considers only people in the labor market may not represent the entire population, producing biased estimates. As a solution, the author proposes first estimating a probit model, in which the dependent variable is participation in the labor force. Based on the coefficients of the probit model, the lambda variable (inverse of the Mills ratio) can be calculated, which, when used as an explanatory variable in the work hours equation, allows correcting the sample inconsistency problem.

To measure the impact of the *Bolsa Família* Program on women's paid working hours, the Heckman model (1979) was used. The model estimates, at first, a probit according to the participation equation of model 3. In a second stage, the paid workday is estimated through the ordinary least squares model, incorporating the selection bias correction described by equation below:

$$y_4 = \alpha + \beta_1 \, BF + \sum \; \beta_i \, S_i + \beta_2 \lambda + \varepsilon$$

where $y_4$: variable representing the weekly paid workday; BF: dummy variable representing participation in *Bolsa Família*; $S_i$: vector of observable characteristics: age; years of study; dummy for those who self-reported identifying as Black;

dummy for head of household; dummy for children in household aged 0–3 years; for children in household aged 4–6 years; for youths in household aged 7–14 years; for seniors aged 70 years and older; for hours of care and household chores; dummy for urban area; λ: inverse of the Mills ratio (derived from estimation of equation 3). The variables used in this study are based on the empirical literature and theory about the determinants of care and paid work.

It is important to note that the results below are true for the universe of the sample analyzed, since the model does not consider the inclusion of the sample weight, nor the complex design of the database (PNAD Contínua). It is also important to highlight the fact that the matching procedure does not consider unobservable variables that may be correlated to both participation in the program and the indicators investigated in this research, which may cause inconsistency in the results. Despite these limitations, the methodology is widely employed for impact assessments of social programs or policies.

## Results

Three distinct propensity score matching modes are used (nearest neighbour, kernel, and radius) to establish the groups of beneficiaries and similar non-beneficiaries. The quality of the match is considered through measures such as Pseudo-$R^2$, Rubin's B, and Rubin's R, as shown in Table 5.3. Regarding the first measure, Theodoro and Scorzafave (2011) point out that a prerequisite for a good matching is that the post-matching Pseudo-$R^2$ be much lower than pre-matching Pseudo-$R^2$, indicating no distinction in the observable variables between matched individuals. Regarding the two other measurements, Rubin (2001) considers that the samples are well balanced when Rubin's B is below 25 post-matching and Rubin's R is between 0.5 and 2. The nearest neighbor method meets the requirements of the three indicators, the kernel is satisfactory in all but one criterion (Rubin's R indicator). The radius method failed in the three quality indicators and, therefore, has not been used.[8]

Assuming that the matching techniques establish counterfactuals that are appropriate for the group of women who benefit from the *Bolsa Família* program, we can analyze how the program affects the two poles of the sexual division of labor. The results are presented in Tables 5.4, 5.5, and 5.6. It should be noted that significant differences in terms of magnitude of the coefficients are present as a function of the matching technique, a situation that according to Dugoff, Schuler, and Stuart (2014) is frequent and natural, since treatment groups are different in each case.

When considering the *Bolsa Família* Program beneficiary dummy as an explanatory variable of participation in the labor force, the coefficients, shown in Table 5.4, are significant and positive using both techniques. Contrary to common sense, this signals that program beneficiaries are more likely to be in the workforce than non-beneficiaries in a similar situation. This result corroborates the considerations of Bartholo, Passos, and Fontoura (2017) – in a comprehensive review of the literature

**TABLE 5.2** Descriptions of the variables used in the estimations

| | *Variables* | *Description* |
|---|---|---|
| | Dummy for participation in the labor force | Informs if the individual is economically active |
| | Dummy for employment | Informs if the individual is employed |
| | Dummy for formalization | Informs if the individual has a job in the formal sector or contributes to social security |
| Dependents | Dummy for caring for residents or non-residents | Informs if the individual takes care of residents at her household or elsewhere |
| | Dummy for caring for child aged 0–5 years | Informs if the individual takes care of children aged 0–5 years both in and out of the household |
| | Dummy for caring for youths aged 6–14 years | Informs if the individual takes care of youths aged 6–14 years both in and out of the household |
| | Hours of unpaid housework | Hours spent on housework activities |
| | Hours of paid work | Hours spent on paid work |
| | Dummy for participation in the *Bolsa Família* Program | Informs if the individual participates in the *Bolsa Família* Program |
| | Age | Informs the age of the individual |
| Explanations | Years of study | Indicates the years of schooling completed by the individual |
| | *Dummy* for skin color | Informs the self-reported ethnic group (i.e. "skin color" in Brazil) |
| | *Dummy* for head of household | Corresponds to an individual who is responsible for the duties that pertain to a head of household |
| | *Dummy* for spouse | Corresponds to an individual who is the spouse or partner of another individual |
| | *Dummy* for children in household aged 0–3 years | Informs if there are children aged 0–3 years who reside in the household |
| | *Dummy* for children in household aged 4–6 years | Informs if there are children aged 4–6 years who reside in the household |
| | *Dummy* for youths in household aged 7–14 years | Informs if there are children aged 7–14 years who reside in the household |
| | *Dummy* for seniors in the household aged 70 years and older | Informs if they have seniors in their household aged 70 years or older |
| | Hours of care and household chores | Hours spent caring for the family and carrying out household activities |
| | Hours of paid work | Hours spent in the labor market |
| | *Dummies* for macro-regions | Indicator variable for each of the five Brazilian regions |
| | *Dummy* for urban area | Informs if the individual lives in an urban area |
| | *Per capita* household income | Reports monthly per capita household income |

Source: IBGE. PNAD Contínua, 2017.

**TABLE 5.3** Matching quality test

| *Indicators* | *Nearest-Neighbor Method* | | *Kernel Method* | | *Radius Method* | |
|---|---|---|---|---|---|---|
| | *Before matching* | *After matching* | *Before matching* | *After matching* | *Before matching* | *After matching* |
| Pseudo-$R^2$ | 0.356 | 0.003 | 0.356 | 0.007 | 0.356 | 0.409 |
| Rubin's B | 98.1 | 13.2 | 98.1 | 15.5 | 98.1 | 95.3 |
| Rubin's R | 0.07 | 0.85 | 0.07 | 0.17 | 0.07 | 0.06 |

Source: own elaboration based on PNAD Contínua microdata, 2017.

**TABLE 5.4** Effects of the *Bolsa Família* Program on women's participation, employment, and formalization, Brazil 2017

| | *Matching* | |
|---|---|---|
| | *Nearest neighbour* | *Kernel* |
| Participation | 0.170*** | 0.366*** |
| Employment | -0.0531** | -0.263*** |
| Formalization | -0.262*** | -0.330*** |

Source: own elaboration based on PNAD Contínua microdata, 2017.
Note: Level of significance: *** $p<0.01$, ** $p<0.05$, * $p<0.1$.

on the *Bolsa Família* Program and its effects on women's lives – that the program enables the expansion of female choices in contexts marked by traditional gender relations, as is the situation of poor women. From this point of view, the *Bolsa Família* Program favors female economic autonomy, as such autonomy necessarily depends on participating in the labor force in a capitalist society whose welfare state is not sufficiently de-commodifying.

The effect on employment goes in the opposite direction.[9] As shown in Table 5.4, the dummy for receiving the *Bolsa Família* benefit as an explanatory variable of the probability of being employed presents significant coefficients with negative signs, using both matching techniques. Thus, apparently the effect of the program on women's economic autonomy is contradictory. In a way, the benefit increases the likelihood that recipients will be economically active, but reduces their chances of being employed.

Greater female economic activity is healthy in the context of gender relations. However, the effect of the *Bolsa Família* Program on the likelihood of employment can also be understood as an expansion of female choices. Although it is a hypothesis still in need of empirical evidence, high levels of unemployment may be due to the fact that the *Bolsa Família* Program's monetary benefit enables women to refuse precarious jobs and sources of exploitation, even if this means spending more time searching for work. According to this interpretation, the program is contributing to female autonomy, understood from the perspective of Sen's (1993) effective capacities and his assessment that people's well-being cannot be considered solely in terms of their access to goods or income.

For the third variable presented in Table 5.4, the counterproductive effect on women's lives is unequivocal, since the findings indicate that the *dummy* for beneficiaries of the *Bolsa Família* Program as an explanatory variable for formalization in the labor market is negative and significant using both matching techniques. This result may be related to the perennial fear of beneficiaries being excluded from the *Bolsa Família* Program, especially in contexts such as the current fiscal crisis, implying a tighter hold on social expenditures. Policymakers are aware of beneficiaries' fear surrounding their exclusion from the program, observing that policies such as "guaranteed return" and the "permanence rule," discussed in section 2, deserve to be more widespread among beneficiaries.

Another interpretation of the greater probability of working in an informal labor market lies in the unequal division of labor based on sex/gender. As women have to find ways to accommodate productive and reproductive work, beneficiaries often choose the informal market because of the flexibility that informal employment can provide. But it must be borne in mind that these preferences may not be undertaken in a context of full freedom and are conditioned by the very discrimination that women, especially less educated women and those who self-reported identifying as Black, face in the labor market.

If the findings indicate that the program to some extent favors female economic autonomy, there is also evidence of an increased burden of care among beneficiaries. As shown in Table 5.5, the *Bolsa Família* Program is an explanatory variable for the dedication to family care in general and to youths in the household aged 6 to 14 years in particular, presenting positive and significant results using both pairing techniques. For care of children in the household aged 0 to 5 years, the results were not robust, since one matching technique proved significant and the other did not.

**TABLE 5.5** Effects of the *Bolsa Família* Program on women who care for children, Brazil 2017

| | *Matching* | |
|---|---|---|
| | *Nearest neighbour* | *Kernel* |
| General care | 0.114*** | 0.172*** |
| Care of small children | 0.0185 | 0.220*** |
| Care of older children | 0.0659** | 0.144*** |

Source: Own elaboration based on PNAD Contínua microdata, 2017.
Note: Level of significance: *** p<0.01, ** p<0.05, * p<0.1.

Criticism of *Bolsa Família*'s effect on female autonomy, especially from a feminist perspective, would interpret this result as a signal of reinforcement of gender stereotypes, a fact that is difficult not to attribute to the program.[10] However, it should be stressed that the results refer to increased care, both for those residing at home and those away from home, so this extra care is not necessarily due to conditionalities, and may represent the formation of solidarity networks in which the beneficiaries, having secured a minimal income – nowhere near enough to thrive – assist other women in care. In this view, it would not be prudent to attribute to this result to signs of worsening conditions of women's lives in the context of gender relations. It must also be considered that efforts to grant the benefit to women mark a recognition of their responsibility for family care and the idea that women should be compensated for such work, as discussed in section 3. Although this perspective may seem optimistic today, many studies have pointed to the need for recognition of reproductive work and its valuation. Estimates by Melo, Considera, and Di Sabbato (2017) and Jesus (2018) show that, in Brazil, care and household activities, performed free of charge by women in most households, represent at least 12% of the Gross Domestic Product (GDP) – an invisible GDP.

Finally, it is worth highlighting the effects of the *Bolsa Família* Program on time use. The data in Table 5.6 show negative and significant coefficients for paid working hours, as opposed to positive and significant coefficients for unpaid hours dedicated to family care and household chores.

The increase in time dedicated to family care and household chores certainly meets the expectations of feminist criticism regarding the reinforcement of gender stereotypes of female caregivers who are *Bolsa Família* beneficiaries, and the reduction in paid work supports this and other interpretations. That this group of women, in general, makes up the lower fringe of the labor market, suggests that the negative effect is reflected in less time dedicated to precarious work, softening women's subjection to exhausting and degrading hours. It is also important to note that increased time devoted to care may be particularly relevant for female single-parent beneficiary families. In these cases, being able to devote less hours to paid activities and more hours to care can be a desirable effect for children and mothers who are pressured between both needs.

**TABLE 5.6** Effects of the *Bolsa Família* Program on women's (paid and unpaid) working hours, Brazil 2017

| | *Matching* | |
|---|---|---|
| | *Nearest neighbor* | *Kernel* |
| Hours of paid work | -6.076*** | -9.261*** |
| Hours of household activities | 1.054*** | 1.151*** |

Source: own preparation based on PNAD Contínua microdata, 2017.
Note: Level of significance: *** p<0.01, ** p<0.05, * p<0.1.

Bartholo, Passos, and Fontoura (2017) argue that the gains in autonomy for women in the *Bolsa Família* Program should not only be weighed by their productive engagement and financial independence, but also be looked at in light of the broader choices recipients have – such as rejecting precarious informal work opportunities, discontinuing oppressive marital relations, acting proactively in the community, pursuing additional schooling – within specific social structures, often marked by deprivation and traditional gender relations.

With ambiguous outcomes, one cannot have a single interpretation – positive or negative – about the effect of the *Bolsa Família* Program on the sexual division of labor. Women beneficiaries of the program compared to their similar non-beneficiary peers: i) are more likely to dedicate their time to care; ii) have a greater likelihood of participating in the labor market; iii) dedicate more hours to family care; and iv) allocate fewer hours to paid labor. This would be the experience of a conciliation model, identified by Hirata (2015) as the model in which women, in general, balance productive and reproductive activities with little help from men and the state. The most eloquent conclusion of this chapter, therefore, is that the *Bolsa Família* program favors the lifestyle afforded by the conciliation model for poor women.

## Final Considerations

*Bolsa Família* is an income transfer program whereby the state transfers a cash stipend directly to families so long as the family meets certain conditionalities. It is the acknowledgment of the failures of a selective and exclusionary labor market, which leads thousands of economically active citizens into poverty. *Bolsa Família* is a last resort in terms of social protection in a welfare state that is still in the process of consolidation, with all the weaknesses inherent to such a state.

In its recent trajectory – over the course of 15 years since its launch – the *Bolsa Família* Program has significantly improved the lives of millions of Brazilians, who were previously out of the scope of the state and who now have a minimum subsistence income. *Bolsa Família* has not proven capable, in and of itself, of entirely eradicating poverty – a goal to which the program has aspired – nor was it able to laudably alleviate the astonishing inequality that marks Brazilian society, but it has contributed to efforts in this vein. Today, in the face of a persistent economic crisis, the relevance of a last resort protection is reinforced.

As it moves towards maturity, *Bolsa Família* is seen as relatively successful, inspiring many similar initiatives around the world. But it is unable, given the intrinsic limitations of targeted cash transfers, to be as revolutionary as some expected it would be, especially regarding such sensitive issues as changes in social relations.

Without disregarding the success of the *Bolsa Família* Program as a social protection policy, this chapter focuses on empirically assessing only the gender dimension. The aim of this work ultimately is to understand the program's effects on women's lives – preferential recipients of the benefits – in terms of changes in the asymmetric sexual division of labor.

The results indicate that the program favors female participation in the labor force, but reduces their probability of being employed in the formal sector. The increased probability of participating meets the process of female economic autonomy, which in a capitalist society whose welfare state is not sufficiently de-commodifying, can only be done via the labor market. The lower likelihood of employment allows for a negative understanding inherent in the unemployment penalty, but also a positive one if it is understood as the possibility of refusal of exploitative work offers. The lower share of female beneficiaries holding formal jobs is negative in the context of gender relations, due to the reinforcement of precarious work.

While the effects on the labor force accommodate different interpretations, the results concerning care work are definitely regrettable, indicating that the *Bolsa Família* Program naturalizes traditional roles.

Regarding time use, the effects of the program suggest a diminishing focus on paid work and an increasing burden of unpaid work in the areas of family care and household chores. Knowing that these women make up the bottom fringe of the labor market, shorter paid work hours may prove be fruitful, representing less time dedicated to precarious labor. This increase in family care time is in line with criticisms of the program's reinforcement of traditional gender roles.

Based on our results, a single interpretation cannot be extracted from the effects of the *Bolsa Família* Program on the gender dimension. It seems to us that considering the program simply as not helpful in improving the lives of women is too reductionist; on the other hand, concluding that the program is at the root of a marked female empowerment is too optimistic.

Finally, it should be noted that October 2018 was a contradictory date for the Brazilian people. At the same time that it marked the 15th anniversary of the edition of the Provisional Measure that gave rise to the largest conditional cash transfer program in the world, an ultra-conservative government was elected, with an agenda far removed from efforts to strengthen this program and support its mission, since 2003, of eradicating poverty and fostering a more just and unified society.

## Notes

1 National representative household survey collected annually offering social economic information of individuals and household in Brazil.
2 Adapted from Barr (2012).
3 So-called "workfare" benefits gained importance in the 1990s, above all with the rise of active employment policies, with Tony Blair in the UK and Bill Clinton in the US, among others.
4 Self-targeting can materialize in a form that does not involve direct income transfer, namely, as an indirect benefit, such as subsidies for over-consumed products such as basic foods or public transport. In addition to the disadvantages already mentioned in the body of the text, this kind of indirect self-targeting can induce distortions in consumer choice, generating inefficiencies.

5 Average annual sales value the commercial dollar in 2018 at BRL 3.65. Source: Central Bank of Brazil.
6 Net hours of unpaid domestic work are defined as the difference between the number of hours of domestic work performed and the number of hours contributed by other members of the household.
7 The literature has several weighting methodologies for estimating the average effect of the treatment on the treated. We employed the nearest-neighbor, radius, and kernel methods. The nearest-neighbor weighting method consists of first estimating the likelihood of being in the treatment group, and subsequently finding, for each unit treated, untreated units with the closest possible propensity, i.e. "its nearest neighbor." The radius method seeks to define a propensity score neighborhood for each treatment unit and to pair it with control units that are within that vicinity. For the kernel method, all treatment units are paired with a weighted average of all control units, where the weights used are inversely proportional to the distance between treated and untreated propensity score values.
8 Although the Radius method pairing was not successful, the effects of the *Bolsa Família* Program on economic performance and care are consistent with the other results.
9 Note the distinction between the concepts of participation and employment. Participation refers to availability for work, which is observed both among those who are actually employed and those who are not working, but are undertaking some kind of effort to find work. Employment is therefore a narrower concept that excludes those who do not work but are actively seeking employment.
10 For a comprehensive review of the Brazilian literature on the subject, see Bartholo, Passos, and Fontoura (2017).

## References


Adler, Patrick and Ozge Oner. 2013. "Occupational Class and the Marriage Premium: Exploring Treatment Mechanisms. " Working Paper. Martin Prosperity Institute; Rotman School Management University of Toronto, Toronto.

Anderson, Deborah J., Melissa Binder, and Kate Krause. 2003. "The Motherhood Wage Penalty Revisited: Experience, Heterogeneity, Work Effort, and Work-Schedule Flexibility." *ILR Review* 56, no. 2: 273–294. https://doi.org/10.1177/001979390305600204.

Araújo, Clara and Celi Scalon. 2006. "Gênero e a Distância entre a Intenção e o Gesto." *Revista Brasileira de Ciências Sociais* 21, no. 62: 45–68. https://doi.org/10.1590/s0102-69092006000300003.

Bartholo, Letícia, Luana Passos, and Natália Fontoura. 2017. *Bolsa Família, Autonomia Feminina e Equidade de Gênero: o que indicam as Pesquisas Nacionais?* Texto de Discussão 2331. Brazil: Ipea.

Bandeira, Lourdes, and Hildete Melo. 2013. "A Divisão Sexual Do Trabalho: Trabalho Doméstico Remunerado e a Sociabilidade das Relações Familiares." *Gênero* 13, no. 2: 31–48.

Barr, Nicholas. 2012. *Economics of The Welfare State*. Fifth edition. Oxford: Oxford University Press.

Besley, Timóteo and Ravi Kanbur. 1993. "The Principles of Targeting." In *Including the Poor*, edited by M. Lipton, and J. Van Der Gaag, 67–90. Washington: Banco Mundial.

Biroli, Flávia. 2018. *Gênero e Desigualdades: Limites da Democracia no Brasil.* São Paulo: Boitempo.

Budig, Michelle J. and Paula England. 2001. "The Wage Penalty for Motherhood." *American Sociological Review* 66, no. 2: 204–225. https://doi.org/10.2307/2657415.

Budig, Michelle and Melissa Hodges. 2014. "Statistical Models and Empirical Evidence for Differences in The Motherhood Penalty Across the Earnings Distribution." *American Sociological Review* 79, no. 2: 358–364. https://doi.org/10.1177/0003122414523616.

Cacciamali, Maria Cristina, Tatei Fábio, and Natalia Batista Ferreira. 2010. "Impactos do Bolsa Família sobre o Trabalho Infantil e a Frequência Escolar." *Revista de Economia Contemporânea* 14, no. 2: 269–301. https://doi.org/10.1590/s1415-98482010000200003.

Carloto, Cássia Maria and Silvana Mariano. 2010. "As Mulheres nos Programas de Transferência de Renda: Manutenção e Mudanças nos Papeis e Desigualdades de Gênero." Work Presented in 13O Congresso BIEN, São Paulo, Brazil, June/July 2010.

Carloto, Cássia Maria and Silvana A. Mariano. 2012. "Empoderamento, Trabalho e Cuidados: Mulheres no Programa Bolsa Família." *Textos & Contextos* 11, no. 2: 258–272.

Carloto, Cássia Maria. 2012. "Condicionalidades nos Programas de Transferência de Renda e Autonomia das Mulheres." *Sociedade em Debate* 18, no. 2: 121–130.

Cherlin, Andrew. 2016. "A Happy Ending to A Half-Century of Family Change?" *Population and Development Review* 42, no. 1: 121–129. https://doi.org/10.1111/j.1728-4457.2016.00111.x.

Costa, Joana. 2007. "Determinantes da Participação Feminina no Mercado de Trabalho Brasileiro." Masters Dissertation, Universidade de Brasília.

Duarte, Gisléia Benini, Breno Sampaio, and Yony Sampaio. 2009. "Programa Bolsa Família: Impacto das Transferências sobre os Gastos com Alimentos em Famílias Rurais." *Revista de Econômia e Sociologia Rural* 47, no. 4: 903–918. https://doi.org/10.1590/s0103-20032009000400005.

Dugoff, Eva, Megan Schuler, and Elizabeth Stuart. 2014. "Generalizing Observational Study Results: Applying Propensity Score Methods to Complex Surveys." *HSR: Health Services Research* 49, no. 1. https://doi.org/10.1111/1475-6773.12090.

England, Paula. 2010. "The Gender Revolution: Uneven and Stalled." *Gender & Society* 24, no. 2: 149–166. https://doi.org/10.1177/0891243210361475.

Esping-Andersen, Gosta. 2009. *The Incomplete Revolution: Adapting to Women's New Roles*. Cambridge: Polity Press.

Esping-Andersen, Gosta and Francesco Billari. 2015. "Re-Theorizing Family Demographics." *Population and Development Review* 41, no. 19: 1–31. https://doi.org/10.1111/j.1728-4457.2015.00024.x.

Folbre, Nancy. 2002. *The Invisible Heart: Economics and Family Values*. New York: New Press.

Goldin, Claudia. 2006. "The Quiet Revolution that Transformed Women's Employment, Education, and Family." *American Economic Review: Papers and Proceedings* 92, no. 2: 1–21.

Goldin, Claudia and Lawrence F. Katz. 2002. "The Power of The Pill: Oral Contraceptives and Women's Career and Marriage Decisions." *Journal of Political Economy* 110, no. 4: 730–770. https://doi.org/10.3386/w7527.

Goldsheider, Frances, Eva Bernhardt, and Trude Lappergard. 2015. "The Gender Revolution: a Framework for Understanding Changing Family and Demographic Behavior." *Population and Development Review* 41, no. 2: 207–239. https://doi.org/10.1111/j.1728-4457.2015.00045.x.

Gomes, Simone Da Silva. 2011. "Notas Preliminares de uma Crítica Feminista aos Programas de Transferência Direta de Renda: O Caso do Bolsa Família no Brasil." *Textos & Contextos* 10, no. 1: 69–81.

Gruber, Jonathan. 2013. *Public Finance and Public Policy*. Fourth edition. Nova York: Worth Publishers.

Guedes, Moema and Clara Araújo. 2011. "Desigualdades De Gênero, Família E Trabalho: Mudanças E Permanências No Cenário Brasileiro." *Revista Gênero* 12: 61–79.

Guerra, Maria, and Simone Wajnman. 2016. "Tendências de Retração e Envelhecimento da Mão de Obra Feminina no Trabalho Doméstico Remunerado: A Escolaridade é mesmo Determinante?" Work presented at XX Encontro Nacional De Estudos Populacionais, Foz do Iguaçu, Brazil.

Guiginski, Janaina and Simone Wajnman. 2016. "Mercado de Trabalho e Relações de Gênero: Associação entre a Presença de Filhos e as Condições de Acesso ao Trabalho das Mulheres." Work presented at XX Encontro Nacional De Estudos Populacionais, Foz Do Iguaçu, Brazil.

Guimarães, Patrick and Cristiane Santos. 2010. "Determinantes da Ocupação no Mercado de Trabalho de Maridos e Esposas." *Revista Brasileira de Gestão e Desenvolvimento Regional* 6, no. 2: 23–43.

Hersch, Joni and Leslie Stratton. 2000. "Household Specialization and The Male Marriage Wage Premium." *Industrial and Labor Relations Review* 54, no. 1: 78–94. http://dx.doi.org/10.2139/ssrn.241067.

Heckman, James. 1979. "Sample Selection Bias as a Specification Error." *Econometrica* 47, no. 1: 153–161.

Hirata, Helena. 2015. *Mudanças e Permanências nas Desigualdades de Gênero: Divisão Sexual do Trabalho numa Perspectiva Comparada.* São Paulo: Friedrich Ebert Stiftung Brasil.

Jesus, Jordana. 2018. "Trabalho Doméstico não Remunerado no Brasil: Uma Análise de Produção, Consumo e Transferência." PhD dissertation, Universidade Federal De Minas Gerais.

Kerstenetzky, Célia. 2012. *O Estado Do Bem-Estar Social Na Idade Da Razão: A Reinvenção do Estado Social no Mundo Contemporâneo.* Rio De Janeiro: Campus.

Killewald, Alexandra and Margaret Gough. 2013. "Does Specialization Explain Marriage Penalties and Premiums?" *American Sociological Review* 78, no. 3: 477–502. https://doi.org/10.1177/0003122413484151.

Lavinas, Lena, Barbara Cobo, and Alinne Veiga. 2012. "Bolsa Família: Impacto das Transferências de Renda Sobre a Autonomia das Mulheres e as Relações de Gênero." *Revista Latino-Americana de População* 10: 31–54.

Lavinas, Lena. 2014. "La Asistencia Social En El Siglo XXI." *New Left Review* 84: 7–48.

Madalozzo, Regina and Merike Blofield. 2017. "Como Famílias de Baixa Renda em São Paulo Conciliam Trabalho e Família?" *Revista Estudos Feministas* 25, no. 1: 422.

Melo, Hildete, Claúdio Considera, and Alberto Di Sabbato. 2017. "Dez Anos de Mensuração dos Afazeres Domésticos no Brasil." In *Uso Do Tempo E Gênero*, edited by Natália Fontoura, and Clara Araújo, 173–188. Brazil: IPEA.

Melo, Hildete and Débora Thomé. 2018. *Mulheres e Poder: Histórias, Ideias e Indicadores.* Rio De Janeiro: FGV Editora.

Paiva, Luiz Henrique, Leticia Bartholo, JoanaMostafa, Juliana PicoliAgatte, Celso Lourenço MoreiraCorrêa, and Walter Shigueru Emura. 2014. "O Programa Bolsa Família e a Luta para a Superação da Extrema Pobreza no Brasil." In *O Brasil Sem Miséria*, edited by Tereza Campello, Tiago Falcão, and Patrícia Vieira da Costa. Brazil: MDS.

Passos, Luana. 2018. "Normas de Gênero: Constrangimentos e Limitações na Atuação Econômica Feminina." PhD dissertation, Universidade Federal Fluminense.

Passos, Luana and Fábio Domingues Waltenberg. 2016. "Bolsa Família e assimetrias de gênero: reforço ou mitigação?" *Revista Brasileira de Estudos de População* 33, no. 3: 517–539. https://doi.org/10.20947/S0102-30982016c0004.

Rubin, Donald. 2001. "Using Propensity Scores to Help Design Observational Studies: Application to the Tobacco Litigation." *Health Services & Outcomes Research Methodology* 2, no. 3: 169–188.

Ruggles, Steven. 2015. "Patriarchy, Power, and Pay: The Transformation of American Families." *Demography* 52, no. 6: 1797–1823. doi:10.1007/s13524-015-0440-z.

Santos, Giselle Maria. 2014. "Gênero, Desenvolvimento e Programa Bolsa Família: Direitos Reprodutivos, Trabalho e Projetos de Vida de Mulheres do Coque (Recife/PE)." PhD dissertation, Universidade Federal De Pernambuco.

Sen, Amartya. 1993. "O Desenvolvimento como Expansão de Capacidades." *Lua Nova – Revista de Cultura e Política* 28/29: 323–334. https://doi.org/10.1590/s0102-64451993000100016.

Silva, Tiago, Caroline Augusta Paranayba Evangelista, Hugo Miguel Pedro Nunes, Marconi Fernandes de Sousa, and Tereza Cristina Silva Cotta. 2018. "Programa Bolsa Família: Uma Estratégia de Focalização Bem-Sucedida." In *Bolsa Família 15 Anos (2003–2018)*, edited by Tiago Silva, 191–224. Brazil: Enap.

Souza, Paola. 2016. "Efeitos da Maternidade e do Casamento sobre o Diferencial de Salários entre Gêneros no Brasil para o Ano de 2014." PhD dissertation, Universidade Federal do Ceará.

Tavares, Priscilla. 2010. "Efeito do Programa Bolsa Família sobre a Oferta de Trabalho das Mães." *Economia e Sociedade* 19, no. 3: 613–635.

Waldfogel, Jane. 1997. "The Effect of Children on Women's Wages." *American Sociological Review* 62, no. 2: 209–217.

# 6

# GENDER AND AUTONOMY OF WOMEN IN POVERTY

## An Investigation into the *Bolsa Família* Program[1]

*Silvana Mariano and Márcio Ferreira de Souza*

### Introduction

The case of Brazilian society is exemplary insofar as it reflects obstacles to the quality of citizenship that result from inequalities, including those based on gender. Faced with a persistent historical structure marked by profound inequalities, society as a whole is unable to equitably access the benefits of economic development. The latter, therefore, tend to favor the best-placed groups in the social hierarchy – holders of social, economic, and political privileges – and produce, or reproduce the asymmetries between men and women, among other forms of inequality. Struggles for greater autonomy and women's rights constitute historical forms of confronting these inequalities and have recently become manifested in the field of public policy, especially social policy.

Since the 1970s, a number of international organizations have contributed to incorporating women's rights issues in Brazil. This phenomenon occurred simultaneously with the resurgence of feminist and women's movements in the country, in a very particular context initially marked by military dictatorship and later by economic crises and the adoption of neoliberal policies. The reciprocity between the resurgence of women's movements, including feminist, and the process of redemocratization in the country has produced a favorable context for women's demands, a process that Sonia Alvarez has called the "engendering of democracy" (Alvarez 1988). These experiences, under these particular conditions, helped produce a strand of feminism in the country distinct from those observed in democracies with developed capitalist systems. While in these last countries the so-called new feminism has more typically addressed themes such as sexuality, family life, and reproductive rights, new feminism in Brazil more clearly confronted topics like democracy, citizenship and poverty. The so-called "feminization of poverty"

(Pearce 1978) was one of the forms assumed by this debate. In another dimension of this scenario, it was also up to anti-poverty policies to provide solutions to the phenomenon of the feminization of poverty.

Income transfer programs inherit some of these concerns and place us in the situation, as researchers, of having to ask how women engage in these programs and the effects of this engagement, given the asymmetrical structures of the distribution of goods, capacities, and freedoms among men and women. Views concerning women's empowerment and the instrumentalization of women in state actions represent one side of the theoretical and empirical debates and are not novel in their own right: feminist works have already discussed issues related, for example, to the foundation and experiences of the welfare state worldwide. Reflecting on the dilemma between women's dependence on their husbands or on the state, Pateman (2000) considers the latter form of dependence preferable since it is established within a political relationship, negotiated in the public arena. Still, the author defends the importance of research revealing the patriarchal structures of state actions, where these exist.

Understanding how gendered patterns are produced or reproduced through state actions like conditional cash transfer (CCT) programs can best be explored through the perceptions and experiences of the women themselves who are targeted by these policies and who have participated in such programs. Positing women as the subjects of such policies is a common approach within the framework of gender-sensitive public policy. In this chapter, we seek to understand how values associated with gender equity and female autonomy are presented in the perceptions of impoverished women who have been beneficiaries of the *Bolsa Família* Program (PBF) (Family Grant Program) in Brazil. The objective is to determine the impacts of the BF program on increasing the autonomy of these women.

Setting out from the feminist literature, as well as works on the sociology of agency, our approach to autonomy encompasses different planes: political, economic, personal, and social. At the political level, we explore women's relationships to the state, especially regarding the recognition of their rights and their own assessment of the implementation of public policies. Economically, we reflect on the relationship between paid work and unpaid work or care. Based on interviews with individuals, we explore data on domestic decisions and individual freedoms. Socially, we analyze the values and practices related to the obligations and freedoms of both men and women.

The analyses developed here are based on data from questionnaires fielded by the authors of the present work at different times, between 2012 and 2015, in three municipalities located in the state of Paraná: Guaraci, Londrina, and Curitiba (a small city, a large city, and a metropolis, respectively). Because they deal with social perceptions and practices, the data are valid despite the time span between the different data collection efforts, since we are dealing with factors that do not generally change over short time intervals.

Data were collected through a standardized script posing closed and open-ended questions. The interviews were conducted with women who are the primary recipients or cardholders of the BF benefit – as opposed to general beneficiaries – at the headquarters of the *Centro de Referência de Assistência Social* (CRAS) (Reference Centers for Social Assistance). The women interviewed were seeking assistance or services at the time that our interviewers were recruiting respondents in the CRAS waiting rooms. These interviews were conducted individually in a separate space, ensuring privacy.[2] The interviews were recorded as notes on the physical questionnaires. The open questions were coded based on content analysis, and the data set was developed using a statistical analysis program for compiling databases. In total, 202 women were interviewed in the three municipalities of Paraná. The analyses consider the sample as a whole, without comparing the three municipalities.

The case study composed of subsamples from municipalities of different sizes allows us to address the experiences of these women with a certain degree of generalization, without characterizing the particular contexts of each of these urban spaces. The municipalities were selected using the following criteria: the metropolis chosen was the state capital of Curitiba; next, we chose Londrina, the biggest large municipality in the state; and finally, Guaraci, a small municipality relatively close to Londrina that accommodated the research team, based at the State University of Londrina.

The state of Paraná is one of the 27 federative units of Brazil and is located in the country's Southern Region, occupying an area of 199,305,326 km$^2$. Its estimated population in 2018 was 11,348,937 inhabitants, with Paraná ranking as the sixth largest population in Brazil, representing a population density of 52.40 inhabitants per km$^2$. The state ranks fifth in the national Human Development Index (0.749).[3]

In order to infer the possible influences of the BF program on women's autonomy, the research compares the respondents, who were all the primary recipients or cardholders of the BF benefit at the time, according to their time engaged in the program. Having calculated the median time receiving benefits as four years, we then divided the total of 202 interviewees into two groups: respondents engaged in the program for no more than four years and those engaged for more than four years. If the program indeed exerts an influence on the variables investigated in our research, this should result in advantages and gains for the female beneficiaries throughout their period linked to the program. By contrast, similarities between the two groups indicate that time engaged in the program does not influence the factors analyzed. The variables related to the female condition investigated here are: most valued rights; degree of respect for the most valued rights; most important factors in guaranteeing rights; participation in paid work; impediments to engaging in paid work; justifications for paid work outside the home; self-assessment of individual freedoms.

Table 6.1 shows some of the information that characterizes our respondents. Just under half (42.6%) of the women in our sample live with a husband or partner. Approximately one quarter of respondents (24.3%) experienced some change in marital status after joining the program, while 13.9% separated after joining the program. Forty-five percent (45%) of these women engaged in paid work at the time of the interview – the employment rate of the female population in Brazil was approximately 55% in 2015.[4] Low education is a common feature among the poor in Brazil, reflecting inequalities related to educational access. Among the interviewees, more than half possess a low level of education, while 63.9% have up to eight years of schooling. In Brazil, in 2015, the average years of schooling of the population aged 15 and over was 8.2 years, with a slight advantage for women, with 8.0 years for men compared to 8.4 years among women.[5] Almost all of the women (93%) lived with dependent children and/or adolescents at the time of the interviews.

Social inequalities in Brazil have shaped a profoundly asymmetrical society, especially in terms of class, race, and gender. The possibilities for thinking about autonomy are thus diverse. Our focus is here on the gender dimension, but it should be emphasized that in examining the topic of women living in poverty, we are connecting poverty and race in advance. The population distribution by race in Paraná is composed of 70.3% of people who identify as white, 3.1% as black, 25% as brown, 1.1% as Asian, and 0.25% as indigenous. Our sample, 48% of which is composed of respondents who identify as black[6] (Table 6.1), presents an over-representation of this group given the overall distribution of people identifying as black and brown in the state.

**TABLE 6.1** Characterization of female respondents in the state of Paraná

| | |
|---|---|
| Total respondents | 202 |
| Average people per household | 4 |
| Lives with partner / husband | 42.6% |
| Does paid work | 45% |
| Lives with children | 93% |
| Up to 8 years of schooling | 63.9% |
| Median Age | 35 years |
| Changed marital status after joining the program | 24.3% |
| Separation after joining the program | 13.9% |
| Median time receiving benefit | 4 years |
| Black Women | 48% |

Source: Author's original work (2015).

In addition to this introduction, the chapter is organized into three complementary thematic sections. The first reflects on female autonomy in a context of poverty and briefly situates the configuration of income transfer programs in Brazil, connecting them to a wider international context. The second section examines the themes of law and citizenship among women assisted by the BF program. The third focuses on perceptions of autonomy and individualization as expressed by the respondents.

## Thinking about Female Autonomy in the Context of Poverty

Latin America experienced alarming increases in poverty and social inequalities in the decades between the 1970s and the 1990s, especially in Brazil. Beginning in the 1990s, CCT programs were created in the region as a strategy for immediate alleviation of poverty, during a period also characterized by the implementation of neoliberal policies. In focusing specifically on the Brazilian case, we must take into account the contradictory tendencies of this time. While, on one hand, there was the importation of neoliberal ideals, there was also the spread of egalitarian values, translated in the so-called "Citizen Constitution" of 1988, and the unprecedented proliferation of the agenda on women's rights.

The 1988 Federal Constitution introduced the country to a new legal framework with significant expansions in social rights, with special relevance for women. These predictions were partly reinforced by the 1993 Organic Law on Social Assistance (LOAS), important for introducing social assistance as a key element of the social security system. In this context, the fight against poverty and the reduction of social inequalities acquired huge importance in political and academic debate, leading to the formulation of new policies, including CCT programs. From the outset of this process of reformulating the political pact in Brazil, women have played a major role (Blay 1982, 1999; Pinto 2003) and have drawn attention to both the importance of social policies to women and the importance of women to social policies (Pateman 2000).

Another important factor in this context involves the actions of international organizations. The Fourth World Conference on Women, held in Beijing in 1995, resulted in a Declaration and Platform for Action that greatly expanded the use of language sensitive to gender equity and women's rights in the wider context of human rights and human development. From this international framework, "gender mainstreaming" or the "gender perspective" has become a guiding paradigm for policies designed to empower women and reduce inequalities between the sexes. Such a paradigm has spread globally in the wake of projects aimed at assisting developing countries. Very often, however, this diffusion has been accompanied by the simplification that creating gender policies is the same as helping women.

Early on, feminists drew attention to the importance of empirically investigating how women are included in state actions, considering the context that interconnects three axes: poverty alleviation, human development, and women's autonomy. In a sense, Latin American CCT programs translate the connection between these three axes. Based on the feminist literature on people's experiences of these programs, we highlight some of their common characteristics: i) focusing; ii) targeting of the benefit to families; iii) prioritization of the transfer of the resource to women; and iv) conditionalities (Fonseca and Roquete 2018). The feminist literature challenges all these factors with particular emphasis on investigating the effects of female ownership and the conditionality of women's citizenship or autonomy, considering issues with gender – i.e. the power relations involved in the distribution of factors such as goods, capacities and freedoms between men and women. These studies are sometimes interested in investigating potential changes to women's status, in the terms formulated by Nancy Fraser (2006; 2007): that is, they adopt participatory parity between men and women as the normative core of the analysis, which leads to the valorization of policies aimed at improving the status of women in areas associated with female subordination. Another perspective that has been influential in this research agenda is the capabilities approach, along the lines of Nussbaum (2002), valuing policies that broaden not only the options available to women, but also the freedoms.

By analyzing social programs targeting poor women in developing countries, feminist research has identified an overall trend towards women's empowerment (Nussbaum 2002; Moser and Moser 2005). This instrumentalization occurs when the focus of the program considers women a conduit to address the needs and interests of others such as the family, the community and the state.

A gender-based perspective in public policies has become a paradigm and a campaigning issue for feminist organizations (Mariano 2009). In addition, research on the experiences of conditional cash transfer programs in Brazil has deepened this research agenda. Considering the size of the population served and its social reach across the country, the BF program has been a privileged object in these studies in the Brazilian context.

Income transfer through the BF program is a poverty alleviation strategy that gives women some gains because it transfers monetary benefits and they can control their use. The preference for women as the primary beneficiaries or cardholders in the program is justified by the social obligations that women assume towards care: they are more dedicated to the education of younger generations and ensure a fairer distribution of the benefit received. These factors are valued in studies that conclude that the PBF contributes to the autonomy of women living in poverty (Morton 2013; Pereira and Ribeiro 2013; Rego and Pinzani 2014; Pires 2012). The focus on the economic dimension as a means to enhance women's autonomy and the derivation for gender relations represent two limitations of these studies. By adopting this approach, these studies make women's instrumentalization a secondary issue and fail to problematize the effects of "familist" and "maternalistic" approaches to women's citizenship.

"Familist" policies are characterized by their valorization of the family as a social institution in itself responsible for ensuring the welfare of its members. When the family is unable to provide sufficiently for their needs, the state steps in to assist the family. There are two basic problems with this approach. First, the "family" always appears indefinitely and abstractly (and even fictively), hiding the fact that it is usually women who provide the necessary care for its well-being (Mariano and Carloto 2010). Second, women are incorporated into the course of state action as representatives of the family group and other family members are rarely challenged or involved. "Maternalistic" policies, in turn, are strongly associated with the familist approach and have the limitation of including women as mothers. The combination of familism and maternalism produces policies that ignore the needs and interests that ultimately pertain to women themselves, and these are included in the programs in an instrumental way. This instrumental use of social responsibilities prescribed to women does not take into account the existing connection between this situation and the conditions of subordination that affect them (Mariano 2010). Policies of this kind do not explicitly stipulate objectives intended to promote women's interests, rights, or autonomy.

Unlike "maternalistic" and "familist" approaches, public policies committed to a gender-sensitive perspective explicitly set goals that aim to promote the equitable redistribution of power and resources between men and women (Guzmán 2000). These are policies committed to reducing gender inequalities, thus promoting women's autonomy. The National Policy Plan for Women (PNPM) of 2008 (Brasil 2008), setting out to direct Brazilian policies, defined the principle of women's autonomy as follows:

> Women should be guaranteed decision-making power over their lives and bodies, as well as the conditions to influence the matters in their communities and country and to break with the historical legacy, with its cycles and spaces of dependence, of exploitation and subordination detrimental to their personal, political, and economic lives.
>
> *(Brasil 2008, 27)*

In focusing on women's autonomy at the political, economic, personal, and social levels, our interest also resides in the analysis of the culture in which social rights are embedded. Research by Inglehart and Norris (2003), based on international data, points to a global trend of an increasing valorization of gender equality, especially among women with higher levels of education and lower levels of religiosity. This process is associated with cultural changes resulting from modernization, especially in urban societies. While we agree with the idea that culture matters, we also recognize that the social structure conditions, rather than determines, the experiences of individuals (Archer 2011).

Based on a national survey conducted in 2003 on gender, work and family in Brazil, Clara Araújo and Celi Scalon (2006) found that there were certain ambiguities in the expected modernization in Brazil. On the one hand, there is the growing presence of values indicating more egalitarian gender relations, such as acceptance of female work and agreement on the need for greater participation from men in raising children and carrying out domestic activities. On the other hand, the understanding persists that the home and motherhood are central to women's lives, indicators of the "strong influence of the traditional dual model whereby the man is the 'provider' and the woman the 'caregiver'" (Araújo and Scalon 2006, 50).

Comparing the findings reported by Araújo and Scalon (2006) and Bohn (2008), it appears that the values associated with gender equality in Brazilian society are more commonly present in perceptions of formal policies than in perceptions of family and care. Based on these contributions, we argue that women's autonomy involves perceptions of both public life and private life, without, however, presuming any dichotomy between these spheres.

The following sections present and analyze the perceptions of women who were beneficiaries of the BF program regarding the conditions and factors surrounding their rights and freedoms.

## Rights and Citizenship among Women Beneficiaries of the *Bolsa Família* Program

Conceptions of law and citizenship are fundamental to the notion of subjects and, consequently, the notion of subjects with rights. These conceptions take shape in the types of public policies formulated for different social groupings. These actions, in turn, have different impacts on people's lives, including social gender patterns, accessible opportunities, and the capacities promoted among men and women. Regarding sexual citizenship, gender-based public policies are also forged. As a result, socio-political frameworks based on gendered conceptions produce the types and objectives of state-promoted policies. The gendered character of citizenship (Pateman 1993) and the generalized character of state actions (Alvarez 1988) have both been widely investigated by feminist research.

The condition that particularly interests us in this sphere is that of women living in poverty in urban areas of Brazil. Excluded from the public sphere due to the complex intersectionality of conditions of gender, class and race/color, women turn to welfare benefits, which tends to constitute a link between these poor women and the state, a fundamental actor in the recognition and expansion of women's citizenship.

Access to rights is a *sine qua non* for women's citizenship. To address this theme in the questionnaire, the women were presented with an open-ended question, asking them to list up to three rights that they consider the most important. The respondents produced a diverse list of options with 397 responses, which were coded into 14 categories, as shown in Figure 6.1.

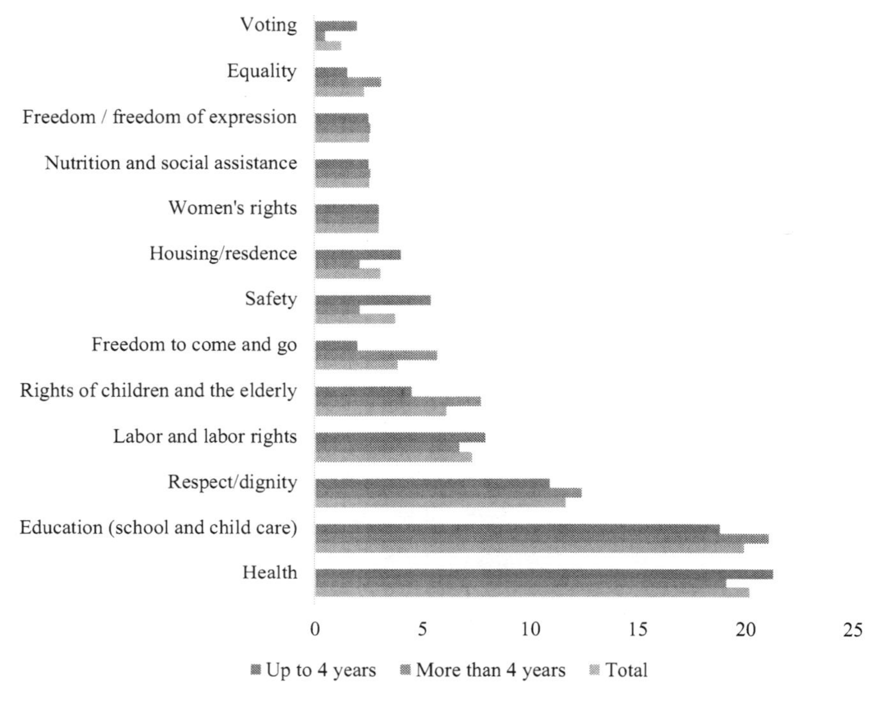


**FIGURE 6.1** Most valued rights, by tenure in the program
Source: Author's original work (2015).

According to the data presented in Figure 1, the two rights most valued by the respondents are health (20.2%) and education (20%), which correspond to social rights and the provision of public services, about which these women complained, reporting poor access to services and services of poor quality.[7] The third most valued right was respect (11.7%), which includes complaints about humiliating treatment by employers, neighbors, and civil servants. The right to work was indicated in 7.3% of the answers. Security and housing appear in 3.8% and 3.1% of responses, respectively. As a whole, rights linked to social policies were highly valued among respondents. This emphasis may be indicative of some politicization among these women regarding the importance of public services.

More individual rights, such as the freedom to come and go, freedom of expression, and women's rights proved less important with rates of just 4% each. These results are indicative of the fact that, faced with conditions of poverty, these women are frequently compelled to accept degrading jobs and precarious public services. Moreover, they complain of a limited capacity to worry about demands that characterize a condition or situation of freedom rather than of survival. Comparing the group engaged in the program for four years or less with the group in the program for over four years, there are no significant differences in the order of importance that women attach to rights. In both groups, we can infer the same pattern of ranking individualizing aspects as secondary elements, despite the fact these would attribute greater value to freedom and could have more positive effects in terms of enhancing women's autonomy.

Access to quality services or goods such as health, education, housing, and public safety is crucial for women's citizenship, especially poor women, because these goods and services directly impact the conditions under which they perform childrearing activities or care work (Machado 1995; 1999). In our research context, the demands of these women in relation to health, education, housing, and public safety concern the needs of their daughters and sons. Their interests are thus formulated from the configuration of responsibilities socially attributed to women. When these interests are adequately addressed, they can theoretically favor the conditions for women to have sufficient time to pursue other interests, including individual aspirations. However, respondents rarely reported that these public services met their needs, meaning it is difficult to promote individualization among women with little to no income, a situation corroborated by all these responses.

After responding to the question about the three rights they considered the most important, the respondents were then asked about their opinion concerning the degree of respect for each of these rights. The response options were: fully respected, partially respected, and not respected. As Figure 6.2 shows, 20.8% did not answer the question. About 7% think that their rights are fully respected; 33% feel their rights are partially respected, and 40% report that their rights are not respected. The predominant perception among the survey respondents, therefore, is one of disrespect or partial respect for their rights. We can infer from these data that women have a critical perception of the material, social, and political context in which they live. This criticism is more pronounced among those women who have engaged in the program for the longest time: 42.3% compared to 38.1% among beneficiaries engaged in the program for up to four years.

Juxtaposing the responses in Figure 6.1 and Figure 6.2, we can identify the gap between the legal existence of right(s), or *de jure* rights, and the substantiality of these right(s), or *de facto* rights. Such a distinction is crucial in the Brazilian case where rights are often elaborated into law but may not concretely develop into policies (Santos 1979). Social protection and many other provisions of the so-called "Citizen Constitution" only exist in a condition popularly known as "on paper." This situation particularly affects women, especially poor and black women, who tend to bear the brunt of care responsibilities with the aid of neither the state, due to their citizenship status, nor the market, due to their class status (Lavinas 1997).

The criticisms raised by the female respondents concerning the precarious conditions of social rights in Brazil present paradoxes in terms of what they consider necessary to guarantee the rights they cite as important to them. The question was presented on a card: 13 possible answers were arranged in a circle to avoid any appearance of preselection or ranking. The options were: family support, access to

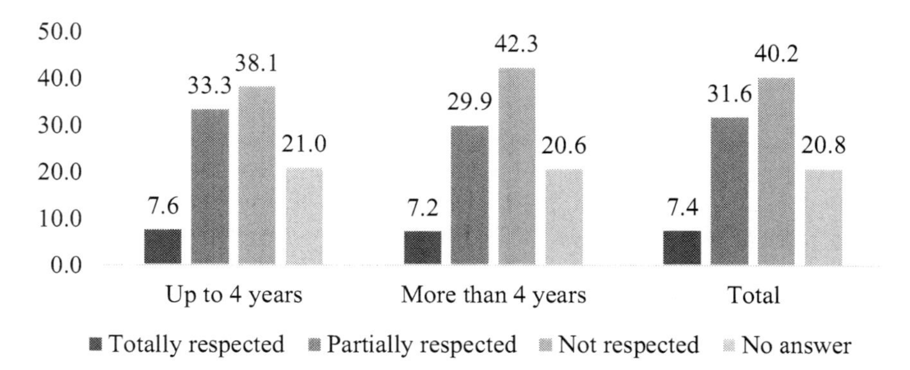


**FIGURE 6.2** Degree of respect for the most important rights, by tenure in the program
Source: Author's original work (2015).

childcare and schools for children, personal endeavour, access to health services, access to education; government policies, access to minimum income, access to justice; support for welfare entities, church support, support from friends and acquaintances, associativism, and access to information. The particular aim of this question was to address the two constitutive dimensions of autonomy: the agency and the political involvement of these women. Reconciling agency and the politicization of social processes is a way to avert the risk of treating agency in an individualized or, in other words, atomized dimension. The results are shown in Figure 6.3.

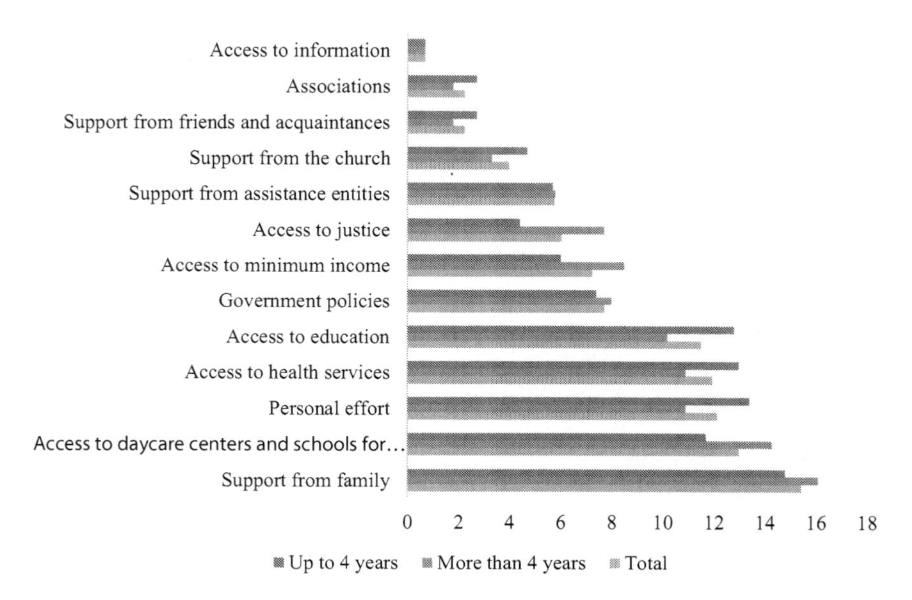


**FIGURE 6.3** Most important factors to guarantee rights, by tenure in the program
Source: Author's original work (2015).

According to the data, 15.5% of the respondents reported that family support is, in their view, the main mechanism for guaranteeing their rights. Together with personal endeavor (12.2%) and support from friends and acquaintances (2.3%), these three areas account for 30% of the total responses. Personal endeavor is the variable with the largest difference between the two compared groups, and its incidence falls significantly among those beneficiaries engaged in the program for a longer period. In this same group, while the personal endeavor response rate (12.2% versus 10.9%) dropped, the rates for access to day care centers and schools for children (13.0% versus 14.3%), access to minimum income (7.3% versus 8.5%), and access to justice (6.1% versus 7.7%) rose. The rate of family support also increased, albeit to a lesser extent (15.5% versus 16.1%). In other words, among the beneficiaries engaged in the program the longest, the importance of the state is reaffirmed, as are policies related to education (for children), income transfer, and justice. On the other hand, the importance of family support is reaffirmed even more strongly. These answers reveal that the support these women receive from the state is insufficient to do without the solidarity networks formed by family relations. The importance of other support networks is similar between the two compared groups. Assistance organizations (5.8%) and churches (4%) account for almost 10% of the responses, 10.4% among the group engaged in the program for four years or less, and 9.1% among those engaged in the program for four years or more.

Slightly more than half of the respondents (51.4%) indicated in diverse ways that state action was necessary to guarantee their rights. Here we consider the following types of responses: government policies, access to education, access to health services, access to day care centers and schools for children, and access to a minimum income. The rates among the groups were 50.9% among those in the program for four years or less and 51.9% among those who had been beneficiaries for more than four years, a striking similarity.

Regarding social policies, 13% of respondents reported access to day care centers and schools for children as the mechanism necessary to guarantee their rights. These perceptions corroborate the importance of these public services to women, since they reduce the time they need to devote to care and thus generate conditions for autonomy and freedom. Comparatively, women with longer time in the program tend to value this aspect more. In a context of scarce public facilities, the criticisms contained in these answers may be indicative of a type of denunciation and demand.

Studies by Bila Sorj, Adriana Fontes, and Danielle Carusi Machado (2007), for example, show that access to day care centers and preschools facilitates a reconciliation between work and family and has a positive impact on women, increasing their participation in paid work and consequently increasing their income. According to the authors, "this positive impact generally occurs among all social classes. But it is the poorest families who benefit most from the mechanism compared to higher income groups" (Sorj, Fontes, and Machado 2007, 576–577). Coverage of early childhood education services thus tends to favor an improvement in women's living conditions, especially those in poverty, and thus contributes to women's autonomy. This is why it was so frequently reported by respondents.

According to the women interviewed, their burden of care work is greatly exacerbated by the absence of full-time schooling and a lack of day care options, not to mention the long distances mothers and their children must travel to reach educational establishments (the case of women living in large municipalities like Londrina and Curitiba in our sample). These barriers tend to deepen in large municipalities, which is why the interviewees in these cities were more critical of the BF program conditionalities, due to the difficulties, in terms of time and cost, of the inconvenient distance of the available school options from their home. They also complained about conditionalities because of the inherent difficulties of monitoring and ensuring their children's school attendance. These difficulties are discussed in detail by Cássia Carloto in this volume.

Based on our data, we also highlight a large group of these women who do not view the state as the primary mechanism for guaranteeing their rights. These data can be interpreted from two angles, not necessarily mutually exclusive. From one perspective, this perception corroborates a shift in responsibility for social issues from the public to the private/domestic sphere, indicating a kind of rejection of the public sphere. This is a problematic situation from the viewpoint of women's citizenship. As Jelin (2004) has pointed out, reducing the activities related to the unpaid care work taken on by women is more likely when they have access to public services and these activities are redistributed among members of the household. From another perspective, these data can also be interpreted as a reflection of the moral and social values of poor Brazilian families (Sarti 1995), which connects, in a sense, with another meaning of familism. Family has a strong appeal both in the formulation of social policies and in the configuration of solidarity networks: in other words, when we focus on the means of providing for the needs of individuals, familism can be interpreted from both a state and societal perspective. Some research suggests that, in the Brazilian case, families assume greater importance as a support network among the lower strata, working classes and populations in poverty (Sarti 1994, 1995; Fonseca 1997).

In Brazil in 2016, women 14 years of age and older dedicated on average 20.9 hours a week to caring for dependents and/or household chores, while men spent 11.1 hours (IBGE 2018). The proportion of children under three years old attending school or day care the same year was 30.4% (IBGE 2018). Such coverage was unevenly distributed across the various regions of Brazil, however, to the detriment of the poorest populations. This additional burden of unpaid work assumed by women reduces the time they can devote to activities such as paid work and political participation.

Scarcity of public services is one of the obstacles encountered by these women, and under these conditions they are less likely to find ways to extend their personal freedoms and autonomy. The respondents show awareness of this phenomenon when slightly more than half of them indicate state action as a mechanism necessary to guarantee their rights. On the other hand, approximately 40% of respondents indicated personal endeavor and the support of family, friends, neighbors, charitable organizations, and the church as important factors in guaranteeing their rights (Figure 6.3). These perceptions may inhibit the engagement of these women with collective demands or claims and their involvement in public action.

It is important to understand the emphasis these women place on the support of family, friends, and neighbors in this same context of scarce public services and the low institutionality of social rights in Brazil. These social ties generate support networks that enable the daily solutions of these women to various situations, such as childcare, food donations, payments of utility bills, housing assignment, and the purchase of gas for cooking. According to reports, these support networks are predominantly made up of links between women, corroborating the results of other surveys of Brazilian working-class families and families in poverty (Sarti 2007).

The needs these women encounter, the obstacles they face, and the opportunities they create are strongly associated with the gender patterns prevalent in Brazilian society. Judging by women's experiences with its implementation, the BF program shows no signs of fomenting any change or innovation in this pattern. Our results corroborate the findings of Araújo and Scalon (2006) regarding the persistence of the view that home care and motherhood are central to these women's lives. We add the caveat, however, that such centrality cannot be understood only in terms of the cultural patterns reproduced by individuals in their daily interactions. We must also take into account the precarity of social protection in Brazil and, in parallel, the familist and maternalistic character of these policies. Faced with the scarcity of state-provided social protection and the fact that existing protection is based on the traditional dual model and its asymmetrical gender, class, and race paradigms, these women effectively depend on their own private strategies to solve their needs. There are not many choices involved in this form of dependence. The intertwining of the institutional and personal dimensions shapes the concrete conditions in which these women act to meet their responsibilities and needs.

The symbolic dimension that characterizes the ways of life and behaviors of poor families helps us understand the construction of the roles and responsibilities of men and women among this social group. At the symbolic level, the cultural association between the male "provider" and the female "caregiver" is still widely validated in these social practices. This symbolic representation assigns the economic domain to men (present in 42.6% of the domestic arrangements in our sample) and the domain of emotions, care and familial affection to women. Man as the "provider" of the family carries an economic and moral significance. Although this division cannot be taken rigidly, it still characterizes social relations among many groups of poor families in Brazil (Sarti 2007).

In the case of biparental families, it is left to women to maintain the bonds of union between family group members and to control the household budget. This attribution is not related to the ability to make money, but to the role of housewife (Sarti 2007), a function reinforced in these women's relationship to the BF program. These attributions favor the election of women as the claimants responsible for the resources passed on through conditional cash transfer programs. Making use of the roles socially assigned to women, these programs seek to enhance their own effectiveness. Pragmatically or instrumentally, the programs thus symbolically reinforce the idea that women are the managers of the home (Mariano and Carloto 2009). Based on the data presented in Figure 6.3, we infer that women in poverty can only perform these social attributions through the support of solidarity networks formed by family relationships in the foreground and the local community in the background.

When it comes to the single parent family, this burden is accentuated further as these women are almost always the sole source of income for the domestic group. As we saw in Table 6.1, approximately 43% of respondents live with a partner. In other words, the majority, approximately 57% of the women, live in single-parent families and generally these domestic configurations are made up of women and children or adolescents. This fact also reinforces the BF program's guidelines specifying that benefits are awarded to women. So far, however, this gender targeting of Brazilian social policies has not involved strategies to reduce the burden that this condition places on women, including the competition between paid and unpaid work, immersing them in a kind of poverty trap produced by the intersection of gender, race, and class.[8] Composing a single-parent family with children and adolescents thus tends to increase the dependency of these women on non-state solidarity networks to meet their needs.

In the next section, we discuss how aspects of paid and unpaid work and forms of freedom are associated with conditions of female autonomy. In so doing, our aim is to discern possible influences on the livelihoods of women beneficiaries based on the length of time they have been engaged in the program.

## Perceptions of *Bolsa Família* Beneficiaries concerning Autonomy and Individualization

As a key aspect of this reflection, we wish to apprehend the perceptions of the beneficiaries of the *Bolsa Família* Program concerning their autonomy and individualization. The sense of individualization adopted here is partly in line with Ulrich Beck's (1992) thesis of individualization. Despite the ambivalent and contradictory character of individualization, it leads to the idea of individuals as agents and, in this sense, their individual and collective ways of life are manifestations of their choices. Since the gender dimension is fundamental to our analysis, we conceive of individualization as the possibility for women to move away from the naturalized and traditional gender roles socially attributed to them in the context of Brazil's patriarchal society.

Firstly, we highlight work as an important element for addressing the autonomy of these women. A connection can therefore be established with data related to a person's individualization. For this reason, we chose to analyze the variables that relate to the reasons presented by respondents as impediments to engaging in paid work and the reasons that justify the performance of paid work outside the home. We also focus on the data related to the interviewees' experiences in the field of gender relations, given that such experiences are significant in terms of interpreting their perceptions of autonomy and individualization.

From a gender-based perspective, considering the national scenario, the participation rate of Brazilian women in the workforce in 2016 for those aged 15 years and over was 52.8% (IBGE 2018). Among the respondents, 45% reported performing paid work, as shown in Figure 6.4. Another 55% were not engaged in paid work, limiting themselves to performing tasks related to childcare and home care.

The breakdown of the data by the respondents' marital status reveals the influence of traditional gender patterns when it comes to paid work and the family. Among the respondents, 42.6% lived with a spouse and 57.4% did not. The predominance of women without a spouse engaged in a conditional cash transfer program stems from the fact that female single-parent families are more vulnerable to poverty, mainly because they are usually households composed of one adult – a woman – infants, children, and/or teenagers. Besides this arrangement representing families with only one adult, the situation is aggravated by the precarious way women are incorporated in the Brazilian labor market to fill the most undervalued and unstable positions.

We cannot ignore the concept of the sexual division of labor (Hirata and Kergoat 2007) as a fact illustrative of the historical and traditional process of labor naturalization. This notion is rooted in women's apparent biological dimension

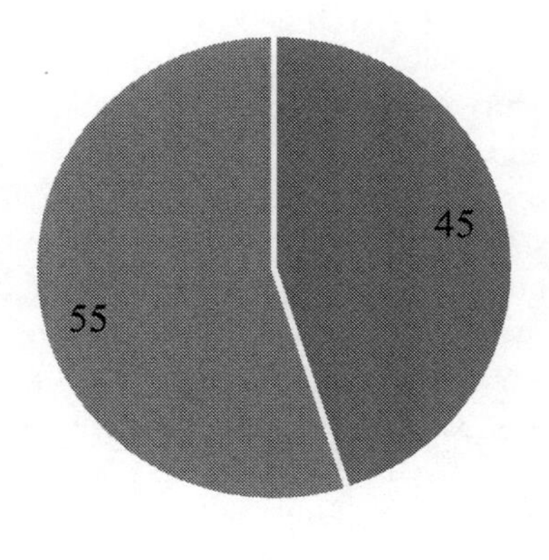


**FIGURE 6.4** Percentage of beneficiaries asked about engagement in paid work
Source: Author's original work (2015).

and their concomitant allocation of responsibility for household and family care tasks. The sexual division of labor is not a phenomenon exclusive to Brazilian society, but it is highly pronounced in Brazil and present across all social strata.

Among the married respondents, 37.2% report being engaged in paid work. Among unmarried respondents, this rate rises to 50.9%. The presence of a spouse is thus an inhibitor for women's participation in paid work, the outcome of a social pattern still based on the sexual division of labor, as we announced in the previous section when citing the situation of biparental families.

Reproductive activities here signify "the set of activities that includes family care and housework. Family care includes: pregnancy and childbirth, child rearing; providing education, health care, and food (including preparation of meals); water and firewood collection; purchasing provisions; doing household chores; engaging in family care" (FAO 2003, 33). Housework, in turn, is also part of reproductive activities and can be defined "as a set of tasks related to the care of people and performed in the context of a family – conjugal union in a domicile and parentage – free work performed essentially by women" (Fougeyrollas-Schwebel 2009, 257).[9]

Despite the economic, cultural, and demographic changes that have reshaped the classic sexual division of labor and affected the organization of care, families and women in particular continue to assume the primary responsibilities of providing protection and care to dependent persons (Aguirre 2005). The role of "caregiver" falls most heavily on poor women, lacking the services offered by the market, deprived of many of the facilities provided by technologies, and recipients of often inadequate services.

The following are the options provided as response choices for respondents to explain the reasons for not being engaged in paid work: child care; care for the elderly, the sick, or disabled; lack of any job offer; low education; lack of qualification or training; pregnancy; health problem(s); age. The option "other reasons" was included to enable voluntary responses not covered in the provided range of alternatives. Figure 6.5 illustrates the percentage distribution of the responses obtained. We have aggregated information from four response groups: (a) care activities, including self-care for pregnancy; (b) lack of labor supply; (c) health problems; (d) other reasons. This last group includes various alternatives that were seldom mentioned, such as low education, lack of qualification, and age.

Among women without paid work (Figure 6.5), approximately 35% explained their situation as the need to take care of children, the elderly, and people with disabilities, and/or care for their own pregnancy/prenatal care. The lack of job offers was selected by approximately 8% of respondents. Personal health problems were indicated by approximately 14% of respondents as the reason for their unemployment. This is a very significant rate, especially considering that health is one of the areas that make up the program's conditionalities (Trevisani, Burlandy and Jaime 2012). In terms of the overall time receiving benefits, there is little percentage variation between the two groups of women. As regards personal health problems, we found a greater variation between the two groups, with a higher incidence among women with longer periods in the program.

In addition to these rates of engagement in paid labor being low for a market-based society, there is also the problem of the overall profile of women's inclusion in the Brazilian labor market. In Brazil, women have more years of schooling and work longer hours (of paid and unpaid work); however, they receive lower wages compared to men (IBGE 2018). Women in poverty are almost exclusively engaged in intermittent work, without formal ties or social security protections, and this work generally requires low qualifications and offers very poor remuneration. Our respondents are predominantly engaged in domestic work, confirming the Brazilian pattern and performing tasks such as cleaning, cooking, washing and ironing clothes, and caring for children or the elderly.

This scenario reveals the limits to expanding the opportunities and freedoms of this female demographic. According to Nussbaum (2002), such an expansion is the normative center of feminist justice theory. Increasing women's capacities, the author argues, is a condition for extending their freedoms. Moreover, social justice is only realized when it is capable of enhancing women's capacities, given that economic, cultural, institutional, and emotional conditions are traditionally unfavorable to women in many parts of the world, especially in poor and developing countries.[10]

In order to understand the significance of paid work for improving their autonomy, women were asked the following question: "in your opinion, which of these reasons would justify a married woman with children working outside of the home?" The question permitted multiple responses including the choice of adding an open response. The respondents' opinions were analyzed based on the response choices offered to them, as shown in Figure 5.6: family financial need (71.3%); personal fulfillment (19.3%); economic independence of women (17.3%); accomplishment of some family project (19.3%); not being confined to the home (11.9%).

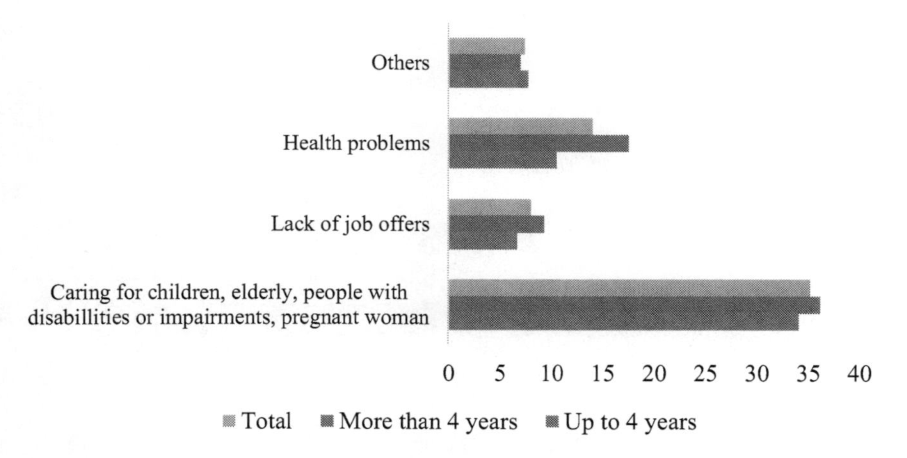


**FIGURE 6.5** Women's impediments to engaging in paid work by tenure as BF beneficiaries
Source: Author's original work (2015).

In Figure 5.6, which shows the percentage breakdown of the answers according to the respondents' time as beneficiaries and concerning their justifications as married women with children for engaging in paid work outside of the home, "family financial need" appears as the most frequent response, comprising 71.3% of the total. In general, there are no marked variations based on women's time engaged in the PBF. The answers from which we were able to infer more personal perceptions of autonomy with an emphasis on the dimension of individuality ("personal fulfillment," "women's economic independence," or "not being confined to the home") appeared to a lesser extent among both of the compared groups (engagement in the program for (a) four years or less or (b) more than four years).

The experiences reported by BF beneficiaries on some emblematic dimensions in the field of gender relations (Figure 5.7) reveal aspects related to perceptions of autonomy. Vera Soares (2011, 281) defines women's autonomy as "the ability to make free and informed decisions about their own lives, so that they can be and act according to their own aspirations and desires in a given historical context." Soares draws attention to three spheres of autonomy: the physical, economic, and decision-making spheres. The first sphere concerns women's "control of their bodies" – that is, their ability to make decisions about their health, reproduction, sexuality, and physical integrity. The second sphere is related to women's "ability to acquire and control economic resources – that is, the ability to generate their own income, control material goods, and make decisions about family assets." The third sphere is related to women's participation in "decision-making that affects their collective and individual lives" (Soares 2011, 281).

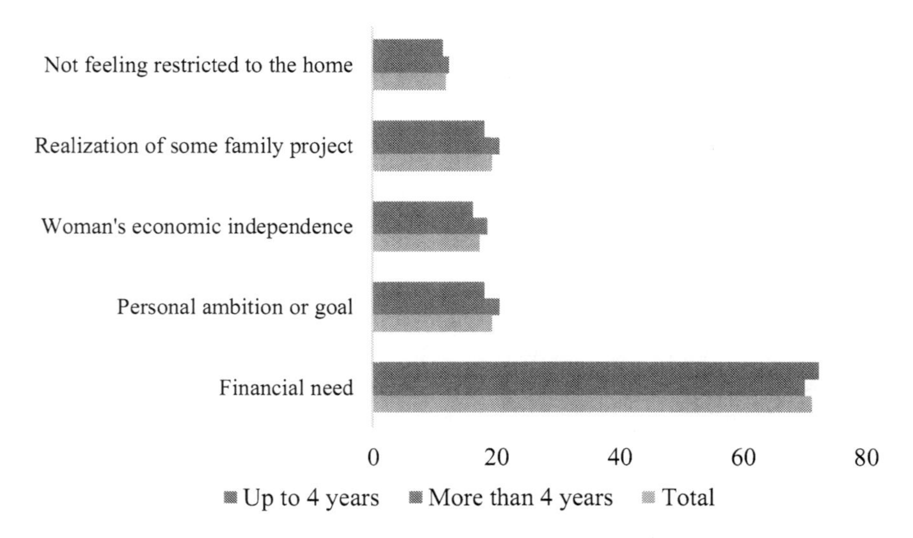


**FIGURE 6.6** Reasons a married woman with children will work outside of the home
Source: Author's original work (2015).

Soares's reflection, while not focusing exclusively on women living in poverty and based on an approach to women included in the labor market, sheds light especially on our data concerning the personal experiences of the women in our sample. Initially, the respondents were asked about the value they attach to certain situations that affect women's lives. These values could range from zero to ten. The questions prompted the women to reflect on the presented themes and assign some degree of importance to each of them. Subsequently, direct questions were asked about personal experiences for which the answers were "yes," "sometimes/so-so," "no," "I don't know/decline to answer." The questions presented were as follows: i) do you suffer domestic violence? ii) in your home, is responsibility for housework equally divided (with your spouse)? iii) do you have credit to pay for goods and services in installments? iv) after receiving the BF program benefit, did your spending power increase? v) do you have good self-esteem? vi) do you have or have you had the freedom to choose how many children you had? vii) are you free to dress as you please? viii) do you have the freedom to attend places/environments you want? ix) are you sexually satisfied? x) do you live in a good and comfortable home? xi) are you free to choose your sexual partner? xii) do you participate in government decisions? The themes addressed in this set of questions are linked to the three spheres of autonomy cited earlier: the physical, the economic, and the decision-making spheres (Soares 2011). The answers presented in Figure 6.7 also allow us to compare political, social, and individual aspects.

Although the time receiving the benefit presents few intergroup variations in terms of the specific items, there is a predominance of reports on experiences relating to individual freedoms or the physical sphere of autonomy, such as: freedom to visit the places and environments one desires (74,3% among women with longer benefit and 73,3% with shorter benefit) and the freedom to dress as desired (82.5% among women with longer periods on benefit and 86.7% with shorter periods on benefit); freedom to choose one's sexual partner (72.2% and 69.5%); achieving sexual satisfaction (47.4% and 60.9%); and the freedom to choose how many children one will have (63.9% and 73.3%). In both groups, more than 60% of women said they had good self-esteem (63.9% and 67.6%). The theme of domestic violence was the least mentioned: 7.2% of women who receive the benefit over a period of four years responded that they suffer domestic violence, while the other group totaled 8.6%.[11]

Regarding the economic sphere, we observed that 56.7% of women who received benefits for more than four years (group A) reported living in a good and comfortable home, in contrast to 49.5% of their peers who received the benefit for four years or less (group B). Regarding the increase in spending power, there is little variation (60.8% of group A and 61.9% of group B). Respondents who stated that they had credit to pay in installments corresponded to 36.1% and 34.3%, respectively. Moreover, 51.5% of women in group A, versus 42.9% of their peers in group B, reported equality in the division of domestic work in their home.

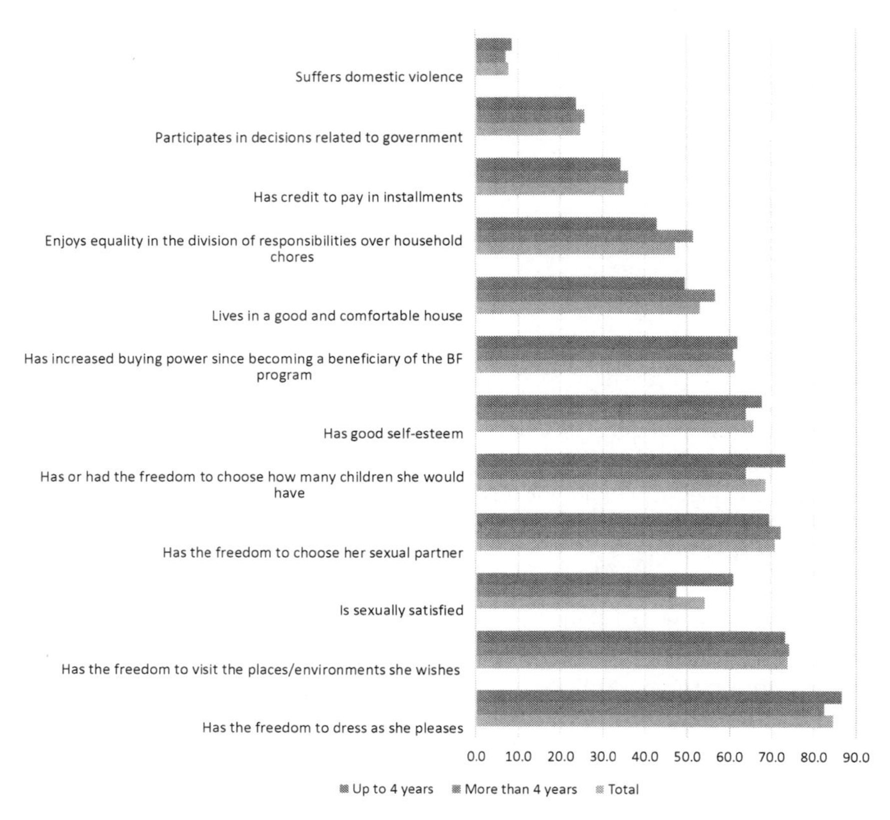


**FIGURE 6.7** Women's self-assessment of their individual freedoms by their tenure as BF beneficiaries

Source: Author's original work (2015).

Based on the responses to their own personal experiences, a significant portion of the women interviewed reported that they do not enjoy the freedom to make choices on questions such as: (i) the style of their clothes; (ii) the environments they visit; (iii) their sexual partner(s); and (iv) how many children they have. Group A in the program has lower rates across all of these categories. This group has a comparative advantage compared to the women more recently benefitting from the program in terms of: (i) spending power; (ii) housing comfort; and (iii) access to credit. In other words, the longer women stay in the program, the more they tend to accumulate economic gains (albeit in small percentages), which, nevertheless, do not translate into increased freedoms in relation to gender-conditioned behavior. We highlight the advantage of the older group in terms of political participation (25.8% of group A *versus* 23.8% of group B). While these women generally understand participation in government decisions in narrow terms as their right to exercise their vote in general elections, these responses indicate a potential among them for greater appreciation of and engagement in politics.

The importance of the role of the state in the socialization of care becomes a means to corroborate the process of individualization itself, as we highlighted in our analysis of rights and citizenship. In line with other analyses carried out on the BF program (Lavinas and Nicoll 2006; Sorj, Fontes, and Machado 2007; Lavinas, Cobo, and Veiga 2012; Carloto and Mariano 2012; Passos and Waltenberg 2016), we consider the importance of providing public care and care services for seniors, day care centers for young children, and full-time schools for youths. These are highly relevant services when it comes to reconciling work and family care and, consequently, the insertion of women living in poverty in the labor market with better paid and full-time jobs.

Arguments critical of the BF program have focused on the question of women being the primary beneficiaries or cardholders by emphasizing the contradictions between the possibility of strengthening women's autonomy through consumption (Carloto and Mariano 2012; Lavinas, Cobo, and Veiga 2012) while reaffirming the traditional sexual division of labor, as most analyses emphasize (Carloto and Mariano 2012; Gomes 2011; Pires 2012). Despite their different analytical focuses and distinct methodologies, as one of the general considerations present in such studies, we can highlight the arguments that the BF program reinforces traditional gender roles by reiterating responsibilities socially assigned to women to the detriment of their autonomy. There is greater dedication to family care (children and the elderly) by beneficiaries than non-beneficiaries (Passos and Waltenberg, 2016). For women with little to no income, the imposition of BF program's conditionalities can generate "excessive responsibilities or obligations related to social reproduction," impacting on their time at home and work (Carloto and Mariano 2010), especially given the fact that "women's insertion [in the labor market] through the domestic space is frustrated by the intermittence of their productive insertion" (Lavinas, Cobo, and Veiga 2012, 51). For these poor women, meeting the BF program conditionalities can lead to "responsibilities or burdens" impacting on their time at home and work (Carloto and Mariano 2010).

One of the aspects revealing the potential autonomy of female beneficiaries of the PBF is the perception of paid work as a source of autonomy. We can note, however, that in the case of women in poverty, it emerges as a primary condition for meeting the family's financial needs. From the viewpoint of class and gender, therefore, we can note a distinct perspective when compared to the perceptions of educated and middle-class Brazilian women about the place and meanings of paid work.

## Final Considerations

This research compared the perceptions of women who benefit from the BF program by dividing them into two groups by the median time of participation in the program, in order to infer the program's influences on aspects related to social patterns of gender relations and women's autonomy. We consider that there are gains for women's autonomy when social values and practices exist that deviate from the patterns that underpin female disadvantages and when an expansion in the possible freedoms for women is evident. The variables investigated were: (i) most valued rights; (ii) degree of respect for most valued rights; (iii) most important factors for guaranteeing rights; (iv) participation in paid work; (v) impediments to engaging in paid work; (vi) justifying reasons for paid work outside the home; (vii) self-assessment of individual freedoms.

Concepts such as freedom, individualization, and the politicization of women's rights emerged as relevant aspects for our analysis, both theoretically and empirically. From reading our data, we were able to observe the existence of situations revealing some differences that, according to our inferences, are favorable to women who have participated in the program for a longer time. While the older group in the program has the highest valorization of public policy, they attach less importance to personal endeavor as a condition for guaranteeing rights than the more recent beneficiaries. The group with the longer period as beneficiaries also has a comparative advantage in economic aspects such as spending power, comfort of housing, and access to credit. We interpret these data as constituting gains in citizenship, and in this respect the program contributes to women's advancement.

The rights most valued by women are those related to social policies, especially education and health. In both groups, the perception prevails that these rights are not respected or are only partially respected, revealing the criticism of these beneficiaries in relation to both the difficulties of accessing public services and the poor quality of these obtained. This criticism is more prevalent among women with longer engagement in the program, who were those who most frequently defended the need for state action to guarantee rights, especially in relation to meeting their demands for services such as public education and health services for their children.

When we turn to the constitutive variables of female individualization, on the other hand, which could have more pronounced effects on the reconfiguration of women's status, the results disfavor the inference of any positive influences of the program on women's autonomy and prosperity. For both compared groups, family support is the primary means of securing rights, often more among more long-term beneficiaries. Regarding impediments to engaging in paid work, the respondents listed: taking care of children, the elderly, and the disabled, as well as prenatal care activities; lack of quality work options; and health problems. In these three cases, the beneficiaries with longer periods in the BF program reported more complaints. Longer participation in the program has thus not helped these women find alternatives to dependence on family or to find better conditions for reconciling paid and unpaid work.

Concerning women's justifications for engaging in extra-household paid work, the respondents from the two compared groups showed similar response rates and a low incidence of responses linked to individualization. As for self-assessment of individual freedoms, significant portions of these women reported lacking the freedom to make the kinds of choices they were asked about. On all these points, the beneficiaries with longer periods in the program showed disadvantages. Because they have been engaged in the program for longer, these women have accumulated economic gains such as spending power, comfort of housing, and access to credit. Yet these gains do not translate as freedoms in terms of women's personal or individual choices.

According to our investigation, therefore, a tension exists between the possibilities of the Bolsa Família program, recognizing women as "an end in themselves," and the adoption of the strategy of the instrumentalization of women to enhance the results of policies targeted at the domestic context, in line with a utilitarian or instrumental perspective.

By expanding the options available to them, themes such as autonomy and the expansion of women's freedoms pose new challenges for social policies directed at women and new demands for the debate on and analysis of how women are inserted in policies like conditional cash transfer programs.

## Notes

1 We are grateful to the State University of Londrina and to the Federal University of Uberlândia, which provided us with the institutional conditions to carry out these researches gathered in this chapter. We are grateful to the National Council for Scientific and Technological Development (CNPq) and the Araucária Foundation to Support Scientific and Technological Development in the State of Paraná (*Fundação Araucária*). We are especially grateful to the students of the State University of Londrina, who at different times and stages contributed to the realization of these researches: Lina Penati Ferreira, Lorena Ingred Moreira Pio, Agnes Félix Gonçalves, Lais Regina Kruczeveski, Samira do Prado Silva, Ana Paula Botão Pereira, and Luís Gabriel Ramiro Costa. We are grateful for the welcome of the municipal administrations and the teams of workers of the Reference Centers of Social Assistance of the cities of Paraná where we carried out the research analyzed in this chapter: Curitiba City Hall, Curitiba Social Action Foundation, Londrina City Hall, Municipal Social Assistance Secretariat and Guaraci Municipality, Reference Center for Social Assistance. Without this support, this research would not have been possible.
2 Women were informed about the research and provided verbal consent for the interview.
3 Source: https://cidades.ibge.gov.br/brasil/pr/panorama. Accessed March 29, 2019.
4 Available at http://www.ipea.gov.br/retrato/indicadores_mercado_trabalho.html. Accessed Sept. 15, 2019.
5 Available at http://www.ipea.gov.br/retrato/indicadores_mercado_trabalho.html. Accessed Sept. 15, 2019.
6 The category "black" includes people who identify as "black" or "brown."
7 For more on the conditions of use of these services, see Chapter 7 in this volume.
8 Josimara Delgado and Márcia Tavares work in this volume deepens the discussions on poverty from the intersectional perspective.

9 Hirata (2016) highlights the change in the understanding of care to its current configuration in professional terms, including elements such as vocational training, promotions, careers and salary. However, the dimension of care to which we refer, considering the contingent of women we analyzed, is still centered on a more traditional notion on unpaid care work activity. In other words, the attention that women give to the home, children, other family members, and so on.
10 Teresa Sacchet, in Chapter 3 in this volume, presents an intensive reflection on *capability* theories and feminist theories of justice to analyze the *Bolsa Família* Program.
11 We are unable to venture deeper into this theme at the present time, given its breadth and the vast literature in Brazil. However, it is worth noting that the results of our sample contrast with Brazilian statistics on the incidence of domestic violence in the country. According to national data, especially based on care provided by public health services and care services for women in situations of violence, domestic violence is widespread in the country. This contrast can most probably be explained by the methodology adopted in our research of presenting the question directly and objectively. According to recent data, "the Ministry of Health records that in Brazil every four minutes a woman is beaten by at least one man and survives. Last year [2018], more than 145,000 cases of violence were reported – physical, sexual, psychological and other – in which the victims survived. Each record may include more than one type of violence" (Folha de São Paulo, September 9, 2019). Available at https://www1.folha.uol.com.br/cotidiano/2019/09/brasil-registra-1-caso-de-agressao-a-mulher-a-cada-4-minutos-mostra-levantamento.shtml. We also emphasize the underreporting of violence against women in instruments employed by public health services, a fact that Brazilian feminist organizations regularly denounce.

## References

Aguirre, Rosario. 2005. "Los Cuidados Familiares como Problema Público y Objeto de Política." Work presented in Reunión de Expertas Políticas Hacia las Familias, Protección e Inclusión Sociales, Santiago de Chile.

Alvarez, Sonia E. 1988. "Politizando as Relações de Gênero e Engendrando a Democracia." In *Democratizando o Brasil*, edited by Alfred Stepan, 315–380. Rio de Janeiro: Paz e Terra.

Araújo, Clara, and Celi Scalon. 2006. "Gênero e a Distância entre a Intenção e o Gesto." *Revista Brasileira de Ciências Sociais* 21, no. 62: 45–68. http://dx.doi.org/10.1590/S0102-69092006000300003.

Archer, Margaret S. 2011. "Habitus, Reflexividade e Realismo." *Dados-Revista de Ciências Sociais* 54, no. 1: 157–206. https://dx.doi.org/10.1590/S0011-52582011000100005.

Beck, Ulrich. 1992. *Risk Society. Towards a New Modernity*. London: Sage Publication.

Biewener, Carole and Marie-Hélène Bacqué. 2015. "Feminism and the Politics of Empowerment in International Development." *Air & Space Power Journal-Africa and Francophonie* 6, no. 2: 58–76.

Blay, Eva A. 1982. "Do Espaço Privado ao Público: A Conquista da Cidadania pela Mulher no Brasil." Work presented at VI Annual Meeting of ANPOCS, Nova Friburgo.

Blay, Eva A. 1999. "Gênero e Políticas Públicas ou Sociedade Civil, Gênero e Relações de Poder." In *Falas de Gênero: Teorias, Análises, Leituras*, edited by Alcione Leite Silva, Mara Coelho de Souza Lago and Tânia Regina Oliveira Ramo, 133–145. Florianópolis: Editora Mulheres.

Bohn, Simone R. 2008. "Mulher para Presidente do Brasil? Gênero e Política na Perspectiva do Eleitor Brasileiro." *Opinião Pública* 14, no. 2: 352–379. https://doi.org/10.1590/S0104-62762008000200004.

Carloto, Cássia Maria and Silvana Mariano. 2012. "Empoderamento, Trabalho e Cuidados: Mulheres no Programa Bolsa Família." *Textos & Contextos* 11, no. 2: 258–272.

Carloto, Cássia, and Silvana Mariano. 2010. "Halfway Between the Private and Public Sectors: A Debate on the Role of Women in Social Welfare Policy." *Revista Estudos Feministas* 18, no. 2: 451–471. https://doi.org/10.1590/S0104-026X2010000200009.

Fonseca, Ana Maria Medeiros and Claudio Roquete. 2018. "Proteção Social e Programas de Transferência de Renda: Bolsa-Família." *Cadernos de Pesquisa* 86, no. 1: 9–31.

Fonseca, Cláudia. 1997. "Ser Mulher, Mãe e Pobre." In *História das mulheres no Brasil*, edited by Mary Del Priori, 510–553. São Paulo: Contexto.

Fougeyrollas-Schwebel, Dominique. 2009. "Trabalho Doméstico." In *Dicionário Crítico do Feminismo*, edited by Helena Hirata, Françoise Laborie, Hélène Le Doaré, and Danièle Senotier, 256–262. São Paulo: Editora UNESP.

Fraser, Nancy. 2006. "Da Redistribuição ao Reconhecimento? Dilemas da Justiça numa Era 'Pós-Socialista.'" *Cadernos de Campo*15: 231–239. https://doi.org/10.11606/issn.2316-9133.v15i14-15p231-239.

Fraser, Nancy. 2007. "Reconhecimento sem Ética." *Lua Nova* 70, no. 1: 101–138. https://doi.org/10.1590/S0102-64452007000100006.

Gomes, Simone. 2011. "Notas Preliminares de uma Crítica Feminista aos Programas de Transferência Direta de Renda: O Caso do Bolsa Família No Brasil." *Textos & Contextos* 10, no. 1: 69–81.

Guzmán, Virgínia. 2000. "A Equidade de Gênero como Tema de Debate e de Políticas Públicas." In *Gênero nas Políticas Públicas: Impasses, Desafios e Perspectivas para a Ação Feminista*, Coleção Cadernos Sempreviva, edited by Nalu Faria, Maria Lúcia Silveira, and Miram Nobre, 63–66. São Paulo: SOF.

Hirata, Helena and Danièle Kergoat. 2007. "Novas Configurações da Divisão Sexual do Trabalho." *Cadernos de Pesquisa* 37, no. 132: 595–609. https://doi.org/10.1590/S0100-15742007000300005.

Hirata, Helena. 2016. "O Trabalho de Cuidado." *Sur, Revista Internacional de Direitos Humanos* 24, no. 13: 53–64.

IBGE (Instituto Brasileiro de Geografia e Estatística). 2018. *Estatísticas de Gênero*. Brasília: IBGE. https://www.ibge.gov.br/apps/snig/v1/?loc=0.

Inglehart, Ronald and Pippa Norris. 2003. *Rising Tide: Gender Equality & Cultural Changes Around the World*. Nova York: Cambridge University Press.

Jelin, Elizabeth. 2004. *Pan y Afectos: La Transformación de las Familias*. Buenos Aires, Argentina: Fondo de Cultura Económica.

Lavinas, Lena and Marcelo Nicoll. 2006. "Atividade e Vulnerabilidade: Quais os Arranjos Familiares em Risco?" *Revista de Ciências Sociais* 49, no. 1: 67–97. https://doi.org/10.1590/S0011-52582006000100004.

Lavinas, Lena, Barbara Cobo, and Alinne Veiga. 2012. "Bolsa Família: Impacto das Transferências de Renda sobre a Autonomia das Mulheres e as Relações de Gênero." *Revista Latino-Americana de População* 10: 31–54.

Lavinas, Lena. 1997. "Gênero, Cidadania e Políticas Urbanas." In *Globalização, Fragmentação e Reforma Urbana*, edited by Luiz César de Q Ribeiro and Orlando Alves dos Santos Junior, 169–187. Rio de Janeiro: Civilização Brasileira.

Machado, Leda Maria Vieira. 1995. *Atores Sociais: Movimentos Urbanos, Continuidade e Gênero*. São Paulo: Annablume.

Machado, Leda Maria Vieira. 1999. *A Incorporação de Gênero nas Políticas Públicas: Perspectivas e Desafios*. São Paulo: Annablume.

Mariano, Silvana and Cássia Carloto. 2009. "Gênero e Combate à Pobreza: Programa Bolsa Família." *Revista Estudos Feministas* 17, no. 3: 901–908. https://doi.org/10.1590/S0104-026X2009000300018.

Mariano, Silvana. 2009. "Cidadania na Perspectiva das Mulheres Pobres e Papéis de Gênero no Acesso a Políticas Assistenciais." *Revista Brasileira de Ciência Política* 2: 119–157.

Mariano, Silvana. 2010. "Cidadania Sexuada Feminina: A Inclusão das Mulheres na Política de Assistência Social." In *Desigualdades de Gênero no Brasil: Novas Ideias e Práticas Antigas*, edited by Márcio Ferreira de Souza, 41–70. Belo Horizonte: Argvmentvm Editora Ltda.

Morton, Gregory Duff. 2013. "Acesso à Permanência: Diferenças Econômicas e Práticas de Gênero em Domicílios que Recebem Bolsa Família no Sertão Baiano." *Revista Política e Trabalho* 38: 43–67.

Moser, Caroline and Annalise Moser. 2005. "Gender Mainstreaming Since Beijing: A Review of Success and Limitations in International Institutions." *Gender & Development* 13, no. 2: 11–22. https://doi.org/10.1080/13552070512331332283.

Nussbaum, Martha. 2002. *Las Mujeres y el Desarrollo Humano: El Enfoque de las Capacidades*. Barcelona: Herder Editorial.

Passos, Luana and Waltenberg, Fabio. 2016. "Bolsa Família e Assimetria de Gênero: Reforço ou Mitigação?" *Revista Brasileira de Estudos Populacionais* 33, no. 3: 517–539. http://dx.doi.org/10.20947/s0102-30982016c0004.

Pateman, Carole. 1993. *O Contrato Sexual*. Translated by Marta Avancini. São Paulo: Paz e Terra.

Pateman, Carole. 2000. "El Estado de Bienestar Patriarcal." *Contextos* 2, no. 5: n.p.

Pearce, Diane. 1978. "The Feminization of Poverty: Women, Work and Welfare." *Urban and Social Change Review* 11: 28–36.

Pereira Milena Cassal and Fernanda Bittencourt Ribeiro. 2013. "No Areal das Mulheres: Um Benefício em Família." *Revista Política e Trabalho* 38: 87–104.

Pinto, Celi Regina Jardim. 2003. *Uma História do Feminismo no Brasil*. São Paulo: Editora. Fundação Perseu Abramo.

Pires, André. 2012. "Orçamento Familiar e Gênero: Percepções do Programa Bolsa Família." *Cadernos de Pesquisa* 42, no. 145: 130–161. http://dx.doi.org/10.1590/S0100-15742012000100009.

Presidência da República Brasil. 2008. *II Plano Nacional de Políticas para as Mulheres*. Brazil: Secretaria Especial de Políticas para as Mulheres.

Rêgo, Walquíria Leão and Alessandro Pinzani. 2014. *Vozes do Bolsa Família: Autonomia, Dinheiro e Cidadania*. Second edition. São Paulo: UNESP.

Santos, Wanderley Guilherme dos. 1979. *Cidadania e Justiça: A Política Social na Ordem Brasileira*. Vol. 1. Rio de Janeiro: Editora Campus.

Sarti, Cynthia Andersen. 1994. "A Família como Ordem Moral." *Cadernos de Pesquisa* 91: 46–53.

Sarti, Cynthia Andersen. 1995. "O Valor da Família para os Pobres." In *Família em Processos Contemporâneos: Inovações Culturais na Sociedade Brasileira*, edited by Ivete Ribeiro, Ana Clara Torres Ribeiro, 131–150. São Paulo: Loyola.

Sarti, Cynthia Andersen. 2007. *A Família como Espelho: Um Estudo Sobre a Moral dos Pobres*. São Paulo: Cortez.

Soares, Vera. 2011. "Mulher, Autonomia e Trabalho." In *Autonomia Econômica e Empoderamento da Mulher*, 281–301. Brazil: Fundação Alexandre de Gusmão.
Sorj, Bila, Adriana Fontes, and Danielle Carusi Machado. 2007. "Políticas e Práticas de Conciliação entre Família e Trabalho no Brasil." *Cadernos de Pesquisa* 37, no. 132: 573–594.
Trevisani, Jorginetede Jesus D., Luciene Burlandy, and Patricia Constante Jaime. 2012. "Fluxos Decisórios na Formulação das Condicionalidades de Saúde do Programa Bolsa Família." *Saúde e Sociedade* 21, no. 2: 492–509. http://dx.doi.org/10.1590/S0104-12902012000200021.

# 7

# CONDITIONALITIES IN THE *BOLSA FAMÍLIA* PROGRAM AND WOMEN'S USE OF TIME IN DOMESTIC FAMILY WORK

*Cássia Maria Carloto*

## Introduction

From the late 1990s and the first decade of the 21st century, Conditional Cash Transfer (CCT) programs began to be adopted in Latin America as a means of combating poverty using a social risk management approach. In most of the CCT programs, women/mothers are the titular beneficiaries. The justification for this is the idea that they are better at managing household funds and are responsible for the care of their children. Therefore, if it is they who receive the benefit then the money will be invested in objects, advantages, and improvements for their homes and children. The analysis of Molyneux (2007) is that in addition to constituting the majority of the poor population worldwide, women are held responsible for being the mothers of future poor people. Therefore, their children need subsidies in order to develop their capacities and in so doing break with poverty. Molyneux points out (2007), however, that the prescriptions of the agencies that promote poverty reduction programs, such as the World Bank, make no mention of specific efforts that should be made in relation to female poverty.

CCT programs began to appear in Brazil in the 1990s, their names varying by state and municipality. These programs were reorganized and amalgamated in 2003, at the beginning of the first administration of President Luiz Inácio Lula da Silva, and what had been *Auxílio Gás* (a program to assist with the cost of cooking fuel), *Bolsa Escola Federal* (a schooling costs assistance program) and *Bolsa Alimentação* (a program to assist with food costs) were rolled together to become the *Bolsa Família* Program (hereinafter referred to by the Portuguese acronym PBF). Upon joining the program, beneficiary families undertook to comply with certain health and education conditionalities, the idea being to help reduce school absenteeism, improve educational performance, promote antenatal health checks, and increase child vaccination rates among the poorest populations. In the event of non-compliance with these conditionalities, beneficiary families are subject to graded sanctions that run the gamut from notification to freeze to suspension to cancellation, in the event that non-compliance recurs over successive periods. According to the 2008 Guidelines for Policies and Programs of the Ministry of Social Development and Fight Against Hunger (hereinafter MDS), the purpose of these graded sanctions is to allow families that do not comply with the conditionalities to be identified and followed up so that the problems that have given rise to the non-compliance can be resolved. As will be seen in this article, many of these problems are related to the absence of a public network of education and health services that is able to meet the demands of PBF beneficiary families.

Public policies in the fields of health and education are fundamental for compliance with these conditionalities and, where found wanting, lead to women having to spend large amounts of time seeking them out. There is an inverse correlation between distance from large urban centers and availability of such services in residential areas. Some authors, such as Cotta and Paiva (2010, 73), argue that it is unreasonable to condition cash transfers on the use of scarce public services that are of poor quality and staffed by public servants who "submit citizens to degrading situations."

The inadequacy of public services designed to support women's care activities penalizes the very women from impoverished families who are the target of the PBF by increasing their (unpaid) work time in the intra-familial sphere and limiting female citizenship in such a way that it becomes impossible for them to participate long-term in the labor market and/or collective decision-making. If race/ethnicity are associated with poverty, we see that black women face the greatest increase in the difficulties they face. The PBF, as is the case in all such programs across Latin America, is based on the idea of a traditional family in which the woman is seen, in a way that has become normalized, as the provider of domestic and reproductive services as well as the person who can expend her time and energy to meeting the program's conditionalities and, frequently, as the sole adult in the family. Women who fail to meet the conditionalities are subjected to dual punishments. Firstly, they are judged as bad mothers who were incapable of taking care of their children properly and for that reason lost their benefits. They are punished a second time by the actual suspension or cancelation of their benefit, which exacerbates the conditions of extreme poverty in which they live.

How much time do these women spend in the administration of health care and access to education for their children? Does compliance with PBF conditionalities increase their burden of responsibility? How do they organize the care of their children so that they are able to go to school? Does their responsibility for meeting PBF conditionalities increase time spent on family and domestic care in such a way as to exacerbate the difficulty of developing personal and economic autonomy? These are the questions that guided the development of the research that is the basis of this chapter.

The objective of this chapter is to consider how female PBF beneficiaries organize their day-to-day childcare, how much time they must spend to ensure that the children under their care have access to school, and the difficulties and obstacles that they encounter. To this end, I have drawn on data collected from reports from women who live in large and medium-sized cities in the two neighboring southern Brazilian states of São Paulo and Paraná. These data are of considerable value in that they depict a country with large regional differences in terms of poverty, employment, education, and health. The southern regions of Brazil are the ones with the best economic development indicators, however, not all of the cities in these regions have achieved the same levels of development, and some places presenting indicators comparable to those from the poorest regions of the country. The research on which this chapter is based took place between 2013 and 2016 in three municipalities in Paraná and one in São Paulo. I organized two data collection focal groups and applied questionnaires to 130 women. More details on my data collection procedures are given in Section 2.

The text is divided into two sections. In Section 1, I discuss family care in the familial-domestic sphere from the perspective of a feminist economics that calls into question the socioeconomic reality engendered by the socio-capitalist formation and its patriarchal components. These contributions help contextualize care in a macro-political frame and break with dichotomies that distort and fragment the social and highlight women's use of time in care activities. The debate on time use is based on feminist approaches that consider the sexual division of labor in families, a key lens through which to understand the limitations on women's effective exercise of their social, economic, and political rights. In the second section, field data from research on care and time use in the domestic family sphere and the conditionalities in the BFP are analyzed from a critical perspective as regards the conditionalities in Conditional Cash Transfer Programs (CCT). This perspective emphasizes the instrumental use of women in maternalist and familist social programs, and how the conditionalities built into these programs, which are in no way reflected in corresponding conditionalities incumbent on the State, add to and even overload the responsibilities and concerns of the beneficiary women.

## Care in the Domestic Family Sphere

The familism and maternalism that underpin Latin American social policies have delegated responsibility for the care of such dependent family members as children, the chronically ill, persons with special needs, the elderly, and other adults in general to women (see chapter 2). This worsens among the poorest women, most of whom are black, as they cannot fall back on the paid care work offered by the market. This means that a large part of the social security provision in the region results from individual and private initiative, is strongly stratified and segmented, reflecting the income of each household, and constitutes an expression of the sexual division of labor – itself one of the main factors behind social inequality.

According to Navarro and Rico (2013, 30), care, as a specific area of study, emerged vigorously in Latin America in the 2000s and built on European debates about unpaid domestic and reproductive work and its links with the economic system. Studies on care tend to include mention of the broadness of the concept and its work-in-progress status as a field of knowledge and an empirical category. Thomaz (2011, 147) asks whether the term "care" is or can even be a theoretical category in and of itself, or whether forms of care are empirical entities that must be analyzed in terms of other social categories. In many of such studies, therefore, "care" is very much description-dependent. This means that explicit specification of the type of care under discussion is always pertinent.

"Care economics" – a sub-discipline of Feminist Economics – deals with the provision of goods, services, activities, social relations, and values related to basic existential and reproductive needs of people in societies. The association between the terms "care" and "economy" implies a focus on aspects that generate or contribute to generating economic value. What is of particular interest in economic terms is the relationship between the way in which societies organize themselves to ensure the care of their members, and the way their economic system functions (Rodríguez-Enríque 2013; Carrasco 2003; Orozco 2014). From the perspective of feminist economics, there is an emphasis on how well-being is created in the everyday, cared-for life. This life is made up of concrete subjects, with sexualized bodies, subjectivities that give rise to partial, contradictory identities, continuously under reconstruction, and in tension between imposed norms and the capacity to resist them with affection and disaffection.

So what *is* care according to feminist economics? The question is not so much one of defining specific activities, but of asking to what extent the socioeconomic system as a whole guarantees concrete, daily well-being via "collective structures that are charged with such care or else by delegation to households, such that the lion's share of these goods and services [are handled] in [invisible] economic spheres" (Orozco 2014, 91). The notion of care thus overlaps with unpaid work and so-called "reproductive work," and relates to activities undertaken outside the sphere of market consumption that are necessary to reproduce and maintain life. According to Orozco:

> care consists of activities residual to those of the market: activities that are essential to clean up after the crimes caused by the logic of accumulation and/or to cover the spaces that the markets leave empty because they are not profitable; activities that are characterized by being subject to reactionary ethics, to be done in a hidden way due to a multidimensional notion of invisibility understood as subalternism and subtraction of the ability to

> question the whole system that contrasts with the full visibility of the markets and their heteropatriarchal accumulation logic.
>
> *(Orozco 2014, 92)*

Care is, therefore, part of social organization and, as Esquivel (2012, 27) states, to understand it, it is not enough to examine the microsocial aspects – one must also understand the role of social policies in the "provision and regulation of care relationships, activities and responsibilities, assigned to different institutions and subjects." The concept of organization of care refers to the configuration resulting from the intersection between the institutions that regulate and provide services and the ways in which households at different socioeconomic levels and their members benefit from them (Faur 2014). Every social policy assumes a social organization of care, even if it is not explicit in its formulations and principles. Care therefore becomes a relevant category for the examination of social policies. Social programs for poverty alleviation, such as CCTs, exist within this framework.

The PBF, as a social program developed within neoliberal frameworks, is based on the care work performed by women for the meeting of conditionalities in an adverse context of provision of free and universal public services. Care activities, in this context of privatization and precarization, demand considerable time, especially for women in situations of poverty.

Research on time use has been the main tool for empirical analysis of the social distribution of care. In Latin America, such research has been conducted in 19 countries in the region. Between 2009 and 2011, at the initiative of the Secretariat for Policies for Women, Brazil undertook a national survey on the use of time with the Brazilian Institute of Geography and Statistics (hereinafter, "the IBGE") (Fontoura and Araújo 2016). These surveys make it possible to reclaim the importance of the distribution of time and work and to identify the domestic unit as a space for production and economic distribution that exhibits great inequality in the exercise of rights and the well-being of families.

The reasons that led to this type of study and the consolidation thereof are related to demographic structural changes and family arrangements, to transformations in the industrial productive structure, to the massive incorporation of women into the labor market, to the invisibility of family-domestic work, to the expansion of an economic leisure and media sector, and to an increase in the time dedicated to travel in large cities. Feminist investigations have played an important role in overcoming a dualistic and androcentric perspective in the so-called reproduction generating times that lie outside the hegemony of marketized time (Carrasco and Dominguez 2003).

These times, necessary for life, include care, affection, maintenance, domestic management and administration, and leisure. More than measured and paid time, these are times lived, donated, and generated, with a component that is difficult to quantify. This new perspective has highlighted the power relations and gender inequality that are hidden behind the mercantile way of valuing time and the unequal sexual division of labor.

There are some limitations to time use surveys. One of them concerns the nature of the concept of time as identified by gender studies, which have questioned the idea of time as something natural. Time is undoubtedly a cultural construction that should not be limited to Western standards that take the physical and timed dimensions as their main references. Both the calendar and the clock are human conventions. Time is also the guiding element in the construction of everyday modes of life. It is, at the same time, abstract, generic, and social, because it is through time that the interaction between social agents or actors takes place (Carrasco and Dominguez 2003, 134).

In its social definition, time drives us objectively towards activity or practice and less towards metaphysical conceptions or universal time. Time is not disconnected from social practices, whether individual or collective; it is these practices that produce social time. Given that only social action originates and manifests itself, the variability of facts becomes the observable criterion for identifying social time. Furthermore, since all social action is interaction, it is in it and from it that time is socially constructed (Lozares, Lopez, and Dominguez 1998).

To define the field of care to be analyzed and the use of time, the research focused on three of the seven dimensions of care, based on Thomaz' typology.[1] The first dimension concerns the nature of care, and it is necessary to define its social content, whose nature is defined as an affective activity or state. The second dimension concerns the social domain in which the care relationship is located. This separation, according to Thomaz (2011), refers to the characteristic division of the social division of labor in capitalist society, which occurs between the public domain and the private or domestic domain. In this research the reference is the domestic family space, for which I have adopted Carrasco's (2003) concept. Carrasco does not distinguish domestic work from care and uses the concept of family domestic care[2] to deal with non-marketable activities performed for the reproduction of human life. For Carrasco (2003), it is difficult to distinguish domestic work from care, because, in the goods and services produced in the home, it is more complicated to separate the affective-relational aspects of the activity itself, as they involve personal elements distinct from market goods. The third dimension demarcated by Thomaz (2011) refers to the institutional framework in which care is provided, the physical location of care activities. In this study, the center is the home, the school, and the health network, due to the conditionalities of the *Bolsa Família* Program, and the care practices and time spent were carried out by the PBF beneficiaries themselves and do not involve paid work done by third parties.

## Compliance with PBF Conditionalities, Care, and Use of Time

In this section, the main research results are presented and analyzed from the data collected through two focus groups and the application of 130 questionnaires to PBF beneficiaries. The focus groups were made up of beneficiaries attended by the Reference Centers for Social Assistance (Portuguese acronym: CRAS)[3] of the regions who were chosen for the research and invited to participate. The main objective in the focus groups was to obtain information on the activities and routines of the beneficiaries in the daily care of children. This information served as a basis for preparing the questions in the questionnaire. The criterion for choosing the CRAS was location in the region/territory of greatest vulnerability, based on the assumption that the greater the difficulties related to the absence of public services and equipment, the greater the time spent by women in carrying out domestic family care activities, and the greater the difficulty of meeting conditionalities. "Vulnerability," in this case, was related to the degree of absence and/or precariousness of public policy provision in terms of education, health, housing, transportation and security.

During my field research for the analysis of time use, I paid special attention to activities related to the education and health conditionalities of the PBF. My intention was not to record and quantify the time spent on such activities in minute detail, but rather to understand what material and non-material activities are performed on a daily basis in order for the children to be able to remain in school, and who undertakes them. Therefore, I sought to identify and quantify the tasks that directly or indirectly benefit the children in a family, even if they also benefit adults, such as food preparation.

For the details of the activities, support was sought in the conception of daily time developed by Lozares, López, and Domínguez (1998). Their conception is centered on daily routines focused on the activities carried out in a time sequence of a 24-hour day with a focus on the care of children and based on the statements of interviewed women. This care is situated within activities and routines necessary to ensure that children can remain at school and retain access to health care. The interview script was based on a care routine that starts in the morning, when the titular beneficiaries wake up, and ends at night, when they go to sleep. In order to capture how day-to-day care for school age children is constructed, activities that in some cases are carried out in the early hours of the morning were also investigated. I took into account the considerations of Javeau (1980), verified whether there were standards of care based on a cultural model, and looked at a relatively homogeneous group of low-income female titular BFP beneficiaries living on the outskirts of medium and large cities. Time was calculated in terms of simple time, which limits the total time per person in a 24-hour period.

The questions were organized into the following modules: food, cleaning, clothing care, daily shopping, direct care for children, and health care. In all questions, they were asked how much time they spent and who performed the tasks. In the food module, I verified how much time they spent preparing breakfast, lunch, afternoon snacks, and dinner. In the cleaning module, I asked about time spent on general cleaning. In clothing care, I asked about washing and hanging out laundry, removing it from the clothesline, folding it, ironing it, and storing it. In questions related to everyday shopping, I asked about trips to the supermarket, the bakery, the butcher, and the street market. In the health module, I asked about accompanying their children to a doctor or hospital, buying medication for and administering it to their children, and having them undergo medical and laboratory exams. In the module on direct care for children, I asked about bathing children, dressing them and brushing their teeth, taking them to school and picking them up afterwards, helping them with homework, going to parent-teacher meetings, playing with the children, putting them to bed, talking to them, praying with them, and care during the night. This detailing of the routine, established according to children's school activities, was based on comments made in the focus groups.

## The Beneficiaries: a Brief Profile

The questionnaire first asks about respondents' age group, race/ethnicity, marital status, occupation, number of children, and household size. It also seeks to verify if there is a pattern in relation to other national surveys of female BPF beneficiaries and in the cities I considered. My results were comparable to those of Bartholo, Passos, and Fontoura (2017), which were based on national data, and did not show great divergences between municipalities surveyed. Most of the respondents (66.15%) were aged between 21 and 40. In terms of race/ethnicity, 28.46% declared themselves to be white and 70% brown or black. 50.77% declared themselves married or in a stable relationship. 49.24% declared themselves to be separated/divorced, single, or widowed. Single-mother households are concentrated in the most vulnerable social groups. In the world of poor single-mother families, the mother is usually black, as there are more black families in situations of poverty and extreme poverty.

Most respondents (69.23%) declared that they did not work outside the home; only 29.23% said they did. The main occupation (40.43%) of those who did work outside the home was freelance domestic cleaning work. These women usually work in different houses and go to each house once a week. This type of work confers no legal protection or labor rights. Other occupations cited also belonged to the precarious category: nanny, recyclable garbage collector, dressmaker, manicurist and hairdresser, general cleaning services, beauty product salesperson, caregiver, waitress, general services in civil construction.

Most respondents (68.47%), excluding those who gave no answer, had between one and three children. A survey released on July 11, 2018 by the United Nations Population Fund (UNFPA 2018), which sought to present a population and development portrait of the country, reported that Brazil has experienced an accelerated drop in fertility in recent decades. The current average is 1.7 children per woman. The survey points out that the rate declined considerably between 2001 and 2015 among the most vulnerable, a group comprising the poorest and black women. According to the survey, the fertility rate among women who make up the poorest 20% of the population fell from 3.92 per woman in 2001 to 2.90 in 2015, which corresponds to almost one child fewer per woman, on average. By comparison, the drop was from 1.41 to 0.77 among the richest 20%. The scenario is similar when considering race/color. The fertility rate of black women fell from 2.75 (2001) to 1.88 (2015). Brown women, who in 2001 had an average of 2.65 children, in 2015 had an average of 1.96. White women, with 2.10 children on average in 2001, now had 1.6 (UNFPA 2018).

These data contradict the common-sense view that poor women have more children deliberately so as to be eligible for the PBF and thus remain dependent on the state. In Brazil, the idea that there is a relationship between poverty and numbers of children is still widely held by civil servants and the general population. It is commonplace for the poverty of poor women to be attributed to their large families. Several respondents reported that they felt embarrassed even before applying for the PBF, as they knew that they would be asked how many children they had and would be judged harshly if the reply exceeded two. Even more embarrassment was involved in cases of children with different fathers. Most (95.50%) of the respondents' children were aged one to 15 years, this being the type of family prioritized by the PBF.

I found some differences between white and black PBF beneficiaries. In a study of PBF beneficiaries Mariano and Carloto (2013, 21) examined data related to gender and race and found that black women had lower incomes, lower education levels, and higher rates of single mother families. Although there was a higher rate of black women in paid work, their occupations were predominantly precarious in nature, which makes economic autonomy difficult. The authors noted that inclusion of black women in the PBF suggests that, even in conditions of poverty and extreme poverty, social vulnerability is experienced at different levels between black and non-black women, with disadvantages for the former. Poor women, however, are seen as a universal category in the design of policies for combating poverty. It is necessary that social policies, including policies to combat poverty, adopt paradigms and develop methodologies capable of considering factors such as gender, social class, color/race/ethnicity.[4]

## Activities, Time Spent and Responsibilities

The titular beneficiaries were the main person responsible for housework and care in 79.23% of responses. Their daughters appear in second place, which only confirms data from studies on the place of women in the public and private spheres.[5] The respondents' stories show that girls are responsible for caring for their siblings, especially minors. Interviewee A reports:

> She (the 13-year-old daughter) stays at home in the morning, arranges lunch for another child who arrives in the morning and then for the two youngest children so they can go to school in the afternoon. If she didn't...
>
> *(Interviewee A)*[6]

This unequal division of domestic tasks reduces the woman's ability to earn an income and can make access to jobs more difficult, contributing to the feminization of poverty. It can also hinder girls' access to formal education, a fundamental criterion for access to the labor market. The perpetuation of a culture that keeps women linked to the private space shows that they are forced/taught to do domestic family work from childhood. Women related to the respondent, such as aunts, grandparents, and sisters, were also sometimes cited as the person responsible for these tasks.

Of the material and physical care aspects carried out within the home, those related to the conservation of clothing (washing clothes, hanging them on the line, ironing them, and putting them away) demand more time than any other. Next come those involving food preparation and, finally, shopping for groceries and keeping the home clean. Regarding food, this starts with breakfast, continues with lunch, then there is the afternoon snack, and it ends with dinner, which is the activity that takes up the most time. As schools operate part-time in mornings or afternoons, all children have to have lunch at home. It is a routine that imposes strict schedules, especially regarding lunchtimes, as reported by one of the women: "you have to be there at the right time, otherwise you hold them up" (Interviewee B). Respondents expended the largest number of hours/minutes on feeding and cleaning activities when the majority of the children in the household are aged under six. Regarding clothing care, the age range associated with the heaviest burden of activity is seven to 11. Indeed, when all activities are considered, this age group features as the most time-demanding.

As for care activities carried out outside the home involving third parties, the ones that demand the most time are those that involve the pursuit of public health services due to the precariousness of services and the care network, the various comings and goings and long waits for health services, in addition to the need to adapt to the opening hours of these services, which in most cases correspond to business hours.

I also asked about caring for children other than their own children or for adults and their familial relationship to them. 16,50% of respondents reported taking care of other people, with care for nieces and nephews being the most cited, followed by grandchildren and neighbors' children. Therefore, in addition to caring for their own children, the women provide care for other people, which confirms the historical role of women as carers for others, be they children, adults, teenagers, or the elderly. Most respondents (80.50%) answered that they perform this function in their own homes. The homes of the families covered by this research consisted of between two and four rooms covering a floor area no greater than 40 square meters and providing shelter for three to five people. 19.23% of respondents care for people with special needs, the elderly, and children. The majority care for children.

The affective aspect of care is frequently anchored in the solidarity networks that are part of the lives of these families, in their survival strategies – especially for those who hold down jobs. In Brazil, the neighborhood plays a central role. Women in a given neighborhood establish a network of help and care aimed primarily at young children.

## Activities Related to School Education

One of the requirements of the PBF is that children attend school. This calls for action in both private and public spheres. In the public sphere, the right to a public, universal, free, and good quality education must be guaranteed before all else. A constitutional provision, such as Brazil's, which states that education is the duty of the state and the right of all must be complemented by public policies that guarantee that the right may be enjoyed. In the private sphere, the care practices that must be guaranteed so children can be educated include but are not limited to personal hygiene, food, sanitary conditions, support for extramural activities, taking children to school, and picking them up afterwards – all of which impose strict daily time management. The responses testified to weaknesses in public education and health policy. They spoke of precarious and/or insufficient free and quality public services, which lead to women being overloaded and penalized in the domestic family sphere, and facing increased time burdens in respect of childcare, performed primarily by mothers, sisters, and grandparents. These are care categories that demand time that can be quantified as well as subjective time that cannot counted in clock hours.

The first thing that came up in the focus groups was taking children to school and picking them up afterwards. All of them took their children to school, with the exception of one respondent whose husband was responsible for the task. Not all of them were able to pick up their children from school, especially those who had jobs. Interviewee E reports:

> In my case, I barely have time. I work three days a week, so in the morning I can drop them off but there's no way I can pick them up afterwards.
>
> *(Interviewee E)*

They all thought it was important to drop off and pick up their children at school, as they were concerned about the risks that the children faced while commuting alone, especially the girls. Interviewee J reports:

> Just the other day my girl was going to school alone and a guy followed her, which made her scared.
>
> *(Interviewee J)*

These comments refer to children aged seven to 11. One difficulty reported by the group at this point is that children from the same family study in different school shifts, one in the afternoon and the other in the morning. Interviewee C reports:

> We have to drop everything and drop the kids off and then go and pick them up afterwards; I have to go myself, and when I can't, it's my other granddaughter who goes and picks the boy up.
>
> *(Interviewee C)*

In most medium and large cities, the Brazilian educational model divides elementary and high schools into separate buildings that in some cases are quite far apart. The women spend a lot of time on these trips as there is no free school transport available to take their children to and from school: "The school is far from home, you know, so it's hard to drop them off and pick them up." This is not a situation unique to PBF beneficiaries, but due to the conditionalities of the program, beneficiaries are under greater pressure. Local schools often lack places for new entrants, as the next respondent attests. Interviewee E reports:

> When I came from another town, it was difficult to find a place here. They wanted to send the children to another neighborhood, the boy in the morning and the girl in the afternoon. There was a fight. We had to go to the Education Center, I went to the Municipal Secretary's Office, I went all over the place, it was very, very difficult, and they missed out on school for a month because there were no places for them.
>
> *(Interviewee E)*

Comments like these reflect the precariousness of the public educational system in the places where these interviewees live. As stated at the beginning of this section, I chose neighborhoods with the highest risk and social vulnerability levels, as these are the places with the greatest difficulties in accessing education and health. In one of the municipalities where my research was carried out, one particular region presents problems and complaints of all kinds, such as construction deficiencies in housing units, land and housing units incompatible with the reality of large families, commercialization and real estate speculation, violence, lack of employment opportunities, and inadequate infrastructure and services (Alves, Rizzoti,Wandereley, and Sposati 2017). Areas with urban and social facilities are far from residential areas, which makes it difficult to access such basic social facilities as schools, early childhood education centers, health facilities, and even for routine activities related to commerce and local services. Thus, people suffer through long commutes to perform daily chores. The distance from employment and other activities makes the location a "bedroom suburb." The various shortages expose the hollowness of the argument, so often used by PBF administrators, that the program would improve beneficiary families' access to health, education and social assistance.

Another activity that was frequently mentioned, and that demands time, was helping with homework. 67% of respondents helped their children with homework. It is not a simple task; it involves aspects that remain invisible and are difficult to quantify. It is the type of activity that can be done, usually in the evening, especially when the mothers work outside of the home during the day, during this period in which the women clean the house, wash clothes, prepare food, and engage in other care activities with other children. Preparing dinner is a food activity that takes up more time, as at night working mothers prepare food for the next day's lunch.

A common guideline in home study encouragement manuals is that the child should have a quiet, individual space or "corner" to do his or her homework, while parents should supervise and make sure the child completes the task. This is a model that assumes that children have their own room and that their parents have sufficient education to help them, which is not the case for children in these families in situations of poverty. The following stories exemplify this aspect:

> Sometimes I had difficulty with homework because I had only done the first year of school. I [decided to] go back to school. I said: "I'm going to go back to school", then everyone at home looked at me and started making fun of me because I went to study after I was old. I took a supplementary course, then I started helping my grandchildren. So I went back to studying to help with the homework because there comes a time when the older ones don't want to help the younger ones, you see.
>
> *(Interviewee C)*

> It was hard for me as I had studied very little.
>
> *(Interviewee F)*

> That's because my parents always lived on a farm, so it was very far for them to take me to school, and when I went to school and the teacher saw that it was going to rain [the next day], I didn't go. So, we went to school only a few times. I came to study as an adult, like you go to an adult school with a child, right?
>
> *(Interviewee F)*

> My boy said that I say things wrong, he said "you are stupid; you didn't study," if you do not study today, you will be called stupid for the rest of your life.
>
> *(Interviewee G)*

The paucity of studies on these women is the result of the historical absence in Brazil of a social policy of universal non-marketized and inclusive education that serves everyone, especially the rural population, in the same way. There are not enough complementary adult education programs that meet adults' needs, such as programs located close to their houses so they don't need to spend money on transportation, greater security in their neighborhoods, places to leave young children, and support from partners who will often do not let them go out at night and make use of violence. The last verbatim revealed the humiliation felt by the mother, provoked by her own son, to which she was submitted for not having completed her studies. As has been much discussed by feminist research, women's lives are dedicated to providing care for others. We see this in the initiative of the grandmother who goes back to school to help her grandchildren and her son. She does this not because of her own interest, which, incidentally, is hard to identify and detached from that of those she cares for, as can be seen in these statements. Interviewees H and I report:

> We have to take care of ourselves so we can stay strong and take care of them. There are times when we can't take care of them. sometimes we dedicate ourselves too much to them and forget about ourselves. We have to be strong and grounded to be able to take care of them.
>
> *(Interviewee H)*

> [...] I think there are issues that are important, motherhood, work is fundamental, but there are other issues that we need to look out for, and that we forget in the light of day.
>
> *(Interviewee I)*

An investigation by Ramón Ramos Torres (2007) on the use of time destined to domestic work and childcare shows how the concept has become a matter for moral judgment and imbued with the idea of good and bad in such way that time use can be seen as a moral resource. Ramos Torres, in discussing the variants of time as a resource, refers to 'donated time' as time offered to others for moral and affective considerations and associated with the mother's time, time that is dedicated to domestic work and care, which has a gendered quality because it is carried out, fundamentally, by women. Donated time has to do with expectations of reciprocity on the part of those who receive care, and tensions may appear in the reciprocity circuit. Ramos Torres (2007) also comments on the association of such time with an almost mystical sacrifice in two forms, one linked to a sacrifice inherent to motherhood in which nothing is expected in return, and the other to the sacrifice of not wanting to lose anything from the growth process of the children.

A school system that had a public network offering childcare facilities and schools that offer full-day curricula would relieve mothers' workloads as well as their care and concerns for their children and would stimulate extracurricular activities with guidance from teachers. Brazil suffers from a huge deficit in terms of this type of free public service. There is a private childcare network, aimed at children aged up to five years old, which manages to meet the demands of those who can afford it. Full-time school days would make salaried work much more available to women in the opinion of my respondents. Interviewees D and G report:

> That's the hardest part for mothers...
>
> Ah, [full-time school days] would be perfect right? Imagine. They stay there all day, [they all speak simultaneously] we would be able to work, we would not have to worry about paying someone to take care of them, it would be great.
>
> *(Interviewee D)*

> Lots of mothers talk about this. I used to leave my children alone quite a lot. I used to leave them alone when they were seven with a lunch box wrapped in a cloth, locked inside the house, so I could go to work.
>
> *(Interviewee G)*

> It's not worthwhile to go out and get a job. You work all day and earn a pittance, you have to pay to go to work and pay to have lunch – you end up paying to work, you still have children with a person you who you can't even be sure will take care of them properly, if at all.
>
> *(Interviewee G)*

In the absence of day care centers or full-time facilities a care network is in many cases established by the people in the neighborhood. In order that mothers can go to work, they pay a small amount to a woman in the neighborhood who takes care of small children. It is a form of paid but informal work done within the home, which is neither quantified nor treated as work in official censuses. Full-time schooling is a right that children have so that they can achieve quality education. As feminist activists have been saying for many years, full-time schooling would be fundamental to increasing the possibilities for women's economic autonomy as well as decreasing time spent on day-to-day care for their children.

The women were extremely concerned about children not wanting to go to school as an interviewee told me:

> The worst thing is when your kid doesn't want to go to school anymore, it upsets all of the mother's arrangements, you know? There is no structure, nothing to hold on to.
>
> *(Interviewee J)*

Both two focus groups showed particularities in respect of the age groups, one concerning younger children and the other concerning adolescents. All but one of the respondents felt that it was easier to leave small children in school than have them at home. The dissenting respondent cited the fact that her son was bullied because of a lesion on his face: sometimes he doesn't want to go to class, because of what the others say. He starts crying and they keep teasing him. In cases such as this one, the time spent by the mother in convincing her son to go to school is not counted in any statistic. Interviewee H reports:

> There are times when he doesn't want to go, but I have to be patient, and we take him and talk to him, because he can't miss class.
>
> *(Interviewee H)*

As Stechi (2015) points out, male adolescents are the group that miss school the most. The difficulty with younger children is taking them to school and picking them up afterwards, whereas the difficulty with teenagers lies in convincing them to go to school and stay there, a cause of considerable suffering and conflicts. The respondents reported that this was a major cause for concern. As one of them commented:

> I'm here (in the focus group) and that makes me wonder: where is he? I feel like I need to be more careful, more concerned in my head.
>
> *(Interviewee D)*

Some adolescents drop out of school after not having advanced through the grade system for several years and, aged 13 to 16, having to go to classes for much younger children – an enormous disincentive. Other compliance factors related to teenagers[7] include involvement with the use of psychoactive substances, early entry into the labor market, teenage pregnancy, conflicts at school, and the need to care for younger siblings. The women's stories also show that the mothers are extremely concerned about bullying and racism in schools. Situations like these also cause school absenteeism/dropout/avoidance. According to the respondents, bullying and racism are practiced both by students and staff. Interviewee I reports:

> [The principal] told my son to go get you-know-what-ed; they called my son a monkey. So I went there and said, "you called my son a monkey."
>
> And he said, "your son quit school because he wanted to." We got into an argument. "Look at me," I said, "I was here. I saw you telling my son that he didn't need to come to school anymore." Who ever heard of a principal saying such a thing? Children need to be encouraged to go to school.
>
> *(Interviewee I)*

The mothers in one of the focus groups, composed mostly of black women, reported that they feel discriminated against by school staff because they are PBF beneficiaries. This was also reported by the Social Welfare administrators interviewed in the survey. Widespread opinion in Brazil holds that welfare benefits are not rights but government favors. For Standing (2007, 2, cited by Lavinas and Cobo 2010), the imposition of conditionalities presupposes that poor families must be irrational or incapable of knowing their own long-term interests or that they lack some type of vital awareness.

The meritocratic and clientelistic characteristics of social policy that, historically, have prevailed in Brazil, have left their mark on the design of public policies and the conduct of state agents.[8] This legacy is in conflict with the notion of universal law and the basic principles of non-discrimination and rights that are characteristic of democratic social security systems. The program's conditionalities are realized as a "conduct control" method that separates the deserving poor (i.e., those who behave in an appropriate manner as expected by the state) from the undeserving poor (those that do not). Behavior control is applied to this group but not to other social and economic categories to whom public policy is also directed. For example, conditionalities are not imposed on financial institutions that use public resources or on taxpayers who pay income tax and who enjoy basic and essential social services (ONU and CEPAL 2013, 59).

Parent meetings at schools are another activity that is treated as an obligation incumbent on mothers. Parents must attend parent-teacher meetings, which are usually scheduled in the morning or the afternoon on working days, on the assumption that there is always a mother available – a homemaker or someone free to be absent from work. Failure to attend parent-teacher meetings can be interpreted as underestimating the importance of and disregarding children's education. In the month before the questionnaire was applied, 70% of the respondents had attended a parent-teacher meeting. Women who work as freelance cleaners do not get paid on the day they attend the meeting, and this weighs heavily on the household budget.

When it comes to identifying women's daily activities, praying with children is frequently overlooked. A certain amount of time is dedicated to the activity of praying with children, and it is usually mothers who introduce religious practices into their children's daily lives. 56.15% of respondents prayed with their children every day. On the subject of another widely ignored activity, 22.31% of respondents reported taking care of children during the night. As Esquivel (2012) reports, the broad definition of childcare activities extends beyond active forms of care and includes passive care, defined as being present and attentive to young children who cannot be left alone. Childcare at night, at sleep time, or when the child needs care or requests the presence of an adult, is also relevant to time spent on care.

Activities that involve preparing children for school deserve particular mention. These were the last to be cited by respondents. The organization of children's school supplies and uniforms, having them bathe and brushing their teeth, putting them to sleep, getting them out of bed, and having them eat breakfast before school were common topics. As they say:

> It's not just putting things in their backpacks – it has to be organized; everything has to be in order for the school; you have to keep everything in order so it's neat and tidy.
>
> *(Interviewee H)*

More than half of the respondents engaged in these tasks every day. Although easier to count in clock time, even though performed simultaneously, these activities are not the ones that most concern women. The activities of greatest concern were those that they could not control, those that involved a sense of time. It is important to remember that this time spent worrying for children is not unique to PBF beneficiaries but is a concern for all mothers in inverse proportion to the resources at their disposal. In the case of these women, however, these are issues that cannot be controlled by means of individual resources and that depend, in large part, on the social resources made available to them. Picchio (2003, 205) comments that, in the statistical accounting of domestic work, reality must be considered as a phase within a process of negotiation about the division of labor and resources between genders, generations, and social classes. For Picchio (2003), the interests at stake generate potentially profound conflicts, as an enormous amount of physical and emotional energy is at stake, as well as people's material safety and their psychological security – their very quality of life. Most women face individual and collective responsibilities in relation to living conditions in the broadest sense.

In the next section, I look at data on time spent on health care for their children.

## Activities Related to Health Care

Children's health care was another hot topic in the groups. The PBF requires that beneficiaries have their children vaccinated and weighed. Respondents reported that these were easy condition to meet as they would have done it anyway.[9] However, engaging in prenatal care was a thing that they would not otherwise have done. It is important to comment on the time and effort women spend on their children's health, since when they are sick, their presence at school is jeopardized and, as has already been demonstrated, missed school days are directly related to difficulties in access to medical care, especially among the youngest children.

The questionnaires asked how often children are taken to primary (Basic Health Unit) and secondary (hospital) services, and how much time is spent buying medication and administering it to children, making appointments, taking children to the doctor, and having laboratory exams performed.

The women in the focus groups had a number of complaints. As mentioned above, they felt that they were being required to meet certain conditions while at the same time being deprived of the means to do so. Health care in Brazil, in spite of having gained the status of a universal and non-marketized public policy guaranteed by the state since the 1988 constitution, has seen no major advances in terms of quality and coverage. A hybrid health care system prevails in the country: the market-based private system and the state-funded Unified Health System (Portuguese acronym: SUS). Those who have enough money can access a better-quality service in the private system, but those who do not have money only have access to the SUS. The generally held view is that there is one service for "the rich" and one for "the poor." The SUS suffers from many deficiencies, including an insufficient public network of primary and hospital care, a dearth of laboratories, scarcity of specialists, other human resources shortages (in terms of medical and auxiliary staff), and insufficient equipment, material, and medical supplies.

In this precarious context, the complaints cited in the focus groups were about waiting times for care at Basic Health Units, especially for specialties, the lack of doctors, and long waiting times for laboratory exam results. There is another anomaly in the system: the difference in coverage between districts in the same municipality. Some neighborhoods have pediatricians and specialists; others do not, as reported by respondents. Thirty-nine or 23% of respondents had taken their children to a basic care unit within the last month, with average wait times of three to four hours. The same amount of time was spent by those who took their children to emergency rooms or for laboratory tests.

In relation to medical care, respondents cited the scarcity of pediatricians in basic units and the many cases where there is a pediatrician but he or she is unavailable on the day they attend, which sees them referred to other services far from the neighborhood in which they live without being in a position to pay for transportation. The following testimony, accompanied by the complaint of a day's work (and thus a day's pay) lost, provides an eloquent illustration of the situation.

> It is difficult, just like what happened to me. My boy was sick with a high fever, so I got up in the morning and took him to the clinic. He was coughing terribly and had a sore stomach. I arrived at the clinic and the girl there said: "ah, the doctor will not be able to see him, because you didn't make an appointment. The only option is Friday and today is Monday; if you come on Friday, we can fit you in." So I said, "Now I'm going to miss a day's work." So what did I do? I took him back home, put on another outfit, took some money and went to the Children's Emergency Clinic in the city center, near the central bus terminal. I had to pay for the bus for both of us and missed a day of work, because there was no way I could work. I couldn't leave him with a fever and a cough to wait until Friday.
>
> *(Interviewee J)*

The search for medical specialties is another source of hardship. The following statement made by a beneficiary in search of specialized care reveals her "pilgrimage" to the primary care unit (the gateway to care in the SUS network). Interviewee L reports:

> You have to wait a long time to see a specialist. My son has one undescended testicle. I've been trying to find a specialist for four years. He has already undergone phimosis surgery, and they didn't operate on his testicle, in fact … they put it in place, but then it ascended again. He went to the Hospital de Clínica [HC], then the HC sent him to the basic unit again, they sent him to something called the Cismepar [the "Intermunicipal Health Consortium"], the Cismepar sent him back to the basic unit, then to the HC, from there to the endocrinologist.
>
> *(Interviewee L)*

Laboratory exams were the biggest complaint in the focus groups, due to the lack of a waiting list, long waiting times, and high demand. Laboratory and specialist medical services are located in the central areas of the municipality, resulting in time spent on public transport on precarious bus lines that connect peripheral districts to the city center. In this context, it is essential to remember that this type of activity cannot be performed in conjunction with any other, such as domestic care. In other words, the time spent is absolute and requires the full presence of the woman-mother-caregiver from start to finish. There is a greater burden of suffering and stress that is caused not only by the children's illness, which is common to all mothers and fathers, regardless of whether they are beneficiaries of the PBF, but by the anguish of not being able to see their children receive dignified care.

As can be seen from the sections on education and health, the PBF conditionalities require individual administration on the part of women. It is their responsibility to keep their children in school in a context of profound social adversity without any corresponding obligation being borne by the state. This responsibility implies considerable expenditure of time, and this involves numerous clock hours and a lot of mental occupation in the form of worry, anxiety, and suffering – a clock that cannot be turned off.

I had no intention of exploring time felt, but in the course of the verbatims in the focus groups, this dimension was brought up in a forceful way. As a subjective dimension, this is more difficult to analyze and refers to so-called invisible time, which concerns worry about children who do not go to school, for instance. It is a mental state of permanent concern, tension, and conflict resulting from having to miss a day's work; a state of continuous availability and of being attentive 24 hours a day. When asked what took up her time, one of the women said: "My time is my mind being kept busy."

In a previous article[10] on the conditionalities of the PBF, attention was drawn, with reference to Carrasco (2012), to a characteristic of this work: that it is not linear, as it follows the life cycle, intensifying when it comes to care for dependents, children, the elderly, or the infirm. Another characteristic cited by Carrasco is that direct care times are more rigid because they cannot be grouped and many of them require very fixed schedules and hours and, as a result, are less readily combined with other activities. It is enough to consider the schedules of the basic health units, the children's schools, and the difficulties of women who work outside the home.

The time dimension, as part of the public/private dichotomy, has some particular characteristics. Only marketable time is valued in our society, i.e., time which becomes money and corresponds to public time. But there is another type of time, which exists in the shadow of the economy. The time that generates reproduction, which, more than measured and paid time, is time lived, dedicated, and generated, with a component that is difficult to quantify and that incorporates intangible aspects, represented by subjectivity of the person herself, incarnate in the lived experience it is necessary to give visibility to the emotional and affective dimension of care (Carrasco 2012, 43).

For Bathianny (2009, 95), an emotional bond, usually mutual, is established between the caregiver and the cared-for, a bond in which the caregiver feels responsible for the well-being of the other and makes a mental, emotional, and physical effort to fulfill this responsibility. Care is the result of many small and subtle conscious and unconscious acts, which cannot be considered completely natural or effortless. There is much more that makes up care than mere nature; there are feelings, actions, knowledge and time. The following account exemplifies the heavy care routine that poor women face:

> I take care of my three grandchildren; it is my responsibility. I take care of my mother and my son. My husband is an alcoholic and takes no responsibility for anything. So I take care of my grandchildren so my daughter can work at the dump so she can pay my bills. I have to clean my house, give food to my grandchildren, go clean my mother's house, give food and medicine to my mother. I cannot be sick. Then there is my other son who is in prison. There is no way I could have a job. So I take care of them.
>
> *(Interviewee M)*

The testimony summarizes what has been observed so far: the excessive load of activities, the family support network that, in a precarious way, replaces the state in programmatic actions that should be socialized so that the burden of care for children and the elderly can be shared, and the impossibility of empowerment of women, especially those in extreme poverty. The story reminds us of a marathon, an obstacle course in which the time lived and felt cannot be timed.

## Final Considerations

With the reconfiguration of the role of the state that began in the 1990s within the framework of neoliberalism, and the crisis of capitalist social formation threatening what feminist economics treat as social reproduction, new sources of support needed to be found for the provision of social security. In this context, the family was "rediscovered" as the primary locus of social protection. The state takes no responsibility and imposes a series of obligations on the family that go beyond people's desires or abilities. The proposal is that the state should only intervene when the family and the market fail. The field of social reproduction is reorganized and reprivatized and within it the woman occupies a central role based on a rigid sexual division of labor.

As research shows and precisely because they occupy a subordinate position in the gender hierarchy and have a fundamental role in social reproduction, women in situations of extreme poverty are the most affected by the overload placed on the family from the reordering of social policies. Without the state as the main agent of social protection through reception services, health care, education or monetary benefits for children, the elderly, and/or the sick, they find themselves once again unprotected and tied to traditional roles and functions. As we have seen, these functions were used and reaffirmed by many Latin American governments when they started to implement their CCT programs. Women ended up having to manage the conditionalities in the programs.

My research shows that PBF beneficiaries, most of whom are black, must, as the main providers of care, engage in a vast array of daily activities involving measurable, felt, and lived time that in many cases cannot be measured on the clock. The fact that the PBF emphasizes female titularity and makes receiving the benefit conditional on children attending school and receiving basic health care increases the responsibilities of women in caring for their children. It is clear that time use is not so much a question of minutes and hours spent, but the breaking up of a day organized according to school hours and distance from the beneficiary's home. The school timetable dictates the schedule of domestic family work and availability for salaried work.

The conditionality related to health is the one that most occupies women's time due to the need to travel for health services and to endure long waiting times, in addition to the need to adapt to the opening hours of these services, which, for the most part, correspond to business hours. Time lived and felt was cited with great emphasis in focus groups. This is time that cannot be measured on a stopwatch, it is time spent in thought, in uninterrupted worry, in anguish, in permanent alertness. It is the feeling of fear and helplessness in the face of the possibility of losing the *Bolsa Família* benefit, of being branded a "bad mother" according to the heteropatriarchal, racist, and capitalist model that is in deep communion with the social security systems in a neoliberal economy.

When formulating income transfer programs, multilateral agencies and government managers were able to anticipate the invisible work to be undertaken by women in caring for children and opted to valorize it as a strategy for breaking the intergenerational cycle of extreme poverty. The argument of this text is not that conditional cash transfer programs should be eliminated. Instead, I argue that programs should be reconceived with an unconditional, non-marketized character in a context of state provision of public policies with a view to socialization of care. In the meantime, it would be cruel to poor, black, young, and old women to deprive them of a benefit that helps relieve their children's hunger.

Finally, I reaffirm the feminist economics argument that social security should be based on an ethics of care for the sustainability of human life.

## Notes

1. The other dimensions are: the social identity of the caregiver; the social identity of the person receiving care; interpersonal relationships between the person who gives cares and the person who receives it; the economic character of the care relationship (Thomaz 2011, 149–151, our translation).
2. These are treated as family care: the action of caring for a child, an adult, or elderly person who is dependent for the development and well-being of their daily life. In addition to material work, there is an affective and emotional aspect that includes activities such as: playing, taking walks, helping with homework, and socializing (children); attention to physiological, medical, and social needs (walking, keeping company) for the elderly and the infirm (Carrasco 2003).
3. Social Assistance Policy in Brazil is managed by the Unified Social Assistance System (Portuguese acronym: SUAS). The national organization of the SUAS is based on a structure of equal primary care for all municipalities in the federation. Direct attention is provided in municipalities through the so-called "CRAS," which act as social welfare portals. PBF applicants must register at their local CRAS unit in order to receive the *Bolsa Família* and take advantage of social work services. CRAS units are distributed within municipalities by district according to population density.
4. For more information on black women in the PBF see chapter 4.
5. See Saraceno 1995.
6. The interviewees were identified with letters.
7. These are measures applied to adolescents who commit such offenses in educational settings as provided for in the Statute of Children and Adolescents (Portuguese acronym: ECA). They may be applied to young people aged 12 to 18. In some exceptional cases, they may be extended up to the age of 21. They are applied by judges from the Childhood and Youth Court.
8. See Chapter 10 in this volume.
9. Reports dating from 2019, collected from staff in the Social Assistance Secretariat in one of the municipalities, indicate that this condition has recently become a source of friction. There are shortages of vaccines and scales in the Basic Health Units (Portuguese acronym: UBS). Staff reports indicate that beneficiaries did not have their children weighed or vaccinated in the PBF control reference month (due to these shortages) which leads to sanctions or non-receipt of the benefit until the situation is rectified.
10. Carloto 2012.

## References

Alves, Jolinda M., M. Luiza Rizzoti, M. Angela Wandereley, and Aldaiza Sposati. 2017. "A Lógica Territorial na Gestão de Políticas Sociais. Universidade Estadual de Londrina, PUC-SP, CAPES and CNPq." PROCAD Research Report.

Bartholo, Letícia, Luana Passos, and Natália Fontoura. 2017. *Bolsa Família, Autonomia Feminina e Equidade de Gênero: o que indicam as Pesquisas Nacionais?* Texto de Discussão 2331. Brazil: Ipea.

Batthyány, Karina. 2009. "Cuidado de personas dependentes y gênero." In: *Las bases invisibles del bienestar social- El trabajo no remunerado em Urugauay*, edited by Rosario Aguirre, 87–121. Uruguay: UNIFEM, Doble clic Editoras.

Carloto, Cássia. 2012. "Condicionalidades nos Programas de Transferência de Renda e autonomia das mulheres." *Sociedade em Debate* 18, no. 2: 121–130.

Carrasco, Cristina and Marius Dominguez. 2003. "Género y Usos del Tempo: Nuevos Enfoques Metodológicos." *Revista Economia Crítica* 1: 129–152.

Carrasco, Cristina. 2003. "A sustentabilidade da Vida Humana: Um assunto de Mulheres." In *Produção do Viver*, edited by Nalu Faria, and Miram Nobre, 22–49. São Paulo: Cadernos SOF.

Carrasco, Cristina. 2012. *Estatísticas Sob Suspeita: Proposta de Novos Indicadores com Base na Experiência das Mulheres*. Translation by Valenzuela Perez. São Paulo: SOF Sempreviva Organização Feminista.

Cotta, Tereza C. and Luis H. Paiva. 2010. "O Programa Bolsa Família e a proteção social no Brasil." In *Bolsa Família 2003–2010: avanços e desafios*, edited by Jorge A. Castro, and Lúcia Modesto. Vol. 2. Brazil: IPEA.

Esquivel, Laura. 2012. "El cuidado infantil em las famílias, um análisis en base a la Encuesta de Uso del Tiempo de la Ciudad de Buenos Aires." In *Las Lógicas Del Cuidado Infantil Entre Las Familias, El Estado y El Mercado*, edited by V. Esquivel, Eleonor Faur, and Elizabeth Jelin, 73–103. Buenos Aires: Ides.

Faur, Eleonor. 2014. *El cuidado infantil en el siglo XXI: mujeres malabaristas en uma sociedade desigual*. Buenos Ayres: Siglo Ventiuno Editores.

Fontoura, Natália and Clara Araújo, eds. 2016. *Uso do Tempo e Gênero*. Rio de Janeiro: UERJ.

Javeau, Claude. 1980. "Sur le concept de vie quotidienne et sa sociologie." *Cahiers Internationaux de Sociologie* 68: 31–45.

Lavinas, Lena and Barbára Cobo. 2010. "Políticas sociais universais e incondicionais: há chances reais de sua adoção na américa latina?" Work presented in 13th Congresso da Rede Mundial de Renda Básica, São Paulo.

Lozares, Carlos, Pedro López, and Marius Dominguez. 1998. "La articulación de ámbitos sociales a partir de la base temporal." *Papers* 55: 115–130.

Mariano, Silvana and Cássia Carloto. 2013. "Aspectos diferenciais da inserção de mulheres negras no Programa Bolsa Família." *Revista Sociedade e Estado* 28, no. 2: 393–417. doi:10.1590/S0102-69922013000200011.

MDS (Ministério do Desenvolvimento Social). 2010. *Guia para Acompanhamento das Condicionalidades do Programa Bolsa Família*. Brazil: MDS.

Molyneux, Maxine. 2007. "The Chimera of Success: Gender Ennui and the changed International Policy Environment." In *Feminisms in Development Contradictions, Constetations and Chalenges*, edited by Andrea Cornwal, Elizabeth Harrison, and Ann Whitehead, 1–11. London: Zed.

Navarro, Flavia M. and Maria N. Rico. 2013. "Cuidado y políticas públicas: debates y estado de situación a nível regional." In *Las fronteiras del cuidado: agenda, derechos e infraestructura*, coordinated by Laura Pautassi, and Carla Zibecchi, 27–58. Buenos Aires: Editora Biblos.

NU (Nações Unidas), and CEPAL (Comissão Econômica para a América Latina e o Caribe). 2013. *Los bonos en la mira: aporte y carga para las mujeres*. Santigo, Chile: Nações Unidas.

Orozco, Amaia P. 2014. *Subversión feminista de la economía: aportes para un debate sobre el conflicto capital-vida*. Madrid: Traficantes de Suenõs.

Picchio, Antonella. 2003. "Visibilidad Analítica y polytica del trabajo de reproducion social." In *Mujeres y Economia. Nuevas perspectivas para viejos y nuevos problemas*, edited by Cristina Carrasco, 201–244. Barcelona: Icaria.

Ramos Torres, Ramón. 2007. "Metáforas sociales del tiempo em Espana: una investigación empírica." In *Trabajo, gênero y tiempo social*, edited by Carlos Prieto Rodríguez, 173–104, Madrid: Hacer; Complutense.

Rodríguez-Enríquez, Corina. 2013. "Organización del cuidado y políticas de conciliación: uma perspectiva económica." In *Las Fronteiras del cuidado: Agenda, Derechos e Infraestructura*, coordinated by Laura Patassi, and Carla Zibecchi, 133–154. Buenos Aires: Editora Biblos.

Saraceno, C. 1995. "A dependência construída e a interdependência negada." In *O dilema da cidadania*, edited by G. Bonacchi, and A. Groppi, 205–234. São Paulo: Unesp.

Stechi, Tatiana O. 2015. "O Programa Bolsa Família e suas condicionalidades: entre o direito e o dever." Master's dissertation, Universidade Estadual de Londrina.

Thomaz, Carol. 2011. "Desconstruyendo los conceptos de cuidados." In *El trabajo de cuidados: Historia, Teoria y Políticas*, edited by C. Carrasco, C. Borderias, and T. Torns, 145–176. Madrid: Catarata.

UNFPA Brasil (United Nations Population Fund Brasil). 2018. "Fecundidade e dinâmica da população brasileira." https://brazil.unfpa.org/pt-br/publications/fecundidade-e-dinamica-da-populacao-brasileira-folder.

# 8

# STIGMAS AND CONTROLS ON *BOLSA FAMÍLIA* BENEFICIARY WOMEN

*Mani Tebet A. de Marins*

## Introduction

Public policies of any kind can be interpreted sometimes as a social emancipation project, and other times as a moral project of the state aimed at shaping moral frameworks, identities, and forms of exclusion (Fraser and Honneth 2003; Butler 2004; Foucault 2003; Bourdieu 2012; Hall 2006). This chapter uses Foucault's (2003) concept of *governmentality*, which expresses public policies as the result of disputes over political projects, interests, and social representations. Thus, it is important to investigate the intervention and local implementation of the policy, that is, what Foucault (1979) calls peripheral power. I then proceed to verify the effects of gender and controls on maternity in the case of the implementation of the PBF at the municipal level. According to Butler (2015), Foucault claims that the state imposes power at different levels of social relations, and that there are citizens who are beneficiaries and who are dependent on the state as well as others who do not submit to state control. For Butler, the state can also produce forms of oppression, violence, and exclusion of certain social groups (Butler 2015).

In modernity, public policies have oscillated between focusing on the individual or the family as the unit on which to act (Fine, Lapavitsas, and Pincus 2001; Schild 2007; Jenson 2009). The ties between the state and family are based on a lasting and complex history of conflicts and moral/legal commitments. Recently, the modern state has redistributed its responsibilities to the family through social policies. In particular, in Latin America, where policies tend to be familist in nature (Esping-Andersen 1999), mediation between public agents and citizens is generally done through the family and/or the community. In the case of the subject under investigation, namely Conditional Cash

Transfers (CCT), mothers mediate between the state and society. This mediation is constructed through the formal (bureaucratic, administrative, and legal) and the informal (moral, social, cultural, and symbolic) rules of the implementation of public policies.

There is a considerable literature (in particular by US and French scholars: Pressman and Wildavsky 1973; Lipsky 1980; Hill and Hupe 2014; Maynard-Moody and Musheno 2003; Dubois 2010; Duvoux 2009; Paugam 2003) on the implementation of public policies. However, there is a gap in the Brazilian scholarship regarding the implementation processes of those policies that may produce social exclusion and/or discrimination. It is even more difficult to find studies that consider intersectionality as a dimension of social policies.

This chapter addresses some of the challenges that affect the implementation process of social policy at the local/municipal levels. These challenges may be related to the performance (with a number of hierarchical, discretionary, and stigmatizing traits) of public agents that assist beneficiaries of the PBF who, in general, are poor black people. My view on implementation is focused on the day-to-day operations of street-level bureaucrats (Lipsky 1980)[1] which may (re)produce discrimination based on gender, race, and/or class, pass moral judgments on beneficiaries, and even exclude groups already considered socially vulnerable. The specialized literature from different theoretical perspectives shows that State agents not only execute politics in a bureaucratic and normative manner, but often make arbitrary decisions that affect the results of public policy. My analysis of implementation practices focuses on the interaction between public agents and women beneficiaries of the *Bolsa Família* Program (PBF).

Another objective of the present study is to discuss the centrality of the categories of gender and race for the formulation and implementation of public policies in general and, in particular, of policies designed to fight poverty. If women (often black) are priority targets in Brazil's CCT program, why not consider increasing efforts to eliminate gender and racial inequalities, which tend to be most alarming in a context of poverty? If black women suffer from sexism and racism on a daily basis, it is likely that this kind of discrimination also manifests in their relations with the state. Qualitative research on the relationship between state agents and the beneficiary population can bring new and more complex data to the research area under discussion.

In order to clarify the relationship between public agents and women beneficiaries, I conducted participant observation in a community of the metropolitan region of Rio de Janeiro, and carried out semi-structured and in-depth interviews with different actors. I conducted some follow-up interviews with the same family to clarify obscure aspects of their first answers and also to probe for depth about certain issues identified in their statements that could help us in the analysis.

## Poor Women between the State and Society: Controls, Moralities, and Stigmas

Within the theoretical framework of Sociology, I analyze the state starting with its social construction, as an institution that frames groups in spaces of power, shapes behaviors, forms groups, and produces identities. In this sense, I investigate the problematic process of public policymaking, departing from the view that the state is a homogeneous and universal institution that indefectibly produces equality and citizenship. The state, in addition to exercising physical violence, also exerts symbolic violence (Bourdieu 2012). This violence often occurs subtly as arbitrary representations and practices detrimental to social groups that depend on state services. For Bourdieu (2012), the state operates by coercion (or domination) and consensus (unconscious agreement on the part of citizens to follow state directives) through symbolic violence practiced by a legitimate power.

For the author, the state is responsible for the production of beliefs and cognitive structures, as well as symbolic systems charged with moralities and discourses produced by the state's "officiality." The idea of consensus, or rather of citizens' acceptance of state-produced norms, would be legitimated starting with acknowledgement that the rule is just in a universal sense, imposing obedience and submission to the rules of the governmental game (Bourdieu 2012, 260–261).

I intend to demonstrate that, despite there being a publicly disclosed and shared formal text of the policy, different understandings of the norms therein and different forms of control operate through the actions of different agents working on behalf of the state. These forms of control will depend on the way local institutions and institutional agents interpret the policy. Foucault (1979) calls this kind of analysis of power a "bottom-up" approach, as it interprets power at the level of the state as being influenced by local institutions and their practices.

Another fundamental point of Foucauldian discussion rests in the idea of surveillance as one of the strongest forms of state control. Surveillance is presented in a masked but permanent way, and without spatial-temporal limits, with individuals being watched on an ongoing basis and internalized in such a way that those being surveilled are unable to realize the extent to which they are being controlled (Foucault 2009). Even if power implies submission, there is room for political resistance and mobilization practices. There are contexts in which the beneficiaries of certain public policies consciously "manipulate" their beneficiary status (Goffman 2012) often in response to certain stigmatizing situations (Marins 2017).

This paradigm shift in public policy is classified in various ways in the sociological literature: the Post-Washington Consensus (Fine, Lapavitsas, and Pincus 2001), the citizen-consumer (Schild 2007), and social investment (Jenson 2009). Thus, various analytical instruments (capability, empowerment, governance, and human and social capital) seem to trigger this new form of citizenship based on cooperation values. These changes become visible in the areas of human development, minimum income, and anti-poverty policy, according to which women beneficiaries must develop strategies, taking advantage of the financial assistance they receive, to overcome their situations of social vulnerability.

From the 1990s onwards, the social sciences literature began to incorporate, more emphatically, gender analyses to understand the assumptions (and social meanings) contained in public policies. Several authors (Esping-Andersen 1999; Orloff 2007; Jenson 2009; Molyneux 2006; Fonseca 2010) bring up concepts such as that of "familist policy" and / or "gendered policy" in order to understand the redistribution of the state's responsibilities. This discussion is part of a broad set of debates held particularly by feminist theorists.

Conditional cash transfer policies see women as endowed with a fundamental role in establishing solidarity ties and producing social capital. At the same time, these policies exempt men (fathers) from being potentially responsible for family care. This view held by the state and the related practices it carries out may reproduce gender inequalities already present in society.

Following Goffman (2012), in order to obtain a broader picture of the beneficiary, it is essential to observe the stigma in the public sphere. In this research, this implied conducting interviews with other actors (teachers, social workers, health-care specialists, entrepreneurs, and members of the neighborhood itself) who interact with beneficiaries of the BF program. I want to analyze if (and how) female beneficiaries of this CCT program, generally characterizable as poor (often extremely impoverished and predominantly black), experience humiliation and prejudice resulting from the actions of public agents and governmental policy implementation processes.

Specifically with regard to the issue of stigma, Goffman (1988) points out that actors, consciously, calculate the social cost of engagement, sometimes deviating from face-to-face interaction to avoid possible discrimination, sometimes facing it head-on, developing strategies to cope with the stigma. I agree with Goffman (2012) that stigma can only be dealt with from a relational point-of-view, which means that it can only be analyzed on the basis of the social relations that are established between the state, the market, local institutions, and social networks.

## Gender and Conditional Cash Transfer Policies

In the 1990s, groups of researchers and policy makers working on cultural analysis of development policies, especially those designed to fight poverty, were growing and legitimizing themselves. In this new scenario, there was an attempt to incorporate gender issues in the international development agenda. According to Bedford (2009), this was done in two ways. The first was related to investing in "family" as a solution to development, since with women as the stewards of the cash provided, the policy could in principle have a greater effect in reducing domestic violence, increasing solidarity between spouses, and improving child development. The second aimed to insert gender into the social policy platform as a social marketing strategy, linked to the negative male images mentioned above. The World Bank has recommended measures to strengthen family ties, particularly in Latin America. This can be seen most clearly in the reports[2] produced since 1998 on gender and development issues, on the impact on gender of the bank's monetary assistance, and on the production of social capital through the family (Marins 2017). In these documents, the family has emerged as an important informal institution to assist the State in ensuring development by reducing poverty.

More substantively, the family has been framed as a crucial institution in the fight against poverty and in the formation of "safety nets" for social development. Such support networks are now valued as a way to adopt the international commitment to "social inclusion." The concepts of female capacity, partnership, and competence have been activated since 1998 (Marins 2017). The speeches of the heads of the World Bank signaled that gender discrimination was impeding development, especially as women could not accumulate social capital when suffering sexual or psychologically abuse.[3] The World Bank (1997) stated that, as women are usually those who provide primary care, they play a key role in the development of social capital. Molyneux (2002, 167) shows in her article "Gender and the Silences of Social Capital" that the World Bank invested in this idea of social capital, especially in the Latin American context. However, attributes to women the role of promoter of this type of capital, since, in the face of adversity, "poor men" tend to act violently and destructively, not establishing the bonds of trust conducive to restructuring their lives.

Conditional cash transfer programs have two main objectives, one in the short term through direct cash transfers, and the other over the long term with the expectation of breaking the intergenerational cycle of poverty. This last objective is structured based on three dynamics: 1) targeting children and adolescents; 2) requiring that health and education be considered; 3) prioritizing women. Even though the objectives of anti-poverty policies are quite similar in different Latin American countries, the reasons and ways in which countries have adopted such policies are distinct. These differences come down to two characteristics: emphasis on each of these objectives, and the way in which the programs relate to social assistance.

Recently, some national and international works (Suárez and Libardoni 2007; Rego 2008; Carloto and Mariano 2009; Marins 2017, 2018; Jenson 2009; Molyneux 2002; Périvier and Silvera 2009; Chant 2015) have been addressing gender and women's status within CCT programs. The main point of the debate revolves around this question: does the fact that the resource is directed primarily to women imply an increase in female autonomy and/or a reduction in domestic violence? Suárez and Libardoni (2007)[4] and Rego and Pinzani (2013) respond affirmatively to this question considering that the task of social reproduction is now more safely managed. Thus, even if the feminine logic of "care" is not changed, women gain relative autonomy only in the domestic sphere because, according to the authors, they now rely less on their husbands and have greater decision-making power regarding how to prioritize spending in the family's best interests. Thus, according to the authors, the possibility of making choices, even if conditioned by a gender bias, could already be considered a "gain" (albeit a small one) for female autonomy.

Also referring to the PBF, Rego (2008, 170) points out that "resource endowments to ensure the livelihoods of the poor can potentially make them effective holders of social rights." According to the author, ensuring social rights would represent a gain for women in the *sertão* (hinterlands) in the northeastern region of Brazil, allowing this female group a little more freedom and autonomy. In another study, in which the authors compare the Indian microcredit policy with *Bolsa Família*, Rego, Baratto, and Oliveira (2010) consider the moral effects on Brazilian and Indian women who are beneficiaries. In the case of the BF program, according to Rego and Pinzani (2013), there is growth in female self-esteem (based on increased buying power and appreciation of oneself as an autonomous subject capable of fostering happiness) even when the premise of social promotion does not seem to be in effect among the group of beneficiaries. In India also generates a sense of "dignity" among beneficiary women (Rego and Pinzani 2013).

Some authors (Carloto and Mariano 2009; Marins 2018; Jenson 2009; Molyneux 2002; Périvier and Silvera 2009; Chant 2015) argue that this type of program does not enhance women's autonomy in the medium and long term. They argue that because programs like BF mainly promote neither the women beneficiaries' educational training,[5] nor their professional development, they are keeping women in a situation of dependence either on their spouses or on the state.

Drawing on the empirical data collected, the present work will contribute to discussions related to the theme of social development, implementation of public policies, and discrimination produced by the state in relation to beneficiaries of public social protection programs. Such discrimination may have an intersectional character (at the crossing of class, gender, and race) in the sense attributed by Crenshaw (1994). Based on national and international studies, my goal is to analyze the daily operations of bureaucrats: their discretionary power, discriminatory practices, and inattention to and mistreatment and humiliation of vulnerable groups of the population.

The subject matter, namely poverty, introduced in this chapter involves a discussion around some specific objectives related to understanding: 1) how public agents interact with beneficiaries and how the different community actors socialize with program beneficiaries; 2) the extent to which these professionals typify the low-income population and those "in need of" the benefit; 3) the logic by which the agents responsible for the program's various implementation processes produce such classifications of the program's target population – that is, what instruments are used to legitimize and validate their classifications. How do social workers (and other professionals) determine the social *status* of a beneficiary? Does the latter negotiate such socio-institutional classifications or accept them *a priori*?

My objective is also to verify whether the poor who do not receive the benefit produce stigmatizing categories and practices in relation to women beneficiaries. Are the perceptions on non-beneficiaries pervaded by work *ethos* with the notion of merit as a guiding principle? Or would there be other moral categories to distinguish "us" from "them"? Here, we analyze processes that stigmatize beneficiaries. Are these stigmas explicit or are they veiled? Are they intersectionally related to class, gender, and/or race? Or is there a variation in the importance attributed to these variables in the context of discrimination against beneficiaries of the *Bolsa Família* Program?

In 2010, I conducted empirical research in the city of Itaboraí, a suburb in the outskirts of the Rio de Janeiro Metropolitan Region. I collected data using two types of methodologies: participant observation and in-depth interviews. Participant observation was carried out in several spaces, such as: a school, a health center, a Reference Center for Social Assistance (CRAS), the *Bolsa Família* office, the BF registration sector, a popular restaurant, and the Nova Cidade district neighborhood. There were also 70 in-depth interviews with families of beneficiaries (35 in total) and non-beneficiaries (28 in total), as well as with institutional actors, including social workers, health workers, teachers, a school principal, and a BF program coordinator. The Municipality of Itaboraí was chosen as the site of this field research for three reasons: 1) due to the precarious living conditions of the local population (in 2010, according to the IBGE, the municipality had a MHDI of 0.693); 2) due to the high population of BF beneficiaries there (according to Cadastro Único,[6] in January 2010, there were around 12,000 registered families among the total population of 218,000).

In 2011, Rio de Janeiro's per capita Gross Domestic Product (GDP) was BRL36,118.57,[7] more than twice the per capita GDP of Itaboraí, which was around BRL13,404.00. In Itaboraí, the unemployment rate reached 11.7% in 2010, more than two percentage points above the average for the state of Rio de Janeiro (8.9%). In addition, in 2010, Itaboraí had 10.2% of its population in a situation of poverty, with 3.3% of its total population being extremely poor, while the state of Rio de Janeiro saw 7.2% of its population in conditions of poverty and 1.9% in extreme poverty. Thus, Itaboraí is characterized by the precarity and vulnerability of its local population.

Most of the residents of the municipality receive assistance from the federal government, accessing programs aimed at curbing poverty. It is estimated that around 80% of the population receives some kind of social benefit (Cadastro Único 2010). I was able to arrange interviews with the beneficiaries by contacting a social worker from this municipality. The interviews, however, were marked by distrust, as the beneficiaries believed that my work would serve as a basis for monitoring their socioeconomic status and for "a supposed follow-up" to determine if they were complying with conditionalities, in order to assess their legitimacy in remaining beneficiaries of the program. Therefore, I opted for referrals from a beneficiary to interview other residents in the neighborhood without the normative problems that referrals from a social worker could generate. Before proceeding to display the research results, it is important to mention here that the names of all of the respondents have been changed.[8] We will start our analysis with the vocational training courses offered to the general population and to the beneficiaries in particular.

## *Vocational Training Courses*

In Itaboraí, emerged the construction of social classifications based on attitudes towards the provision of vocational training courses (Pronatec[9]) for families in *Bolsa Família*. With regard to one of these courses, located in the Rio de Janeiro Petrochemical Complex (Comperj), Paula (a Social Services intern) stated that:

> At Comperj, it was quite a challenge putting together a class. It was a problem, because they would call the beneficiaries and such, nobody was very interested, and they had to have a high school diploma, which is not very common among the beneficiaries.

In this case, we can point out that it is the requirements of the courses that prevent the beneficiaries from engaging, as they (mostly) do not have the required degree of education to be eligible to enroll in courses. It is noteworthy considering that, among BF program beneficiaries nationwide, most have not completed high school (89% according to Cadastro Único, 2010). The courses offered by the Municipality were to train electricians and welders, courses typically directed to the male gender, which to some extent hinders women's engagement in vocational training. Regarding the courses, according to Paula:

> [...] It seemed really good and it was actually an expensive course to pay for, but it had this criterion: a high school diploma. [...] I do not remember how many seats were available for enrollment in the course, but few beneficiaries looked into it. Enrollment had to be opened to the entire community. They are complacent. Most of them are not interested. They are very poor people, most of whom do not want to study; they don't want to take courses.

Paula's speech on accommodation (particularly regarding course drop-out rates) is inconsistent. On the one hand, she says that a high school diploma is mandatory, on the other hand, she points out the poor announcement of the course offering to the community: "The course was promoted only by word of mouth. The high school course, for example; sometimes they send a paper for us to share with *Bolsa Família* recipients. And we do so during home visits. But there were no posters." Nevertheless, Paula states that the beneficiaries have unconvincing justifications for not engaging in professional development opportunities: "They make up excuses...like they had a prior commitment or an appointment with a doctor. I already warned them twice. It's their responsibility."

Although there are other reasons for beneficiaries not to engage in the courses offered, the requirement of a high school diploma, rare educational capital among the beneficiaries, and the lack of promotion and disclosure of the course(s) are attributed by the intern Paula to the lack of interest and low enrollment numbers among the population. The fact that the assistance policy offers in the vocational training courses in the municipality open to the general public (but mainly catering to men) gives rise to a feeling of social injustice among those who are not beneficiaries (especially poor workers) who, in principle, would not qualify to take the course free of charge. According to Salvador (non-beneficiary), this type of course should be offered to those who are really interested in learning; he dismisses the idea of opening the course to people who enroll because they must meet a program requirement.

## Representations, Distinctions, and Symbolic Borders in Relation to the Beneficiaries

In the course of my fieldwork, I noticed the emergence of various social classifications that produce symbolic boundaries between social groups. I use here the concept of symbolic boundaries that refers to distinctions between people and practices that work as a set of rules that conduct the social interaction (Lamont and Fournier 1992). In the research, in a context of poverty, two distinct categories were brought up: "worker" and "vagabond." A similar classification was also observed by Anderson (1999), in the United States, in a Philadelphia ghetto, where the distinction occurred mainly between "decent families" (those who have secured formal employment) and "street families" (those who are subject to a world of crime, drugs, or underground economies). Another empirical study by Newman (1999), based on interviews with fast-food restaurant employees, found that the respondents constructed categories to classify the poor, calling them the "unemployed poor" and "vagabonds," thus distinguishing themselves from their impoverished peers based on merit.

Regarding the idea of deserving the benefit, it seems that regardless of group status (beneficiary and non-beneficiary families and institutional actors), people believe that those most in need of this financial support from the state are deserving – that is, only those most "in need" should be allowed to apply for this aid and should use the resource to find a way out of a condition of dependence on the state. For Mara (non-beneficiary), for example, families facing starvation are "families in need." She chose not to apply for the benefit because, even though she could use the cash, she thinks that the benefit should be for "those families who can't even afford to put bread on the table." Both retirees and workers believe that beneficiary families and in particular their cardholding heads of household (predominantly women), who are not "starving," are "opportunists." In general, people who see beneficiaries as "deserving" tend to be those who have suffered most from fluctuations in the labor market.

Particularly, with regard to the category of "opportunists" taking advantage of the social protection system, Jucélia (beneficiary) states that: "There are people who keep saying that the government is giving generously, but no one here owns a car or has a nice house; we ask for help because we really need it." This opposition in attitudes as regards classification reappears: there are those who are "deserving" ("in need") vs. those who are deemed "opportunists" ("not in need"). This latter category is also expressed by the attitude that many women will spend the money on themselves instead of investing in their children, which suggests that these women take advantage of state aid in an opportunistic way, implying that they are somehow morally obligated to direct the resources they secure, not to mention their care and selflessness, to their children and others rather than taking care of themselves.

A beneficiary named Edilceia reports that her family needs to "fit the profile" (investing in her children), otherwise the neighborhood will come to judge her and question her poverty. Edilceia is required to behave in agreement with the moral conditions of the "good mother" (proving herself to be supportive, altruistic, and responsible in view of her role as a parent / head of household). She should not spend money on unnecessary products or services, but rather buy school materials and food for her kids. She says, "if you buy something else (for yourself), [people] really judge you."

As for specific constraints suffered by this population, Raquel, a teacher, suggests that beneficiaries invest the money in the wrong way and, in doing so, attract negative moral judgments. According to her:

> I've heard, "Oh, so you're starving…" "Instead of asking for money, why don't you do something else?" I don't particularly like it because I like programs that encourage people. I just don't like how they spend the benefit. So I think [the program] could have greater oversight. Because [the benefit] may be being used to buy drugs.

Interestingly, Raquel (a teacher from the municipality) stresses that social control should be greater over the poor female population, pointing out that closer scrutiny would avoid the risk of the policy financing beneficiaries' "addictions." It seems that the legacy of the long tradition of food distribution assistance still lingers in the Brazilian social imaginary.

With respect to the way that the beneficiaries spend their grant, Cristina (nonbeneficiary) perceives spending differently. She believes beneficiary mothers spend their benefits on themselves: "I see that they spend that money on themselves. The other day, I saw one drinking and ignoring her son, instead of going out and getting a job." This opinion can also be contrasted with that of Carla, a beneficiary who claims to use the money to "pay for groceries, crackers, and meat for the children. Then, if I can, I buy some clothes."

In this context, there is the production of a symbolic and moral distinction: separating "irresponsible mothers" from "responsible mothers." Salvador (non-beneficiary) seems to make an even clearer contrast between beneficiaries who are "good" and "bad mothers." Salvador criticizes the latter (who spend the money on themselves) because, in his view, they are not fulfilling the duties assigned to all women in the traditional role of mother. His understanding of a "good mother" is based on an attitude aligned with the BF program's moral assumptions: that beneficiary women must be supportive and invest primarily in their children and dependents. This conception of the program is also present in the program guidelines published by the municipality of Itaboraí, offered to the beneficiaries upon registration, indicating how the legal recipient (the woman/mother) should manage the family's benefit. There are also suggestions aimed at guiding the nutritional development of children by recommending the ideal kinds of food mothers should buy and feed their families.

## Stigmatization, Shame, and Control

From the time she first learned of the program to the moment she signed up and started receiving the benefit, Carla[10] (beneficiary) had to pass through various institutional spheres and witness situations in which clerks and other professionals treated her as though they were suspicious of her efforts to access the benefit. The following excerpt traces the path Carla had to take to become a BF recipient and the embarrassment she experienced.

> I first went to the old hospital. Once there, they said registration was closed. I was going to give up. Then my friend took me to the brick house.[11] But registration was closed there too. Finally, after six or seven months, there was a group registering at the college. I was able to apply there, and I received the benefit three months later. I was embarrassed because they asked me how I was able to support myself on R$60. I said I had a health worker who gave me some assistance. When I left, [the clerk] told a woman: "Her story is a little strange, isn´t it?" I felt really embarrassed, you know? Because they thought I was lying. Then I spoke with a friend of mine about this situation. I was there for a while because I was waiting for my friend. I saw a man take one girl´s form, tear it up, and throw it in the garbage. I thought: well that girl is definitely not getting the benefit. They scrutinize the person, checking if s/he is neatly dressed or not; they immediately give you a suspicious look, you know?
>
> *(Carla, beneficiary)*

Judgment (of the way these individuals speak, dress, and behave) and distrust in the self-declared incomes of *Bolsa Família* applicants are recurrent themes in interviews with the employees who process program applications (those trusted to enter the applicants' information into the system). By means of participant observation for four months in the registration sector, I noticed that this type of treatment actually is reproduced in the daily lives of those who seek only to access their right to social assistance. As we shall see, enforcing the rules of the program always entails people in positions of power passing normative moral judgments and reducing applicants to classifications (Maynard-Moody and Musheno 2003) which may reflect prejudiced attitudes towards and outright discrimination against beneficiaries, especially black women. Although most female beneficiaries identify as women of color, they complained less of race-based discrimination, and more of discrimination based on social class.

For example, Adelir (beneficiary) states that, at the time of registration, she was humiliated:

> On that day, I felt humiliated. There are a lot of people who give up on applying, you know? I said I am in need… and they immediately treated me with suspicion; they think you're lying, that you're trying to trick them. They ask several times: Do you really earn just that? Doesn't your husband work?

In the registration sector, two types of domination emerge in relation to beneficiaries: symbolic domination (construction of social distinction and classificatory judgment) and bureaucratic domination (compliance with social control through administrative rule). It is important to recall here the idea of Weberian domination to think about relations with beneficiaries of social assistance policies. For Weber, in a contractual situation, the principle of equality can never be fulfilled, since it establishes a relationship of domination. In fact, it is noted that the social class position of the actors involved, coupled with the bureaucratic domination, gives rise to a situation of hierarchy and arbitrariness that may turn into concrete discriminatory treatment.

For the beneficiary, Luciana, the most problematic issue related to interactions with the state is related to her financial dependence. This is a factor that bothers beneficiaries. As she explains:

> It´s humiliating to be unemployed and receive assistance from the government. You feel useless. People want to work and earn money through their own efforts and not just go to the bank to withdraw money the government gives them. It seems like they are doing you a favor, right? While waiting in line to withdraw [their benefits], a lot of my peers hide their benefit cards out of shame, you know? They don´t want to look like starving people. Sometimes, we hear comments like: "Here they come, counting on other people's money." It's awful.

In the US literature, camouflaging one's position translates into what Small, Harding, and Lamont (2011) term "framing." This term refers to efforts by beneficiaries, in their everyday experiences, to conceal their beneficiary status so as not to be publicly humiliated by being reduced to "poor people who depend on government aid." As Duvoux (2009) has shown in France, internalizing the norm of autonomy (through labor) allows beneficiaries to resist stigma and the feeling of social disqualification, but the line between rights and handouts in Brazil seems not to be as clear as in the French case. During my observation of the *Bolsa Família* office, Naiara (beneficiary) noted that the humiliation that she experienced was mainly at the hands of the bureaucrats in the registration sector.

> They say the government isn't going to give you a thing! You have to work! There's nothing else! So I am no longer even going to try to address the issue of my son missing school [she received a notification that her son had missed school, but he actually was in attendance]. I am not going down there anymore because I don't want to be mistreated. The administrators will comment out loud for everyone to hear: "You spend the whole night partying and don't aspire to anything, get pregnant, and just collect easy money!"

There is a set of problems that involve the interaction of beneficiaries with professionals working in the administration and coordination of the program: gender and class prejudices, moral judgments, humiliation, and stigma, which are reported by beneficiaries as well as by the technical staff linked to the program, individuals who corroborate that the attendants at the "front desk" engage in discriminatory practices. The health worker Cacilda, for example, classifies some beneficiaries as: "[…] parasites, who latch onto the government and never let go. They don't look for work; they want things the easy way. They leach off others." Informal social control induces a moral classification process, making public the negative image of the beneficiary. The idea of a "bad reputation" in Goffman (1988, 80) helps to better understand the development of many evaluative categories of beneficiaries: they "neglect their children," "are opportunists," "sluts," or even "parasites."

At the same time that a relationship based on embarrassment and humiliation develops, in some contexts there is only a bureaucratized relationship. The applicant's (registration) or beneficiary's (re-registration) request is processed quickly, without the attendant's interference. The latter simply fulfills her bureaucratic function of entering data. An example related by Maria explains: "She just asked questions and jotted down my answers, and then I asked when I would receive the benefit and she said: 'That's something you'll have to ask the federal government.' When she finished, she gave me a paper with a phone number and said, 'You can leave. We're done.'"

Here it is possible to see how the institutional actors perceive the trajectories of the applicants to the BF program, from the registration phase until the moment they begin to receive benefits and comply with the policy conditionalities. How do these actors view their interactions with the beneficiary group? What do they highlight as most important in the context of interacting with poor women? Is there a process of degradation of the image of beneficiary women whereby they are disqualified on a moral and social basis? Such questions have guided this part of my analysis.

Regarding the emergence of prejudices related to the "figure" of the beneficiary, Élida (a social worker) states:

> Receiving *Bolsa Família* is humiliating, and the person receiving the benefit begins internalizing this idea that they're in dire need, you know? I think when the government came up with the program, it didn't anticipate that it could be humiliating to people. It was to help meet their needs. Then again, the value is so small. And to receive it, you need to do so much...

The social worker affirms that humiliation is an unintended consequence of the state's well-intentioned offer of social assistance. She adds in another part of the interview that they did not like when the program was initially called *Programa Fome Zero* (Zero Hunger Program) because the title suggested that they were "in extreme poverty." Cacilda (the health worker) perceives a difference in the degree of humiliation related to the value of the benefit: the lower the value, the greater the chance that beneficiaries may feel ashamed or will go through humiliating situations. Cacilda also notes that beneficiaries are especially ashamed when their names appear on the social work attendance form. She says:

> In everyday life, beneficiaries are more ashamed than afraid of denunciation, because the moment they are put on the spot they feel like, "Great, now [people] will treat me like some poor little thing." [...] The humbler people often feel even more ashamed to be receiving the benefit. There is the case of a woman, who receives a little over BRL30, who went to solve a problem with her card. However, she is afraid of closed spaces. So, she went to the BF office one day, and it took longer than she could bear, so she left and came back the next day. Again it took too long, so she said: "I am not going to stand in this line for a little more than BRL30. I need the money, but I can't stand this anymore." She felt humiliated in that situation. The government deposited the money anyway, but she had already given up on collecting it.

Thus, Cacilda, corroborating Duvoux (2009), seems to point out that the feeling of shame and the incorporation of stigma do not arise randomly among beneficiaries. The humbler, to use Cacilda's expression, people are or the more resilient in Dubois's terms (2010), the greater the chances of being subjected to and forced to accept humiliating processes and stigma. This may be related to the lack of a minimal formal educational repertoire for curbing stigma and promoting coping strategies. Silence, especially among the humblest, often entails accepting their condition, which can be observed in the BF program's registration lines.

According to the perceptions of the institutional agents, humiliation usually relates to the precarious position of the subject who, when finding herself needing to apply for assistance program, is classified as extremely impoverished or *miserável* (a word that is frequently confused with "hungry"), which produces a feeling of shame and constant embarrassment. For Paula (social work intern), the beneficiaries do not feel humiliated because they receive the benefit due to their class status; rather, they are humiliated by the attendants and poor services to which they are subjected, especially in the coordination and registration sectors of the *Bolsa Família* program. According to Paula:

> (...) People who work [at the front desk] feel like they own the place. They're always questioning the beneficiaries, like: "Oh, don't you have a husband? So you've got that ring on your finger, but no husband, right?" They treat people with suspicion. These are commissioned political positions, right? Well, most of these clerks have no college degree and are hired as social workers. There's a lot of prejudice here at the front desk. They even go so far as to call women bitches. For example, I've already met a person here who started talking to me and started crying. Then I asked, "What is it?" And she said, "I lost my mother less than two months ago. I wanted to try to get her benefit transferred to me, changing my dependent status, to see if I could receive the benefit for my family, and we get to the front desk and are already mistreated. I just came here to see if I had some right to assistance as a young mother; I'm only 19 years old." And I asked, "What did your mother die of?" Then she said, "Look at the death certificate." Then I looked at the death certificate, and it was "malnutrition." She died because she didn't have enough to eat. She said: "Damn, we get here, they mistreat us, and the first thing we get is a threat based on a law protecting public agents from harassment; if you mistreat them, you go to jail for defiance."

As in Goffman's work, Vincent Dubois, in *La vie au Guichet* (2010), points out that economic dependence on social assistance ends up playing a key role in the game of interactions that beneficiaries will set up with staff at the "front desk." It also emphasizes that this power, characterized by the author as asymmetrical, produces a relationship that is not merely formal / bureaucratic, but carries normative judgments that can ultimately lead to stigmatizing practices that discriminate against people's nationality, gender, race, and class. Dubois, for example, points out that in France there is great resentment of beneficiaries (social suffering, jealousy, and hostility), especially those who are ethnically and socially different from the majority. There, the family allocation policy produces symbolic boundaries, especially between "immigrants" and the "French" (Dubois 2010, 39–40).

In Brazil, it is clear that this symbolic branding seems to be consolidated between those classified as "honest" and those deemed "opportunists." Similar classifications also appear in the United States, particularly in research by Van

Hook and Bean (2009) and Lamont and Molnár (2002). To evade the demoralizing category of opportunist, those seeking benefits claim that the resource is temporary (denying their dependence on the program), or they embody the image of the "victim" to demonstrate that they are truly in need of the resource transferred to them, contrasting the notion of necessity with that of personal interest. Even non-beneficiaries are aware (or hear reports) of beneficiaries having humiliating experiences. Vilma (non-beneficiary), for example, reports a case in which a young woman experienced humiliation:

> One day a girl who lives here came crying over this humiliating situation. She said that the clerk treated her so rudely and that she would not go back there … So I said: "Go tomorrow because, maybe, there will be another clerk there to help you … Maybe this one has love in her heart." And then, when she went back, they said, "You don't need the assistance; you only have one child, you're young, and you can still work." See, here there are a lot of people struggling to get assistance.

Despite suffering clear economic restrictions in her life, Mara chose not to apply for the benefit, precisely to avoid possible humiliations and prejudices that could be exercised by representatives of the state. "I would rather be in need than ask for assistance. I'm ashamed, alright? I'm already poor; do I really need to humiliate myself in front of others asking for money?" Dayane has also resisted applying for the benefit, given that, in her mind, becoming a "beneficiary" would mean going through a process of moral humiliation:

> I will not sign up for *Bolsa Família* because I will not stand in line for hours with my children to apply for the program, so that I can maybe earn and receive some miniscule amount. I will not humiliate myself for crumbs, no. I'm not going down there every month for, what, BRL44. So you can see me there; my colleagues go out in the hot sun on foot to stand in line to receive BRL40 for the month and to be mistreated. I'll pass on that.

Because of the stories of humiliation and embarrassment resulting from interactions with attendants at the *Bolsa Família* office, as reported by beneficiaries throughout the neighborhood, some people give up on asking for assistance. This issue of a material nature may introduce "barriers to access or selection criteria not formally foreseen and that affect the most vulnerable segments of society" (Pires 2017, 10). Some program applicants and beneficiaries avoid face-to-face interaction with clerks in order to protect themselves from possible discrimination. This happens when the person resists participating in certain social settings where they could be the target of harassment. I found out among the group of beneficiaries that they develop strategies that will guide their social encounters, protecting themselves or not (depending on the context).

The feeling of shame would be less related to the position of "failure" in professional life and more linked to the receipt of a very low income. This is why beneficiaries often shy away from assistance, for fear of negative associations (being called "hungry," "accommodated or comfortable," or "vagabond") to which others subject themselves when they apply for assistance. The explanation for this hesitance to pursue assistance is not the same in North American cases, where the fear of being framed in the context of assistance is more due to the recognition of a notion of individual failure in the face of the labor market (Schneider and Ingram 2005).

When candidates have friends or family members who already receive *Bolsa Família*, they ask for help with the application and ask to be accompanied to avoid stigmatizing situations. Based on the experiences of other women in the neighborhood, they calculate how much they stand to earn and analyze if it is worth wasting time in line attempting to apply, always at the risk of being subjected to discriminatory practices.

## Final Considerations

Based on the empirical work carried out in this study, it is possible to state that the spaces studied are subject to a wide system of surveillance (in the Foucauldian sense of the term) and governmentality over beneficiaries. Firstly, surveillance is political because there is specific, albeit mild, oversight as well as sanctions against conditionalities. Secondly, the surveillance / monitoring system is also social because it is based on controlling the conduct and behaviors of beneficiary women. Finally, it is equally moral and corporal in that others use judgment to arrive at stigmatizing conclusions and categorizations about the behaviors and conduct of beneficiaries.

The controls exercised over women beneficiaries are multiple and complex and spread across diverse environments through direct demands, especially because of the moral demands that have been framed in the discourse of public agents. In addition, institutional actors assume an unofficial symbolic charge of framing the beneficiary based on the notions of the "good mother" with the "right conduct" or the "responsible" mother. Contrary to the clear incorporation (hence naturalization) of policy rules, institutional agents adhere to specific moral values that reduce people to the status of poor yet "good" and "deserving."

Among the three groups of respondents (institutional actors, non-beneficiaries, and beneficiaries), two fundamental categories emerged as a form of moral judgment of the beneficiaries, namely: people who are "deserving" and people deemed "opportunists." The first refers to the understanding that the beneficiary is entitled to the benefit because she is considered a "good mother:" altruistic, fair, and responsible. As for the "opportunist" category, it signals that the beneficiary is seen as a "bad mother:" selfish, deviant, and irresponsible. The closer a woman comes to being classified as a "bad mother," the more likely she is to be seen as undeserving of the benefit. The closer she comes to the "good mother" category, the greater her legitimacy as a *Bolsa Família* beneficiary. In this sense, we clearly see the existence of a gender evaluative tension in the judgment of beneficiaries that also reproduces the process of hierarchization of the "good" and "bad" poor.

Applicants to the PBF fearfully confront face-to-face interactions with attendants in the registration sector, primed by the stories of discomfort and embarrassment that their peers have experienced and shared with them. The repercussion of the offensive behavior of clerks and attendants in the registration sector is their reputation among people in the neighborhood as being "rude," a notoriety that causes many potential applicants to deviate from pursuing *Bolsa Família* on the grounds that they are not willing to subject themselves to "humiliation" to receive minor assistance from the state.

This research aimed at highlighting some of the political, moral, symbolic, and gender-based consequences of the implementation of a Brazilian social protection program designed to fight poverty, namely *Bolsa Família*. The empirical results indicate that it is essential to include the state and its public agents as important actors in the creation and modeling of the practices of the poor. Although most of the interviewed women declared themselves as black, the main categories that appeared related to stigmatization and discrimination processes were "woman" and "poor." In fact, surveillance, discrimination, and controls endured by the beneficiaries in the Brazilian urban context are clearly associated to the role of women as poor mothers.

## Notes

1 Lipsky claims that street-level bureaucrats (public service agents), in their daily work, create rules and procedures that deviate from policy directives, frequently drawing on the moral values and personal or group beliefs with which they identify in their decisions related to policies that should be treated objectively. This implicit bias may impact the outcome of the public policy in question.
2 See the report by Banco Mundial (1998), pp. 64–70.
3 This idea appears in particular in the World Bank (2000a, 200b) and (2001) reports.
4 The author conducted semi-structured interviews with 145 (women) respondents who are legal beneficiaries and 45 interviews with government agents (managers, municipal secretaries, CRAS employees, and other public servants). In addition, the present work also analyzes data from 30 focus groups.
5 Importantly, in 2010, according to the National Secretariat of Income and Citizenship (Senarc) of the Ministry of Social Development and Fight Against Hunger (MDS), most female beneficiaries (65.1%) did not complete their elementary education.
6 The *Cadastro Único para Programas Sociais* (*Single Registry* for Social Programs) (CadÚnico) is an instrument used to collect data and information in order to identify all low-income families in the country. Families with monthly incomes of up to half a minimum wage per person must be registered. Families with income above this criterion may be included in CadÚnico, as long as their inclusion is linked to the selection or monitoring of social programs implemented by the Union, states, or municipalities.

7 The average annual sales price of the commercial dollar in 2018: BRL 3.65. Source: Central Bank of Brazil.
8 In addition, they were informed that this was an academic research and that their responses could be used in publications and other media. All of them gave verbal consent to participate in the research.
9 Programa Nacional de Acesso Técnico e Emprego (National Program for Access to Technical Education and Employment (Pronatec) are courses offered to beneficiaries of social policies and people registered in the Single Registry.
10 As already pointed out, the names of the interviewees have been changed.
11 "*Casa de tijolinho*," which means little brick house. It is the name used by beneficiaries to refer to *Bolsa Família* program's local coordination office.

## References

Anderson, Elijah. 1999. *Code of the Street: Decency, Violence, and the Moral Life of the Inner City*. Nova York: W. W. Norton.

Banco Mundial. 1998. *World Development Indicators*. Washington, D.C.: The World Bank.

Bedford, Kate. 2009. "Gender and Institutional Strengthening: the World Bank's Policy Record in Latin America." *Contemporary Politics* 15, no. 2: 197–214. doi:10.1080/13569770902858137.

Blondet, Cecília. 2002. "'The Devil's Deal:' Women's Political Participation and Authoritarianism in Peru." In *Gender Justice, Development, and Rights*, edited by M. Molyneux, and S. Razavi. Oxford: Oxford University Press. doi:10.1093/0199256454.001.0001.

Bourdieu, Pierre. 2012. *Sur l'État: Cours au Collège de France (1989–1992)*. Paris: Seuil.

Brockling, Urlich, Susanne Krasmann, and Thomas Lemke. 2010. *Governmentality: Current Issues and Future Challenges*. London: Routledge.

Butler, Judith. 2015. *Quadros de Guerra: Quando a Vida é Passível de luto?* Translation by Sérgio Lamarão and Arnaldo Marques da Cunha. Rio de Janeiro: Civilização Brasileira.

Butler, Judith. 2011. *Violencia de Estado, Guerra, Resistencia. Por una Nueva Política de la Izquierda*. Madrid: Katz Editores.

Butler, Judith. 2004. *Lenguaje, Poder e Identidad*. Madrid: Síntesis.

Carloto, Cássia and Silvana Mariano. 2009. "Gênero e Combate à Pobreza: Programa Bolsa Família." *Revista Estudos Feministas* 17, no. 3: 901–908. https://doi.org/10.1590/S0104-026X2009000300018.

Chant, Sylvia. 2015. "Gender and Poverty in the Global South." In *The Routledge Handbook of Gender and Development*, edited by Anne Coles, Leslie Gray, and Janet Momsen, 191–131. Abingdon: Routledge. doi:10.4324/9780203383117-31.

Crenshaw, Kimberlé W. 1994. "Mapping the Margins: Intersectionality, Identity Politics, and Violence against Women of Color." In *The Public Nature of Private Violence*, edited by Martha Fineman Albertson, and Roxanne Mykitiuk, 93–120. Nova York: Routledge. doi:10.4324/9780203060902-12.

Dubois, Vincent. 2010. *La Vie au Guichet. Relation Administrative et Traitement de la Misère*. Paris: Économica Études Politiques.

Duvoux, Nicolas. 2009. *L'autonomiedesassistés. Sociologie des Politiques d'Insertion*. Paris: PUF.

Esping-Andersen, Gøsta. 1999. *Social Foundations of Postindustrial Economies*. Nova York: Oxford University Press.

Farah, Marta. 2004. "Políticas Públicas e Gênero." In *Políticas Públicas e Igualdade de Gênero*, edited by Tatau Godinho, and Maria Lúcia Silveira, 127–142. São Paulo: Coordenadoria Especial da Mulher.

Fine, Ben., Costas Lapavitsas, and Jonathan Pincus. 2001. *Development Policy in the Twenty-first Century: Beyond the Post-Washington Consensus*. London: Routledge. https://doi.org/10.4324/9780203418796.

Fonseca, Ana. 2010. "As Mulheres como Titulares das Transferências Condicionadas: Empoderamento ou Reforço de Posições de Gênero Tradicionais?" Work presented at the 13th International Bien Conference, São Paulo.

Foucault, Michel. 2009. *Vigiar e Punir: Nascimento da Prisão*. 37th edition. Petrópolis, RJ: Vozes.

Foucault, Michel. 2003. "Governmentality." In *The Essential Foucault: Selections from Essential Works of Foucault 1954–1984*, edited by Paul Rabinow, and Nikolas Rose, 229–245. London: New Press.

Foucault, Michel. 1979. *Microfísica do Poder*. Rio de Janeiro: Graal.

Fraser, Nancy and Axel Honneth. 2003. *Redistribution or Recognition? A Political Philosophical Exchange*. New York; London: Verso.

Goffman, Erving. 1988. *Estigma: Notas Sobre a Manipulação da Identidade Deteriorada*. Rio de Janeiro: Guanabara.

Goffman, Erving. 2012. *Ritual de Interação. Ensaios sobre o Comportamento Face a Face*. Petrópolis, RJ: Vozes.

Hall, Stuart. 2006. *A Identidade Cultural na Pós-Modernidade*. Rio de Janeiro: DP&A.

Hill, Michael. and Peter Hupe. 2014. *Implementing Public Policy: An Introduction to the Study of Operational Governance*. London: Sage.

Jenson, Jane. 2009. "Lost in Translation: The Social Investment Perspective and Gender Equality." *Social Politics, International Studies in Gender, State and Society* 16, no. 4: 446–483.

Lamont, Michèle and Marcelo Fournier. 1992. *Cultivating Boundaries and the Making of Inequality*. Chicago; London: The University of Chicago Press.

Lamont, Michèle and Viràg Molnár. 2002. "The Study of Boundaries across the Social Sciences." *Annual Review of Sociology* 28: 167–195.

Lipsky, Michael. 1980. *Street-level Bureaucracy: Dilemmas of the Individual in Public Services*. NewYork: Russell Sage Foundation.

Marins, Mani Tebet. 2018. "O 'Feminino' como Gênero do Desenvolvimento." *Revista Estudos Feministas*, 26, no. 1: 1–14. https://doi.org/10.1590/1806-9584.2018v26n139010.

Marins, Mani Tebet. 2017. *Bolsa Família: Questões de Gênero e Moralidades*. Rio de Janeiro: Editora UFRJ.

Marins, Mani Tebet. 2014. "Repertórios Morais e Estratégias Individuais de Beneficiários e Cadastradores do Bolsa Família". *Sociologia & Antropologia* 4: 544–562.

Maynard-Moody, Steven and Michel Musheno. 2003. *Cops, Teachers, Counselors: Narratives of Street-level Judgment*. Ann Arbor: University of Michigan Press.

Molyneux, Maxine. 2002. "Gender and the Silences of Social Capital: Lessons of Latin America." *Development and Change* 33, no. 2: 167–188.

Molyneux, Maxine. 2006. "Mothers at the Service of the New Poverty Agenda: Progresa/Oportunidades, Mexico's Conditional Transfer Programme." *Social Politics and Administration* 40, no. 4: 425–449.

Monnerat, Giselle Lavinas, Mônica de Castro Maia Senna, Vanessa Schottz, Rosana Magalhães, and Luciene Burlandy. 2007. "Do Direito Incondicional à Condicionalidade do Direito: As Contrapartidas do Programa Bolsa Família." *Ciência & Saúde Coletiva* 12, no. 6: 1453–1462. https://doi.org/10.1590/S1413-81232007000600008.

Newman, Katherine S. 1999. *No Shame in My Game: The Working Poor in the Inner City*. Nova York: Russell Sage Foundation: Vintage Books.

Orloff, Ann Shola. 2007. "Farewell to Maternalism? State Policies and Mothers' Employment." Working Papers Series. Institute for Policy Research, Northwestern University.

Paugam, Serge. 2003. *Desqualificação Social: Ensaio Sobre a Nova Pobreza*. São Paulo: Cortez.

Périvier, Hélène and Rachel Silveira. 2009. "Généralisation du RSA: rien à signaler sur les femmes?" *Travail, genre et sociétés* 22, no. 2: 155–158.

Pires, Roberto Rocha. 2017. "Implementando Desigualdades? Introdução a uma Agenda de Pesquisa sobre Agentes Estatais, Representações Sociais e (Re)produção de Desigualdades." *Boletim de Análise Político-Institucional* 13: 7–13.

Pressman, Jeffrey and Aaron Wildavsky. 1973. *Implementation: How Great Expectations in Washington are Dashed in Oakland; or, Why it's Amazing that Federal Programs Work at All, This Being a Saga of the Economic Development Administration as Told by Two Sympathetic Observers who Seek to Build Morals on a Foundation*. California: University of California Press.

Rego, Walquiria Leão and Alessandro Pinzani. 2013. *Vozes do Bolsa Família: Autonomia, Dinheiro e Cidadania*. São Paulo: Editora da Unesp.

Rego, Walquiria Leão, Marcia Baratto, and Lucas Oliveira. 2010. "Direitos Humanos, Relações de Gênero e Cidadania: Programa Bolsa Família e Microcrédito Indiano em Perspectiva Comparada." Work presented at the International Conference of the Basic Income Earth Network (Bien), São Paulo.

Rego, Walquiria Leão. 2008. "Aspectos Teóricos das Políticas de Cidadania: uma aproximação ao Bolsa Família." *Lua Nova* 73: 147–185.

Schild, Verónica. 2007. "Empowering 'Consumer-Citizens' or Governing Poor Female Subjects? The Institutionalization of 'Self-development' in the Chilean Social Policy Field." *Journal of Consumer Culture* 7, no. 2: 179–203.

Schneider, Anne L. and Helen M.Ingram. 2005. *Deserving and Entitled: Social Constructions and Public Policy*. New York: State University of New York Press.

Small, Mario, David Harding, and Michele Lamont. 2011. "Reavaliando Cultura e Pobreza." *Sociologia & Antropologia* 1, n. 2: 91–118.

Soares, Sergei and Natália Sátyro. 2009. *O Programa Bolsa-Família: Desenho Institucional e Possibilidades Futuras*. Texto para discussão 1424. Brasil: IPEA.

Suárez, Mireya and Marlene Libardoni. 2007. "O impacto do Programa Bolsa Família: Mudanças e Continuidades na Condição Social das Mulheres." In *Avaliação de Políticas e programas do MDS: resultados*, vol. 2, edited by Jeni Vaitsman, and Rômulo Paes-Sousa, 119–162. Brasil: MDS/Sagi.

Van Hook, Jennifer and Frank Bean. 2009. "Explaining Mexican-Immigrant Welfare Behaviors: The Importance of Employment-related Cultural Repertoires." *American Sociological Review* 74, no. 3: 423–444.

World Bank. 1997. *Toward Gender Equality: The Role of Public Policy*. Washington, D.C.: World Bank.

World Bank. 2000a. *Vozes dos pobres* (Voices of the poor). Brazil: World Bank.

World Bank. 2000b. "Poverty Reduction and Economic Management Network." Brazil: World Bank.

World Bank. 2001. *Engendering Development through Gender Equality in Rights, Resources, and Voice*. Oxford: Oxford University Press.

# CONCLUSIONS

*Silvana Mariano and Cássia Maria Carloto*

Studies analyzing the effects of Conditional Cash Transfer (CCT) policies like the *Bolsa Família* Program (PBF) have highlighted various dimensions of poverty and human development, including the economic, moral, and social. When these studies turn to examine the impacts of these policies on women, especially vis-à-vis gender and racial inequalities, they need to take into account the combinatory effect of these different dimensions. In the chapters of this book, we have sought, through research and studies with beneficiaries of the BF, to present and analyze the effects, gains, problems and challenges of an income transfer program in which the family – and women within it – assume a central role. In this final chapter we present a synthesis of the reflections and conclusions presented over the course of the book, as well as some considerations of current trends.

What is the most adequate framework of social protection to reduce inequalities between men and women, prevent female poverty and promote women's autonomy? This question has animated feminist debates, studies, and proposals for decades, with different political and ideological positionings, and forms the background to the chapters in this book. Despite the divergences among researchers from this field, convergences also exist in various diagnoses of the social protection experiences which we discuss below.

One convergence relates to the debate on the family. The family, as a social organization hierarchically divided by gender and generation, is an institution that frequently poses obstacles to women's interests in enhancing their independence insofar as it concretizes those responsibilities deemed to be female in the form of demands on women to provide unpaid reproductive work and care. In effect, it limits and controls the opportunities and possibilities for women's autonomy to expand their rights, disputed in the world of work and politics. Another convergence concerns the debate about the labor market, which assigns men and women to distinct occupations with inequalities in qualitative and quantitative terms to the disadvantage of women.

There are also convergences in the interpretations of how the state actions in the areas of rights and public policies affect the everyday life and citizenship of women and men in distinct ways. Universal access to quality public services in the area of social reproduction contribute more significantly to alleviating the time spent by women on care work. Expanding and consolidating public policies with a gender and racial/ethnic profile is a strategy crucial to improving women's living conditions. From the viewpoint of feminist political demands, among the pillars that constitute social organization, the state is the most strategic institution for ensuring and expanding women's rights. However, state action needs to be reframed to achieve what feminists at the Fourth World Conference on Women held in Beijing denominated gender mainstreaming.

Advocacy of this feminist perspective encounters the challenges accentuated by the crises of capitalist accumulation and the social, cultural, and political changes observed in developing countries, where large sections of the population find themselves in poverty. For women living in poverty, the defense of a state that promotes social rights is even more relevant.

Women living in poverty are those most harmed by the work overload assumed by the family in the new social policy framework installed in the wake of the series of economic and fiscal crises since the 1990s, primarily because they occupy a subaltern position in the gender hierarchy and perform a fundamental role in social reproduction, as shown by the research presented and discussed in this book. Without the state as the main provider of social protection through services of shelter, healthcare, education, or monetary subsidies for children, senior citizens, and/or the sick, women find themselves unprotected and trapped in traditional functions and roles. In various Latin American countries, the CCTs utilized and reaffirmed these functions as an instrument to fight poverty, as shown in various chapters of this book. What defines poor women-mothers as functional elements in the objectives of social policies is the naturalization of their role as carers in the domestic-family sphere, which makes them one of the social groups most disadvantaged by the excluding neoliberal model. This interpretation has been corroborated in diverse circumstances in the chapters presented in this book.

The situation of Brazilian women living in poverty is exacerbated when income transfer policies impose counterpart requirements, or conditionalities, that reinforce the responsibilities traditionally considered female and hinder women's autonomy. The BF is no exception. In the book, this debate has informed the various chapters and traversed different moments of the analyses. Several questions surface in the development of the arguments: What limits do focalization, selectivity and conditionalities impose on the BF? What do women gain from the BF? What problems exist? How to meet the challenge faced by programs to fight poverty in contexts like Brazil and to construct new approaches and proposals that respond to gender and racial inequalities? These debates have become even more conflict-ridden in the current political and economic moment in Brazil with the resurgence of conservatism, public expenditure cuts, and a reduction in funding for social programs like the BF, in the name of fiscal adjustment, as discussed in the introduction. This is a moment of uncertainty for the BF.

The theme of focalization involves the debate on the program's operational, social and economic advantages and disadvantages, its capacity to focus accurately on its target public, and the effects that this type of policy has on the intended beneficiaries. The proportion of poor families receiving benefits remains unclear, though, since poverty figures in Brazil vary considerably, depending on the many different methodologies used. Brazilian scholars of the area have stressed the need to establish a unified set of criteria for measuring poverty in Brazil, enabling a standardization of the parameter adopted for the design and evaluation of public policies. But while some kind of unification fails to appear on the country's political horizon, the BF continues to adopt a low poverty line compared to the criteria used, for example, by the *Benefício de Prestação Continuada* (BCP) (Continuous Cash Benefit) and *Cadastro Único de Programas Sociais do Governo Federal* (Cadastro Único) (Single Registry of Social Programs of the Federal Government). This implies a focalization that excludes significant portions of the population in poverty according to the criteria of other programs run by the same federal government. This group includes women who assume responsibility for the social roles imposed on them, especially those living in poverty, but who lack adequate state support to perform these functions. Hence, this focalization excludes of women.

Variations in the research units add another layer of difficulties to poverty measurement. Government research bodies generally make use of two possible units: the individual or the household. The BF, though, adopts the family as its unit of reference. Innumerable operational and social difficulties arise from the BF's choice of criterion, as explored, for instance, in Cássia Carloto's Chapter 7.

The size of the informal economy is another problem when it comes to measuring poverty, since it hinders identification of income, especially when the informal economy accounts for half of the employed population, at least, with higher levels among the poor, as in the Brazilian case. The difficulties of measuring poverty with the aim of supporting focalization coexist with the problem of actually defining poverty. Brazilian social welfare policy is ambiguous in how it defines what poverty is. In official documents poverty is treated from a multidimensional perspective. However, in establishing the objective and criteria of the BF, poverty is defined as the absence of income and limited to the simple equation poverty=hunger.

Stigmatization is another factor of concern for professionals and specialists. In this book, we have seen how the system of state and societal monitoring of women receiving the benefit results in stigmatization and self-focalization. As Chapter 8 by Mani Marins argues, it amounts to a system of social surveillance, founded on the control of women's conducts and behaviors and framed within a dichotomy of the deserving 'good mother' and the selfish and opportunistic mother, reinforced in the attitudes of state professionals. Especially in small municipalities where most of the population know each other, many women who need the benefit do not apply for it so as not to expose themselves to humiliating situations and becoming stigmatized. In other words, as Teresa Sacchet argues in Chapter 3, the program's lack of concern with cultural issues can deepen economic injustices. Stigmatization occurs in all variety of contexts, in municipalities of all sizes. These risks are very well known in the literature on focalization.

The BF combines focalization with selectivity and, as a result, an additional problem becomes ascertaining the target public in the municipalities and determining the benefit quotas for each municipality. Consequently, the rate of coverage of the BF in proportion to the number of poor people or families varies considerably between Brazilian municipalities.

As the second chapter explored, focalization and universalization, as strategies for fighting poverty, have not been approached in coordinated form. On one hand, it is accepted that, in situations of extreme poverty, focalized actions need to be created that reach all the people below the determined poverty line. On the other hand, the state has a duty to promote universal access to the right to a dignified life for all, precisely to ensure people do not fall below the poverty line.

The possibilities of implanting proposals with a universal vision confront at least two major political difficulties. First, the intense competition for public funds, a small portion of which is left over for social welfare. Second, income transfer is not in fact seen as a right of members of the public or the target population. What social assistance users always repeat is that income transfer should be targeted "at those who need it," given that it comprises a form of "help." While this conception is situated as a necessity, universal policies are situated in rights. Focalization and universalization, in Brazil, are not approached in a satisfactory way, and ever more rights have been lost due to the neoliberal measures intensified under the new government. A major obstacle for reversing this trend was the approval, in 2018, by Brazil's National Congress of an amendment to the Federal Constitution that freezes public expenditure for the next 20 years.

As for the conditionalities, this is a factor that directly affects the organization of the everyday life of women receiving the benefit. The absence or precariousness of public policies and programs for care provision, principally in the areas of health and education, are what most hinders women's search for financial independence and a reduction in the excessive workload of day-to-day intra-family care. These are policies that women who have been in the program for more time define as rights and that are not respected, as Silvana Mariano and Márcio Souza have shown in Chapter 6. The scarcity of social services also has an impact on the time that women spend trying to meet the program's conditions. By foregrounding various issues related to the program's conditions, the book has made evident the paradox between the obligation to meet certain counterpart requirements to receive the benefit and, on the other hand, the provision of a network of health and education services without universal coverage, which punishes and penalizes women by cutting their benefit, holding them responsible for failing to meet the conditionalities. It should be noted that even where an absence of conditions alleviates women's worries, they still remain responsible for domestic care, especially when there is no network of universal and quality public services in the area of social reproduction.

A second question, investigated by Cássia Carloto in this volume, Chapter 7, is the use of the time needed to meet these conditions, insofar as women-mothers have to go in search of schools and health services and ensure that their children are able to meet the demands of the courses. This research also highlighted the permanent feeling of dread of losing the benefit, which leaves women in a constant state of anxiety.

Although this book has not presented comparative studies of the country's regions, in Chapter 4 Josi Delgado and Marcia Tavares show that in the Northeast – along with the North, the poorest region of Brazil – there is higher work precarization, a higher number of black women who have faced the process of exclusion from jobs and access to goods and services for various generations. If improving the actions to fight poverty is a government objective, managers must consider the intersections between gender, class, and race in the production and reproduction of inequalities.

In relation to the gains that the women obtain from joining the program, what most stands out are those relating to the increase in consumer power, which provides significant improvements, taking as a parameter the condition of family poverty and deprivation. In this sense, the program's objective of improving living conditions, especially those of children, is achieved by increasing access to food, clothing, school materials, better housing conditions, and credit. These gains do not translate into personal and economic independence for women, but do help women-mothers to obtain more tranquillity in their lives in terms of meeting their material and emotional responsibilities to their children, especially single mothers – i.e. those without a partner. As Luana Passos, Simone Wajnman, and Fábio Waltenberg underline in this book, in Chapter 5, overall there has been an improvement in women's lives, but this does not mean that an increased female empowerment. The authors highlight the paradox that women receiving the BF reduce the time dedicated to paid work and increase the time dedicated to care work and domestic tasks.

Returning to one of the questions formulated at the start of this text: can extreme poverty, in which black women are a majority, be fought with focalized, selective, and compensatory programs that impose conditionalities?

Answering this question is difficult since it is both related to and produced by a social and economic system based on exploitation and domination, exacerbated over recent decades, and that, as Teresa Sacchet discusses Chapter 3 in this book, operates across three dimensions: distributive, cultural, and representative. It is also difficult because it needs to be examined in the context of a country that has still to free itself from its past of slavery, which only began work on building a welfare state with the 1988 constitution, which has been steadily dismantled since and now, under the new government, has witnessed an acceleration in the privatization and commoditization of social rights.

As all the chapters indicated, for the BF to assist in achieving the economic, political, and social independence of the recipient women, the program needs to build strategies to confront the gender and racial inequalities from its formulation to its implementation and evaluation. A program designed to fight poverty cannot ignore the fact that the poorest people are black women. To respond adequately to the challenges faced, the state must transform the program into a social policy to be developed in articulated form at all three governmental levels: federal, state, and municipal. The state, notably the federal government, must also increase the quantity of resources given that poverty has increased. Another strategic question is the investment in care programs and policies, under state responsibility, for children, young people, senior citizens, and people with special needs.

Some advances are also possible at municipal level where there is greater autonomy for the construction of less discriminatory and more inclusive approaches for women receiving funds from the program, socio-educational initiatives, and projects that can contribute to economic independence and help confront domestic violence, for example. However, budget cuts to the different social programs developed at municipal level and primarily involving women benefitting from the BF and their children are already being made by the federal government, jeopardizing various projects in course. The difficulty of hiring qualified professionals as social assistants and psychologists and the constant turnover of professionals at *Centro de Referência de Assistência Social* (CRAS) (Reference Center for Social Assistance) also negatively affects this work in many municipalities.

As reiterated earlier, this is a particularly difficult moment in Brazil to make progress in these strategies. The program is still seen by sectors of the Brazilian middle class as a form of encouraging idleness, disincentivizing paid work and increasing dependence on the state. The notion of a right to a dignified life and even the right to have rights is still very fragile among the oppressed and most exploited classes in Brazil, due to the country's past of dictatorships and its patrimonialist, clientelist, and meritocratic history. The BF is mostly seen as a favor and help. Conditional cash transfer in Brazil, so far in the shape of the BF, presents certain gains in terms of alleviating poverty and grants some facilities for women to manage this poverty. Nevertheless, this type of policy has limitations in terms of being able to remedy the structural issues that produce and reproduce the connections between the conditions of gender, class, and race and that result in the kind of alarming poverty seen in Brazil. Promoting policies from a gender perspective – that is, committed to reducing the inequalities between men and women, including adequately designed direct income transfer programs – continues to be a challenge for Brazilian society.

# INDEX

Note: **Bold** page numbers refer to tables and *italic* page numbers refer to figures; Page numbers followed by n refer to notes.